MYTHOLOGY

Greek and Roman

MYTHOLOGY
Greek and Roman

Robert J. Gula

Thomas H. Carpenter

Longman

New York & London

CONTENTS

ILLUSTRATIONS

MAPS AND CHARTS

INTRODUCTION

Mythology is not for children. Though myths can be defined in the broadest sense as traditional stories and though some myths can be entertaining, there are vaster dimensions to them. The people through whose minds the myths evolved saw the world charged with divinity; their gods were alive and powerful; and their myths reflect an energy of imagination coupled with a genuine belief. It is this energy that is missing when the myths are reduced to nothing more than entertaining stories.

Myths deal with certain fundamental concerns that human beings have about themselves and about the world around them, and those concerns were unsettling to the ancients as they are often still unsettling to us. Violence — the violence of the natural world, but particularly man's inclination toward violence — is a concern that appears with considerable frequency. Hence many myths deal with treachery, murder, and destruction. The mysterious forces of passion and sex also appear frequently. Any attempt to purge the myths of these unsettling qualities not only distorts the true nature of the world that they reflected, but also deprives the reader of the integrity of the mythic vision. The ancients were willing to wrestle with these issues and the modern reader must be willing to meet the myths on their own terms.

There have always been thinkers who have tried to explain the meanings of myths. As early as the fourth century B.C., the writer Euhemerus proposed a theory that all myths describe actual historical events. The Roman Lucretius in the first century B.C. claimed that myths were merely camouflages for deep-seated fears that man has. In modern times, many theories have been proposed, but perhaps the most dominant one today is the psychological interpretation in which myths are seen as expressions of man's unconscious self. The writings of Jung and his followers are among the most significant in this area. While most theories have some degree of validity, no one theory can embrace the vast complexities of myth.

Ancient art and literature are our primary sources for ancient myths. The *Iliad,* the *Odyssey,* the *Aeneid,* and the Greek tragedies are core works. They are available in translation to everyone; hence we have purposely avoided retelling all the plots of these works. We have, however, tried to provide background that will be helpful in understanding them.

Sculpture and painting on vases are the other rich sources of myths. These also are available to everyone, not only through photographs, but in' the collections of many museums throughout the world. All of the illustrations in this book are of ancient works in American museums.

Rarely is there any one set version for a myth, and even the casual reader of myths will soon notice inconsistencies. Therefore, a reader should be aware that a story told by one author may differ in some details from the same story told by a different author. This point is so important that it is repeated quite frequently throughout this book, and often we have cited some of the more important variations. Similarly, there is no set spelling of names in translations of ancient Greek words. For example:

        Cassandra — Kassandra
        Teiresias — Tiresias
        Cronos — Cronus

A third possible source of confusion results from the fact that the Romans gave their own names to many Greek gods, and some translators use Roman rather than Greek names. For example, Zeus may be Jove or Jupiter, and Eros may be Amor or Cupid. We have used the Greek names when referring to Greek myths and the Roman names only when applying to specifically Roman myths. A list of the major Greek/Latin equivalents appears in Chapter XIX.

Rarely is any myth told in its entirety in an ancient source. Our knowledge of a myth often comes from piecing together details from several different writers.

In presenting the material in this book, we have had two purposes in mind. The first is to provide information essential to the reader who wants an overview of classical mythology. The second is to convey some of the flavor of the myths as stories. Hence some chapters tell stories while others simply present information. Furthermore, we realize that some readers may want to read the book from cover to cover, others may want to read selected chapters, while still others may want it as a reference tool. Therefore, to accommodate these various uses, we have intentionally included some duplication of information and have provided cross references where they may be helpful. Many sections are followed by a series of remarks in smaller type. These remarks are intended to provide additional information or insights.

Frequent mention throughout the book is made of the various sources from which we derive our knowledge of the myths. The major names that we refer to are listed below. All dates are approximate.

Homer (ninth century B.C.) — the name given to the poet who united ancient tales of the Trojan War into two epics, the *Iliad* and the *Odyssey*. His use of myth usually reflects more the world of the gods and the heroes than the world of the common man and reflects an aristocratic/heroic tradition.

Hesiod (eighth century B.C.) — poet who wrote of the origins of the gods and of the creation of the world and whose major interest was the average man and his behavior.

Pindar (518-438 B.C.) — poet who wrote odes celebrating the victors of the four major Greek athletic festivals. He refers to portions of myths but rarely tells the complete story.

Aeschylus (525-456 B.C.) — Athenian tragedian, seven of whose ninety plays survive. Gods are live and powerful forces in his works.

Sophocles (495-406 B.C.) — Athenian tragedian, seven of whose plays survive; interested as much in the nobility of man as in the power of the gods.

Euripides (485-406 B.C.) — Athenian tragedian, eighteen of whose plays survive complete; ridiculed popular religion and was the first dramatist to take an interest in the psychology of his characters.

Apollodorus (dates unknown) — Greek writer who provides the most complete source of myths that we have. His work is straightforward and unimaginative.

Ovid (43-18 B.C.) — Roman poet who provides what is often the most complete single version of a myth. He frequently varies details in individual stories to fit his own purposes.

Vergil (70-19 B.C.) — Roman poet who provides background on the Trojan War and the foundation of Rome.

Pausanias (second century A.D.) — a tourist who traveled throughout Greece and wrote down everything he heard, never questioning whether his information was accurate or whether it made any sense.

Many of the illustrations in this book are paintings on ancient pottery. On the earlier vases, the figures are in black on the natural red background of the clay. This is called black figure painting. Later, artists painted the background black and left the figures the natural red of the clay. This is called red figure painting. On occasions both black and red figure artists used a variation in which they painted on a white background. This is called white ground painting. Since the names of most of the painters have not survived, they are often identified today by the location of an important piece — for example, the Providence Painter, the Berlin Painter and the Agrigento Painter. Sometimes they are named for a subject frequently found in their work — for example, the Pan Painter and the Danae Painter. Vase painting, as an important art form, flourished from the end of the seventh century B.C. to the beginning of the fourth.

MYTHOLOGY

Greek and Roman

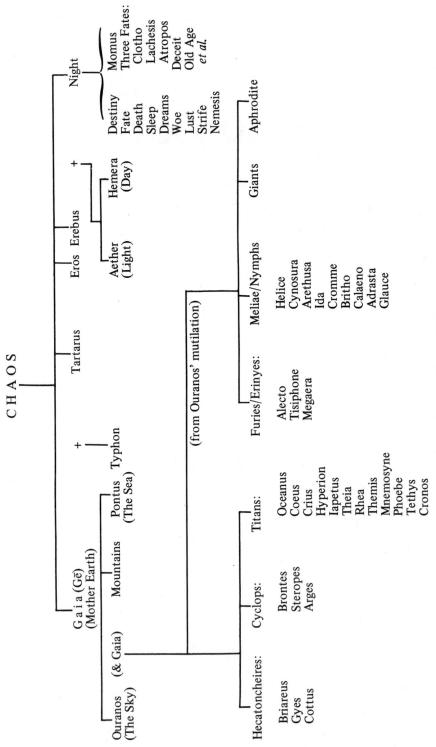

Genealogy of Primal Forces

CHAPTER I

CREATION

The creation of matter and principal forces

At first there was Chaos, a void, shapeless, lightless, formless and lifeless. Then came the broad-bosomed Mother Earth, **Gaia**, and the dark and murky **Tartarus**, the region under the Earth. Also came **Eros**, the most beautiful force there is. Eros relaxes the limbs and overcomes the sense, discretion and judgment of both gods and men. Then from Chaos came Erebus, the darkness under the Earth, and Night, the darkness above the Earth. Lonely darkness was now everywhere. But eventually Night and Erebus, having joined together in mutual attraction, gave birth to Aether, the light of the heavens, and Hemera, the Day. The force of Eros also affected Gaia, and she consequently gave birth to **Ouranos**, the star-filled heavens, and to the huge mountains, and to Pontus, the Sea. The earth, now with her mountains and seas and light and stars no longer being dull and flat and shapeless, appealed to Ouranos, and the two of them joined together. From this union came the Hecatoncheires, giants with a hundred hands and fifty heads, whose names were Briareus, Gyes, and Cottus; there were also the Cyclops, creatures who had only one large eye in the midst of their forehead and hence often called Goggle-Eyes; they were Brontes the Thunderer, Steropes the Lightning-Hurler, and Arges the Thunderbolt, and they were full of strength, violence, and both craftiness and resourcefulness. Finally there were the **Titans**, enormous and powerful creatures, elemental forces in the universe. There were twelve of them: Oceanus, the Ocean, the source of rivers; Coeus; Crius; Hyperion, or Light, who fathered Helios the Sun, Selene the Moon, and Eos the Dawn; Iapetus, later to become important as the father of Prometheus, Epimetheus, and Atlas; Theia; Rhea; Themis, or Justice; Mnemosyne, or Memory; Phoebe; and Tethys. Finally, there was **Cronos**, the youngest and most dreadful of the brood.

Now, the first descendants of Ouranos and Gaia, the Hecatoncheires and the Cyclops, were horrors. Revolted by them, Ouranos hated them. Whenever any of them were born, Ouranos would take them and hide them in the recess of the Earth as if he were shoving them back into Gaia's womb. He took delight in this deed, while Gaia groaned from pain and seethed with anger. Sensing that this was perhaps not the best plan, he settled for casting these children into

1

Tartarus. But mother Gaia, still deprived of her children, was not assuaged. She called together her other children, the Titans, and, although being very much torn by misery and sorrow, she put on a show of confidence and good cheer and tried to enlist their support:

"Sons and daughters, your father is arrogant and reckless; listen to me and do what I ask, and we will be able to avenge the horrible outrages that he has committed; for he has done abominations."

So she spoke; but fear clutched all her children, and not one of them dared to utter a sound . . . no one except Cronos, for he hated his father.

"Mother, this I promise you: I will do what you ask, for I care not one bit about him; for he has done abominations."

So he spoke, and his mother Gaia was pleased. She then took him aside, explained her plan to him, hid him, and had him wait in ambush. Soon Ouranos, drawing the night behind him and overcome by desire, came upon the Earth. He enveloped her and as he was thus diverted and off his guard, Cronos sprung upon him with a sickle, quickly castrated him, and threw his organs over his back. There was thus and forevermore a severing of connections between the sky and the earth.

As Cronos threw off his father's organs, drops of blood were spilled upon the Earth. From these drops came a race of Nymphs, a race of Giants, and three creatures called **Furies** or **Erinyes**: Alecto, the Relentless; Tisiphone, the Blood-Avenger; and Megaera, the Grudge-Bearer. These Furies were agents of vengeance, pitiless, inexorable but just; horrible creatures, winged with snakes in their hair, black, their eyes dripping with blood, and wretchedly foul. They avenged a variety of crimes — murder, violation of oaths, incivility to guests, the aged, or the poor — but their most active avenging concerned crimes against kin and especially against parents. They would pursue their victim relentlessly with whip in hand and afford him no peace whatsoever.

Ouranos' organs themselves landed in the sea. They were taken by the waves for a long time and a white foam formed from the friction of flesh and water. This foam floated by the island of Cythera to the island of Cyprus where from it came a beautiful young maiden, the goddess **Aphrodite,** the "foam-sprung" goddess, who is sometimes called Cytherea because she touched Cythera and at other times called Cypris, Cypria, or the Cypriate because she actually took shape on Cyprus.

a. Thus ends the first great dynasty in the story of creation. There is no religion yet. All we are dealing with is elemental forces. There are no gods, merely representations of archetypal power and of the broadest functions of nature. The stories are crude, violent, and rugged, but there does seem to be some sign of a cause and effect relationship, suggesting basic principles of order and purposefulness. Certainly at this point there is no correlation between man and the powers above, except perhaps for the principle of sex, sexual desire and instinct — i.e., for union — which seems to be a prime motivating factor in these early stories.

b. There are other versions and addenda to the various stories that are worth mentioning:

1. The Nymphs who were born from the blood of Ouranos were called the Meliae.

2. Sometimes the order of the offspring of Ouranos and Gaia is reversed, the Titans coming first. It is unlikely that the Greek mind would have noted the inconsistency; if a Greek did note it, he probably wouldn't have cared; and if he cared, he would most likely have selected the version that most appealed to him; and that is what has been done here.

3. You will remember that Chaos bore Erebus, Night, and Tartarus. Night in turn supposedly bore a host of correlative beings: hateful Destiny, Doom, black Fate, Nemesis, Death, Dreams, Sleep, Momus (who always complains, finds fault, and grumbles), the Three Fates, Woe, Misery, Deceit, Lewdness, Destructive Old Age, and Strife. You can see how most of these qualities in an imaginative way do come from Night: qualities relating to Night directly, such as Sleep and Dreams; qualities relating to Night as the termination of life, such as Doom, Fate, Destiny, Old Age; and qualities relating to the temptations that Night can bring upon us, such as lust, deception and sneakiness . . . i.e., Night, offering seclusion and a feeling of security, may encourage us to let down our guard.

4. The Three **Fates**, mentioned above as daughters of Night, feature prominently in classical mythology. They are usually pictured as three aged crones: Clotho as spinning the thread of life, Lachesis as giving man a certain length of that string, and Atropos as cutting that thread. They are collectively often referred to as the **Moirae**, or the Parcae in Roman thought.

5. Some sources say that Eros was directly descended from Chaos instead of being the offspring of Erebus and Night. It really makes no difference; the principle is the same: Eros, representing an impersonal attraction of forces, results from a need for a figurative union, and both this need and this union effect a highly vital force, one of the most elemental of all forces. At this stage in Greek cosmology, Eros is totally impersonal. As time goes on, however, his function will change. For instance, some later Greek writers represent Eros as the son of Aphrodite. As her companion and son, he later assumes the function of passionate love and desire, and at that point he is an entirely personal force. Eventually he is stripped of all his power and dignity as he becomes the flaccid, chubby, cute and precious little baby whom the Romans called Cupid or Amor and who can still be found with his puffy little cheeks, his bow and his arrow on Valentine cards.

3

The reign of the Titans and the ascendancy of the Olympians

We are now in the age of Cronos, the period of the Titans. The Cyclops and the Hecatoncheires, having been momentarily released from Tartarus when Ouranos was ousted, have been cast down again. Ouranos has apparently disappeared from the scene; at least he no longer appears in the stories. Before he disappeared, however, he prophesied that one of Cronos' sons would some day surpass Cronos himself. Hoping to avoid that prophecy, Cronos took each one of his children as soon as they were born — for he had married his sister **Rhea** — and swallowed them. For each of five years Rhea bore him a child and huge Cronos consumed each one of the five. Rhea was becoming more and more distressed and angry. Consequently, when she realized that she was ready to give birth to another child, she devised a stratagem. She sneaked off to Crete and gave birth to her sixth child in secret. She then entrusted that child to two Nymphs of the region, the Meliae, Adrasta and Ida, who cared for it in a deep cave and brought it up; the baby was fed by a goat; armed guards, called the Curetes, protected the entrance to that cave and clashed their weapons whenever the baby cried so that Cronos might not be able to hear the sounds and become suspicious.

Rhea then returned to Cronos. Realizing that she had had the child, he immediately demanded that she hand it over to him. But she gave him a stone the size of a baby, carefully wrapped in swaddling clothes. Not being very perceptive, he gulped down the rock just as he had gulped down his former five offspring and never gave the matter a second thought.

Meanwhile Rhea's newest son was thriving in Crete, having grown up very rapidly, as is the way with gods. His name was **Zeus**. When he came of age, he went to Metis, his cousin, to obtain advice on how to take vengeance on his father. Metis was the daughter of the Titans Oceanus and Tethys and she was known for her wisdom. She devised a potion which caused Cronos, having been tricked by Rhea into drinking it, to have such stomach trouble that he vomited. And, lo and behold, up from the depths of his belly came the rock and each of his first five children, fully grown, having managed somehow to survive intact inside him during all these years. Their names were Hestia, Demeter, Hera, Hades, and Poseidon.

Needless to say, these five had no affection for their father and they wanted to get rid of him. Hence, they declared war, the great **Titanomachia**, or War between the Titans and the children of Cronos. The battle raged for ten years, the Titans fighting from

4

Mount Othrys and the companions of Zeus from Mount Olympus. Cronos enlisted his fellow Titans and their offspring, putting Atlas at the head of his forces. Zeus led the opposition.

At this time there was a Titan called **Prometheus**, or Foresight, son of the Titan Iapetus, an extremely clever and resourceful being. He had been told by his mother that it would be wit, not physical violence, that would settle this conflict. Consequently, during this battle he tried to give ideas to the Titans, but they had no appreciation for the subtleties of his strategies; rather, they expected that brute strength and force was all that was needed. Prometheus suggested, for instance, that Cronos recall his brothers who had been banished to Tartarus and enlist the aid of these mighty beings. But Cronos refused, perhaps out of native stupidity, perhaps out of pride, perhaps because he feared the power of these creatures.

At any rate, realizing that Cronos had no sense, Prometheus went to Zeus and offered the same advice. Zeus agreed and freed the three Cyclops; they in turn were so grateful that they each gave Zeus a gift to express their appreciation: Brontes the Thunderer gave Zeus thunder; Steropes the Lightning-Hurler gave him lightning; and Arges gave him the thunderbolt. They then gave a gift to the other two males: to Hades they gave a cap which, when worn, made him invisible; and to Poseidon they gave a trident, or three-pronged spear. Then Zeus freed the Hecatoncheires, those hundred-handed, fifty-headed aberrations born of the Earth and the Sky.

Now the tide of battle began to change. Zeus unleashed his wrath, for his heart was filled with rage; lightning and thunder flew everywhere. The Earth shook and screamed from the pain of flames, the forests crackled with fire, all the land and the streams of the Ocean and the Sea boiled. There were wild winds and earthquakes. Hot smoke enveloped the Earth-born Titans, their eyes were blinded by lightning, and thunder deafened them. The Hecatoncheires threw stones, and with their hundred hands they could throw a hundred stones for every one that Cronos could throw, and their volleys were like those of a machine gun. They totally overshadowed the Titans with their barrage.

All this offensive was too much for the Titans. They retreated farther and farther away, until they ended up beneath the Earth in Tartarus, a place as distant from the Earth as the Earth is from the Sky: a piece of metal would take nine days to drop from the Sky to the Earth and another nine days from Earth to Tartarus. Here in Tartarus are the Titans now shut, overcome by the cohorts of Olympian Zeus. Poseidon placed metal gates above them, and a wall surrounds them on all sides; in addition Gyes, Cottus, and Briareus, the fifty-headed ones, loyal to Zeus, guard them. All the Titans, therefore, have now been banished to Tartarus — all except Prometheus, of course, who had been loyal to Zeus, and Atlas, who because of his enormous strength was assigned to hold up the world.

Now that the Titans were disposed of, the three brothers, sons of Cronos, cast lots for the division of the universe: Zeus got the sky, Poseidon the sea, and Hades the Underworld. The earth remained neutral, common ground to all of them.

a. Thus the second great dynasty ends with a restoration of order. This second stage, like the first, still represents one of basic primeval forces of nature. There is still no hint of deity, and the Titanomachia itself sounds very much like violent natural disorders such as volcanos, earthquakes, and storms.

b. What Cronos as a force actually represented to the Greeks is puzzling. It is tempting to assign him some sort of allegorical interpretation, but such a treatment cannot be justified. Either in late Hellenistic or in early Roman times, he was confused, through a false etymology, with the Greek word *chronos,* which means Time. From this confusion came the modern concept of Father Time, that aged creature with a scythe over his shoulder and even now a common symbol of the passing of the old year.

c. There are some curious similarities between various details of these first two dynasties, and many of the motifs appear in other mythologies: (1) the overbearing husband and father, autonomous, peremptory, and dogmatic; (2) the father whose destiny is to be overcome and supplanted by his son; (3) the youngest son rising against the father; (4) the youngest son gaining supremacy over his older brothers; (5) the mother whose maternal instincts are thwarted by her crass consort; (6) the mother who enlists the support of her available offspring to vanquish that consort; (7) the contrast between the crudity of the father and the trickery and subtlety of the mother; (8) the eventual restoration of order.

d. What a reservoir for psychological interpretation these early stories afford: castration, incest, overbearing father figures, sneaky mothers, separation anxieties, patricide, fathers intimidated by sons, sons who hate their fathers, wives who hate their husbands, husbands who are insensitive to their wives, youthful rebellion, fathers disgusted by sons, sons who grow up resenting the father, and even cannibalism.

e. According to some Roman traditions, Cronos, when he was vanquished in the great war, settled in Italy under the name of Saturn and founded a golden age there.

6

f. The following are some of the offspring of the Titans:
  Cronos and Rhea: Hestia, Demeter, Hera, Hades, Poseidon, Zeus
  Hyperion and Theia: the Sun (Helios), the Moon (Selene), the
            Dawn (Eos)
        Clymene?
  Iapetus and Asia?   : Atlas Menoetius, Prometheus, Epimetheus
        Themis?
  Tethys and Oceanus: the rivers of the world
            the Oceanides — i.e., the Daughters of the Ocean,
                among whom are Europa, Metis, Eurynome,
                Asia, Calypso, Tyche, Styx
          the Ocean Nymphs
  Crius and Eurybia: Astaeus, Pallas, Perses
          Astaeus and Dawn: the four winds:
                    Agrestes or Eurus, the East Wind
                    Zephyrus, the West Wind
                    Boreas, the North Wind
                    Notus, the South Wind
                      the stars of the Heavens
  Coeus and Phoebe: Leto, Asteria

7

ZEUS. 4th Century B.C. marble head. *Courtesy, Museum of Fine Arts, Boston.*

CHAPTER II

THE OLYMPIANS

Once the three realms had been determined, the tumultuous times of the Titans quickly gave way to a clearly ordered world. The time of dark, primal forces in violent conflict gave way to the rule of wholly anthropomorphic gods with Zeus as their undisputed leader.

The home of the new generation of gods was Mount Olympus. Rising from a plain between Macedonia and Thessaly, its highest peaks are snow capped throughout the year and often rise through the clouds. It is the highest mountain in Greece and was considered sacred by the ancients; therefore, mortals would never dare to climb it, and its peaks filled them with awe and stimulated their imaginations. There, twelve members of the divine family lived — five children of Cronos: Zeus, Poseidon, Demeter, Hera, and Hestia; and seven of their offspring: Apollo, Hermes, Ares, Hephaistus, Athena, Aphrodite, and Artemis. In Homeric times the identity of the twelve Olympians was clear; however, by the classical period Dionysus was often included as the thirteenth or as a replacement for Hestia. Heracles, according to some later writers, also vied for the thirteenth position. Hades, though one of the sons of Cronos, was never included as one of the Olympians. His realm was beneath the earth.

The gods lived in luxury on Olympus. Hephaistus, the master craftsman, built a palace for Zeus, and in the folds of the mountain he built separate houses for the other members of the divine family. The homes and assembly halls were decorated with gold and silver; the roads were paved with marble. The food of the gods was ambrosia, their drink was nectar, and in their veins flowed ichor rather than blood. They were deathless, and they could never grow old.

While theirs was a life free from want, it was not a life of perpetual harmony. Though immortal, they were not immune to injury and pain both physical and emotional. As in any family, mortal or divine, quarrels and petty feuds were not uncommon. Tempers often flared and jealousies abounded. Brothers and sisters and uncles and aunts struggled against each other for Zeus' favor, and there seldom seems to have been a time when all the Olympians were on speaking terms with each other.

Zeus (Jupiter)

Though the sons of Cronos had divided creation into three equal parts, they did not remain equal in power and majesty. Zeus, the youngest of the brothers, was the undisputed head of the family. On Olympus he was the final judge in disputes among the gods; his anger was feared by all, and his power was limitless among mortals and immortals alike. To the ancients he was the symbol of order and justice and, above all, he upheld the sanctity of the oath.

Zeus always appears in ancient art as a dignified, bearded man in the virile prime of adult life. Often he is clothed from the waist down, and often he holds a scepter or thunderbolt in his hand. In Homer, one of his most distinctive possessions is the aegis. There it appears to be a tasseled garment that could be worn over the shoulders, but it could also be used as a weapon or shield. When Zeus shook it, it caused panic in armies, and when Athena wore it, she took on some of her father's power. It was an embodiment of his authority.

The eagle and the oak tree were sacred to Zeus. At times he was said to take the form of an eagle, and at other times eagles accompanied him. At his sanctuary at Dodona in northern Greece, oracles were given through the rustling of the leaves of a sacred oak tree. The majesty of the eagle and the longevity and strength of the oak made them natural symbols for the most powerful of the gods.

The skies were the specific domain of Zeus. His name literally means "to shine", and he controlled the weather, both as the sender of favorable winds and as cloud gatherer or thunderer. To some he was the sky itself, and his glory was such that mortals could not look on him in his true form. When one of his lovers, the mortal Semele, tricked him into appearing before her in all his splendor, she was instantly destroyed by his brilliance.

Zeus had an insatiable sexual appetite and was a tremendously successful lover with both mortals and immortals. Even before he assumed his place as ruler on Olympus, he had begun his conquests with Metis, the daughter of Oceanus and Tethys. But when Zeus' grandmother, Gaia, recognized his intentions toward Metis, she warned him that an offspring from that union was destined to oust him as ruler of the gods just as he had ousted Cronos and as Cronos had ousted Ouranos. Determined to foil this prophecy, Zeus swallowed the pregnant Metis before she could give birth to their child. Yet the child continued to grow inside him and when it came to term, it burst fully armed from his head as the goddess Athena. Having thus been born without a mother, Athena became one of Zeus' most beloved and loyal offspring.

Themis was Zeus' second mate, and she bore him the Horae, the Fates (Moirae), Order, Justice (Dike), and Peace (Eirene). Eurynome was his third, who bore him the Charities. His sister Demeter followed Eurynome and bore him Kore or Persephone. Mnemosyne bore him the Muses, and then Leto succumbed to his charms and bore him Apollo and Artemis.

Each of these romances were brief one-night encounters, and Zeus realized that a man of his position needed a respectable wife as an example for those he ruled. Thus he chose his sister Hera, the patron of marriage and childbirth, to be his spouse. But Hera was not an easy conquest. Though she clearly wanted him, she realized that she would be far more valued if she played hard to get.

After much frustration, Zeus finally devised a ploy by which to conquer his newest love. One day, when he knew that she was wandering alone on a mountain in Argolis on the Peloponnesus, he brought a storm to the mountain and transformed himself into a cuckoo bird. When Hera took shelter, he flew down to her and dropped exhausted onto her lap. She felt sorry for the poor shivering bird and covered it with her robes to warm it. Finding himself just where he wanted to be, Zeus transformed himself back to his normal form. Hera tried to resist him, but once he promised to marry her, she gave in.

Though properly married, Zeus continued to have many affairs with mortals and goddesses alike. Hera, the epitome of propriety, found her husband's philandering disgusting and devoted much of her energy to foiling his plans and, when that failed, to punishing his lovers.

a. The Olympian gods, as we know them, clearly evolved over a long period of time, well before the age of Homer and Hesiod, and were the end result of hundreds of years of blending and borrowing. Invading tribes brought their own gods with them and, in time, fused them with local divinities. Increased trade and travel brought new gods to the attention of the Greeks, and traits and stories were unabashedly borrowed.

b. One of the most complicated issues in the story of Greek mythology is the movement from the matriarchal to the patriarchal perspective — from a dominant mother goddess, whose realm is the earth and who embodies fertility, to a dominant male, sky god who embodies vast powers above the earth. We will see the importance of this change both in the transformation of older fertility goddesses into virgin huntresses and warriors, such as Artemis and Athena, and in the conquest of sacred places by Olympian males who expel earlier earth goddesses, such as Apollo's expulsion of the earth goddess from Delphi.

c. According to some accounts, notably Homer's, Zeus married Hera before his other exploits. The Greeks had some trouble in making his various wives fit into acceptable myths. Zeus, as the embodiment of order and justice, had to be monogamous, as the society of the Greeks was unequivocally monogamous. Yet, from early, unrecorded times, each of these divine conquests was, at one time or another, called his wife. Ultimately the conclusion seems to have been that unfaithfulness is better than polygamy.

d. Zeus' many lovers seem to fall into two groups. First, many of them were early fertility goddesses who, of necessity, mated with the sky god. Second, many of them were mortals who produced offspring who were founders of cities, families, or clans.

e. Important cities and, later, important families felt the need to trace their ancestry back to a god. This process continued into the nineteenth century of our era, with royal families in Europe tracing their ancestry back to Aeneas, the son of Aphrodite and Anchises. In a similar way, the Stuart kings of England traced their ancestry back to the figure of Banquo.

Hera (Juno)

Hera's central position in Greek mythology is a result more of her role as divine consort of Zeus and of her ritual connection with female life than it is of the stories associated with her. While she was the patron and guardian of marriage and childbirth, her marriage was, by any standard, an unhappy one. She was in constant conflict with Zeus and spent much of her time fuming over his extra-marital affairs. She was most creative when she was trying to foil his endeavors or to seek revenge afterwards. Sex to her was a duty or a means toward an end, while to Zeus it was a great pleasure.

At times Hera could be crudely brutal as she sought revenge. At other times she could be cleverly subtle. Matching her wits with Zeus', she could often manipulate him to pursue the course of action she wanted. Homer tells the story of one particular occasion during the Trojan War when she tricked him into sleeping with her so that Poseidon could turn the tide of the war against the Trojans. At times Zeus would take no more of her nagging and jealousy. Sometimes he beat her, and on one occasion he even hung her from Olympus with anvils tied to her feet.

Though she promoted fecundity in others, Hera had only three children of her own: Hebe, Ares, and Hephaistus. Hebe was the cupbearer of the gods until Zeus replaced her with the beautiful youth Ganymede. As goddess of youth, Hebe was known for her beauty and was sometimes given the epithet "the fair ankled one." Eventually she became the wife of Heracles when he was admitted to the ranks of the Olympians. Ares was the most warlike and most hated of the Olympians, and Hephaistus was the master craftsman. By some accounts, Hera produced Hephaistus without male help as an angry response to Athena's birth from Zeus. Eileithyia, goddess of childbirth, was also sometimes said to be a daughter of Hera, but other traditions say that Hera and Eileithyia were one and the same person.

In ancient art, Hera almost always appears as a stately, fully mature woman. She is always robed and often has a scepter in her hand and wears a wreath or a crown on her head. In literature she is often referred to with the epithet "cow eyed" or "ox eyed." The cow, as a symbol of fertility, is associated with her, as is the peacock and the pomegranate.

> a. Hera was definitely a pre-fertility goddess; her realm was probably the fertility of humans rather than the fertility of the earth. She is a good example of a major female gooddess who, in the evolution of a male-dominated hierarchy, loses her prestige and takes a back seat to the man.

> b. Her marriage to Zeus almost seems to be the attempt of early story tellers of myth to make a symbolic union of the ideas of marriage and order.

Poseidon (Neptune)

When the three sons of Cronos drew lots to divide the universe among themselves, Poseidon received the seas. Though he too had a dwelling on Olympus, his most splendid residence was a palace beneath the Aegean Sea. When he drove his horse-drawn chariot across the waters, its wheels barely touching the crests of the waves, the creatures of the deep accompanied him and bowed before his majesty.

He was a mighty god. When in anger he stormed down the slopes of Olympus, the earth shook, and Hades himself feared that the earth might split, exposing his realm to the heavens. Yet, mighty as Poseidon was, he had little of the power that his brother Zeus commanded. He might rage and stamp and shake the earth, but he would always remain subservient to Zeus. His physical strength paled before the wisdom and authority of his younger brother.

Poseidon's realm included fresh waters as well as salt seas, and he was also the god of horses. White caps racing across an angry sea were sometimes called "white horses" by the ancients. The bull too was often associated with Poseidon, and as "earth shaker" he was responsible for earthquakes. When Hippolytus fled from the false accusations of his step-mother Phaedra, it was to Poseidon that Theseus prayed for revenge, and it was through the bull and the shaking of the earth that Hippolytus was destroyed.

Ancient artists made little distinction between Poseidon and Zeus when they painted or sculptured representations of them. Both appear as bearded adults in the prime of life. Poseidon has one distinctive possession, however, that usually allows him to be identified. While Zeus often holds a thunderbolt in one hand, Poseidon holds his trident, a long-handled, three-pronged fork.

Though no god could equal Zeus in amorous exploits, Poseidon tried, but he was usually unsuccessful in his attempts. Once he fell in love with his sister Demeter when she was mournfully seeking her daughter Persephone. Needless to say, a grieving mother is not interested in sexual overtures, and Demeter tried bravely to escape Poseidon's advances. Fleeing to Arcadia, she turned herself into a mare and grazed in a field with other mares. Poseidon figured out what she had done, turned himself into a stallion, and had her there. Demeter's anger at the rape was famous with the ancients, and at times she was called "the Fury" because of it. The offspring of this union was the fabulous, black-maned horse, Arion.

When Poseidon decided to settle down to married life, he chose the nymph **Amphitrite** to be his wife. Unfortunately she found him repulsive and fled to Atlas, or in some versions to Oceanus, at the far reaches of the world to escape him. But Poseidon was persistent and after much pleading and bargaining, he finally persuaded her to accept him, and she was escorted back to the Aegean by a school of dolphins. Aside from being Poseidon's wife, Amphitrite does not play much of a role in mythology, and when she does appear, she is usually seen as a personification of the sea.

The only important offspring resulting from the union of Poseidon and Amphitrite was **Triton**. Man from the waist up, fish from the waist down, Triton was the original "merman." Blowing on his conch shell, he signalled the beginning and the end of storms. Originally a single creature, Triton was conceived of as a type in later times. Hellenistic and Renaissance representations of Poseidon often have him surrounded by Tritons and Nereids.

Proteus was another of Poseidon's company. Often called "old man of the sea," he tended Poseidon's seals. He spent his mornings in the sea, and during the afternoons he slept in a cave with his seals. He could foresee the future but he was very elusive. He would

14

use every trick at his disposal — and there were many — to evade anyone who wanted to consult with him, and the only way to get an answer from him was to sneak up upon him as he slept and hold him down, even as he changed his shape from water to beast to fire. Finally, if the petitioner held on long enough, Proteus would return to his normal shape and give an answer.

After his marriage, Poseidon continued to try to have affairs, and Amphitrite became another of the jealous wives of the Olympians. He was successful with Medusa, from whose trunk, after Perseus had decapitated her, the winged horse Pegasus and the giant Chrysaor sprang. Another of his lovers was the nymph Thoosa, who bore him the Cyclops Polyphemus. Odysseus' blinding of Polyphemus provoked Poseidon's anger and led to many of the problems the Greek hero had in returning to Ithaca after the Trojan War. Gaia later bore him Antaeus, who was killed in a wrestling match with Heracles. The vainly handsome giant Orion was yet another of Poseidon's offspring.

Nothing seemed to work out right for Poseidon, and both he and his offspring are usually characterized as violent and ill-tempered. Yet, in spite of his violence and quarrelsomeness, he still wanted to be accepted and worshipped by mortals, and many myths describe his efforts toward this end. Attica in particular attracted him. Once he entered into competition with Athena to be patron divinity of that region. Both of the gods were to give a gift, and the gifts were then to be judged. Poseidon struck a rock on the Acropolis with his trident, and a spring of salt water gushed out. Athena presented an olive tree, and immediately she won the competition with her far more useful gift, for the olive was to become one of the staples of the Greek economy. Poseidon was a poor loser and, in anger, flooded the Thriasin plain outside of Athens.

At one time, Poseidon was involved with several other gods and goddesses in a plot to overcome Zeus. The attempt was unsuccessful and, as punishment, both Apollo and Poseidon were required to serve King Laomedon of Troy for one year. During that year they built the walls of Troy, but when they had completed the task, Laomedon refused to pay the agreed-upon price. As a result, Poseidon firmly allied himself with the Greeks during the Trojan War.

a. Poseidon is an excellent example of a god who came to Greece with early invaders and took on new attributes and characteristics necessary in a new environment and social climate. He was originally "the earth shaker," the god of horses, and "the earth surrounder," probably the spouse of an early fertility goddess. Inland people could not conceive of the seas and thus had no mythology of the sea. Poseidon's role as a sea god is clearly a later addition. He gradually superseded Pontus, the earlier god of the Mediterranean, who faded into a vague and unimportant divinity. Poseidon's unions with Demeter and Gaia are reminiscent of his earlier role as a land god.

b. Ancient artists had a difficult time distinguishing between the physical appearance of Zeus and Poseidon. The best example of this problem is the life-size bronze statue in the National Museum in Athens, of which there is a copy in the lobby of the United Nations building in New York. The god stands naked, with his left arm cocked, ready to throw — what? — a thunderbolt or a trident. Scholars still aren't agreed on who the god is.

c. Though Poseidon was rejected as the patron divinity of Athens, he was still worshipped there as an important god, and even today one can be shown the marks of his trident on the rocks in the Erectheion on the Acropolis. He shared that temple with Erectheus, a legendary founder of Athens, in ancient times.

Demeter (Ceres)

As "bringer of seasons" and "giver of good gifts," Demeter was one of the most important divinities in the lives of men. Where her sister Hera was instrumental in human fertility, Demeter controlled the fertility of the land — at times she was even envisioned as the embodiment of the fecund earth. When angered, she could keep the seeds hidden and bring dreadful suffering through famine to man. When happy, she could cover the whole earth with leaves and flowers and long ears of corn.

Demeter's most important offspring was **Persephone,** or Kore, a result of her union with Zeus. Zeus secretly promised their brother Hades that he could have Persephone as his bride. So when she had matured into a beautiful girl, Hades came to claim her; but, since Demeter knew nothing of the arrangement with Zeus, he had to take her by stealth. He knew that Persephone often spent her days outside picking flowers and running through the fields; therefore, he prevailed upon Gaia to sprout a magnificent flower, like no other flower that had ever existed. When Persephone saw the flower, she was struck by its beauty and approached it. As she drew near, however, the earth opened up and Hades caught her in his chariot and swooped her away to his realm underground.

Later, when Demeter went to look for her daughter, she could find no trace of the girl. Distraught, Demeter went into deep mourning and scoured the earth for a trace of her daughter. Night and day she wandered on, holding flaming torches in both her hands. Disguised as an ancient woman, she passed through many fields and towns in her search. When finally she came to Eleusis outside of

16

Athens, she sat down by a well. Having come for water, the daughters of Celeus, lord of Eleusis, found her there and, impressed by the old woman's wisdom, they brought her to their father's house. There, Metaneira, Celeus' wife, also recognized the wisdom of the old crone, and she entrusted her youngest child, Demophon, to her. Demeter, maintaining her disguise, doted over her charge, anointing him with ambrosia each day. Each night she buried him in the heart of the fire on her hearth to burn away his mortality. But one night Metaneira discovered Demeter in the midst of this process and in horror demanded that the old nurse stop. Demeter was furious at the mother's lack of faith and, dropping the still mortal child, she revealed her true identity and rushed from the house. In some versions of the story Demophon was consumed by the fire when his mother interfered with the goddess. Later, after her fury had cooled, Demeter commanded that the Eleusinians build a temple to her and establish rites in her honor and she taught her mysteries to Triptolemus, Polyxeinos, and Diocles.

Through Hecate, a divinity who had heard the screams of Persephone when she was abducted, and the rather vain and lackadaisical Helios, the Sun who sees all, Demeter finally learned what had happened to her daughter, and she brought famine to the earth, announcing that she would neither return to Olympus nor allow the earth to bring forth crops until her daughter was returned to her. This would bring death to humans and in turn would deprive the Olympians of the sacrifices they so dearly loved. The gods sent Iris, the messenger, to plead with Demeter to change her mind, but she was adamant. Thus, the god Hermes was sent by Zeus to try to work out an agreement with Hades. He found Hades in the Underworld in his palace, sitting on one of his couches with Persephone, but there was no joy. The girl had no love for Hades and she missed her mother and all the joys of the earth. Hades listened to Hermes, and knowing the power of his brother Zeus, he agreed to release the girl. But he was unable to bear the thought of losing her forever, so he gulled her into eating seeds of a pomegranate. Having thus eaten of the fruit of the Underworld, she could never be wholly free. Consequently, Hermes returned to Demeter with a compromise solution. Persephone would spend one third of each year with Hades, during which time the earth would be fruitless, and she would spend two thirds of the year with her mother and the other gods, during which time the crops would be grown and the fruits would flourish.

At another time Demeter had a brief affair with Iasion, the giant son of Zeus and Electra. During the marriage feast for Cadmus

17

and Harmonia, she gave way to her passions and lay with him in a thrice-plowed, fallow field. When the two returned to the feast with mud on their clothes, Zeus understood what had happened and, embarrassed by his sister's indiscretion, he destroyed Iasion with a thunderbolt. Demeter, however, was already pregnant, and the offspring of this coupling was Plutus, the god of wealth, particularly the wealth within the earth: its mineral fertility.

a. Demeter appears to have been one of the few original gods of mainland Greece who retained her primacy. She was clearly not brought in by the invaders from the North.

b. The story of Demeter's search for Persephone was an integral part of one of the most important mystery cults of the ancient Greek world, the Eleusinian mysteries. Initiation into the mysteries at the sanctuary in Eleusis must have carried with it the promise of some form of life after death, though the actual details of the initiation were one of the best kept secrets of the ancient world.

Hestia (Vesta)

The three daughters of Cronos were, with the exception of Demeter and her brief indiscretion with Iasion, models of womanly virtue. Of the three, Hestia was by far the most virtuous. After the war with the Titans, both Apollo and Poseidon sought her hand; yet she vehemently refused both of them. Rather, she turned to her brother Zeus and, touching his head with her hand, swore an oath that she would remain a virgin forever. Zeus, the embodiment of the male chauvinist double standard, congratulated her on her decision, and as a reward he made the center of the house sacred to her and commanded that the first offerings of sacrifices be given to her.

Thus Hestia became the protectress of the home and of domestic life in general. As a logical extension of this, she became the protectress of public buildings and even of the state. Her name simply means "hearth."

First born of Cronos — and last born in that the first were regurgitated last — she was truly the spinster aunt of the Olympians. She never left Olympus but was content to spend her days in her family's home, taking care of domestic duties and trying to keep the peace among her more aggressive brothers and sisters and nephews and nieces. According to some late writers, she gave up her position as one of the twelve Olympians so that the newcomer, Dionysus, could take her place.

a. In ancient art Hestia was seldom represented in anthropomorphic form. It seems that she was regarded as the embodiment of the hearth and the home itself, and even of the fire on the hearth. Of the Olympians she is the least mentioned in myths.

b. In the *Homeric Hymn to Hestia* she is associated with Hermes, but the nature of the association is not clear. The *Homeric Hymn to Hermes* attributes the invention of the kindling of fire to him, and perhaps this is the connection.

Apollo

Second only to his father Zeus in splendor and power, Apollo was the embodiment of male beauty and of the essence of civilization. He was the interpreter of his father's will to men and, as such, was the giver of many of the constitutions of the city states throughout Greece. He was the god who supervised purification for blood guilt and on his temple at Delphi were carved the sayings "know thyself" and "nothing in excess." Moderation was his byword. Though concerned with mortals' behavior, he was to them the most distant of the Olympians. He was the "far shooter." He was the champion of no mortal in particular and was the patron of no particular city or group of cities. He was always a bachelor and his various amorous pursuits were almost always ill-fated. He was truly close only to his mother Leto and to his twin sister Artemis.

Apollo was the son of Zeus and Leto, the daughter of the Titans Coeus and Phoebe. When Hera heard of the affair, she was typically furious and sent word to all places on earth not to accept the pregnant Leto, who wandered from place to place trying to find a spot to bear her children. Finally Leto convinced the floating island, Ortygia, later identified as Delos, to shelter her, promising that her offspring would make the barren island sacred and wealthy. All of the goddesses came down to be with Leto in her labor — except for Hera and Eileithyia, who aided in childbirth and whom Hera had managed to keep from knowing of Leto's imminent labor. The assembled goddesses, taking pity on Leto, sent the messenger Iris to bribe Eileithyia if necessary with a splendid necklace. She came and immediately Leto, hanging onto a palm tree, was delivered of twins. Artemis, the first born, helped in the delivery of her brother, Apollo.

Leto did not nurse Apollo in the normal, maternal fashion, but rather Themis wrapped him in white cloth and a gold band and fed him nectar and ambrosia. Within minutes, Apollo outgrew his swaddling, burst the golden band, and claimed the curved bow and

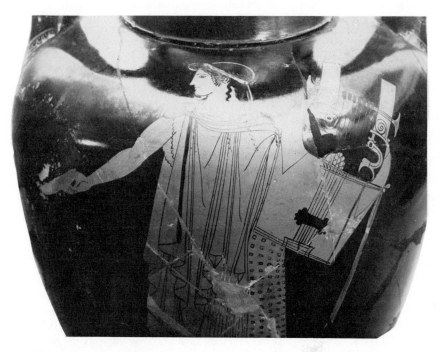

APOLLO. Attic Red-Figured Vase by the Providence Painter, 5th Century B.C. In Attic Red-Figured vase paintings, Apollo almost always appears as a young adult and holds either a lyre or a bow. *Courtesy, Museum of Art, Rhode Island School of Design; gift of Mrs. Gustave Radeke.*

the lyre as his own. Then he promised always to tell mankind of the will of his father.

The perpetually frustrated Hera was still determined to punish Leto, even after she had been delivered of her children. Thus she encouraged the giant **Tityus,** son of Gaia, to rape her. Tityus was willing, but when he made his attempt, Apollo heard his mother scream and, rushing to her aid, he killed Tityus with his arrows. In some traditions Artemis helped him. At any rate, Zeus was outraged at Tityus' attempt on Leto and consigned him to Tartarus where two vultures endlessly devour his liver.

Apollo's most trusted friends were the **Hyperboreans,** a sacred race of beings who lived beyond the north wind and were free from disease and old age. Each year, usually during the winter months, Apollo escaped from the world of the Olympians and went to live with them.

In need of a place where he might establish his oracle to convey to mortals the will of Zeus, Apollo wandered across the earth. When he came to Crisa, the ancient Delphi, he knew that he had found the proper place. But Crisa was controlled by the monster **Python**, a female, snakelike dragon. Apollo fought with Python, finally destroying her with his arrows. As a result, however, blood guilt was on his hands and he had to purify himself by going to the Vale of Tempe. Because of this episode he is sometimes given the epithet "the Pythian."

After having purified himself, Apollo returned to Delphi, but he realized that he couldn't establish an oracle unless he had priests to administer it. One day he became aware of a Cretan ship from Cnossus sailing in the Aegean. Turning himself into a dolphin, he swam to the ship and jumped onto its deck. The terrified sailors tried to throw the mighty fish overboard, but after many unsuccessful attempts they realized that it must represent some divine will. Still on deck in dolphin form, Apollo directed the ship up the coast of the Peloponnesus and into the Gulf of Corinth. The sailors beached the boat just below Delphi and the fish leaped from the ship like a shooting star and vanished. Soon, Apollo returned to the sailors in the form of a handsome youth. He revealed his true identity to them and commanded them to become the keepers of his sanctuary, which they did.

Apollo was unsuccessful in most of his love affairs. Though he was the epitome of physical perfection in a male — and fell in love with several males as well as females — his affairs almost always ended in disappointment. One affair that came close to being fulfilling was with the mortal Coronis. She accepted his love and they were happy — until Apollo learned that she also had a mortal lover, Ischys of Arcadia. Humiliated at being upstaged by a mortal, the furious Apollo sent his sister Artemis to destroy the fickle girl. But then, when the initial anger had passed, he realized how much he did love Coronis, and he tried to stop his order; it was too late. Heartbroken, he went to the corpse of his lover and realized that their child was still alive in her womb. He rescued the child and gave it to the centaur Chiron, whom he ordered to be its guardian. The child, **Asclepius**, grew up under Chiron's watchful eye and learned from him the art of medicine. In time Asclepius excelled everyone else on earth in his ability to cure. Whoever was suffering from sores or from wounds or from broken limbs or from disease came to him and he used balms, herbs, and even surgery. Ultimately, however, he overstepped his bounds and began reviving the dead. Zeus was outraged at this. A mortal was performing a feat that was the exclusive prerogative of the immortal gods. The ancients had a word for such actions; they called it **hybris** and it almost always brought about the mortal's fall. To punish Asclepius for his hybris, Zeus threw down a thunderbolt and killed him. But Apollo, when he learned what had happened to his son, was so angry that as a revenge he killed the Cyclops who provided Zeus with thunderbolts. As a result, however, Apollo had blood guilt on his hands again. This time, to purify himself of his guilt, he indentured himself to Admetus, King of Pherae in Thessaly, and served as a shepherd for nine years. Admetus treated him so well that at the end of the nine years Apollo wanted to give the kindly king a gift. Thus he went to the Fates and, learning from them that the king's death was imminent, he convinced them to let someone else die in his place.

Apollo had a vicious temper and often sought brutal revenge for offenses. At one time the mortal **Niobe**, daughter of Tantalus, carelessly bragged that she, with her seven sons and seven daughters, was better than Leto, who had only one of each. Apollo with Artemis responded to this hybris by destroying with their arrows all of her children.

On another occasion the satyr **Marsyas** foolishly challenged Apollo to a music contest. Marsyas had found the flute discarded by Athena. The goddess had invented this instrument, but when she had realized how silly she looked playing it — her cheeks all puffed up — she threw it away in disgust. Apollo agreed to the contest with the stipulation that the victor might do what he liked to the vanquished. When Marsyas lost, Apollo had him flayed alive. In another musical contest, Apollo defeated Pan and punished one of the judges who had dissented, King Midas, by giving him the ears of an ass.

Apollo was one of the first gods to be anthropomorphically represented in Greek sculpture. In both classical sculpture and painting he came to be seen as the ideal male figure, the model of physical perfection. In sculpture he is always beardless, and he is usually fully grown, yet not having lost the suppleness and beauty of youth. In paintings he usually holds either a lyre or a bow.

While Apollo was the avowed enemy of barbarism, he was never a friendly god. As god of medicine, he was the healer, but he was also "the destroyer" and the god of pestilence. He was the protector of flocks but he was also the "wolf god." He was the god of athletes, of music and of poetry.

a. Among scholars there is considerable difference of opinion as to the origins of Apollo. Some trace him from Asia Minor; others bring him down from the North with the early invaders. There is general agreement, however, that Leto, Artemis, and Apollo were originally unconnected divinities and only came together as an amalgam of the Greek mythic genius.

ATHENA TRIES THE FLUTE. South Italian Red-Figured Vase, 4th Century B.C. Athena, sitting on her aegis, has just invented the flute and is trying it out. A young man holds a mirror for her and she is about to see how silly she looks. To the left of her, Marsyas is intrigued by the new invention and will pick it up with disastrous consequences when she discards it. To the far right a satyr, and to the far left a maenad, holding a thyrsus, watch. Behind Athena, a shepherd looks on. *Courtesy, Museum of Fine Arts, Boston.*

b. The details of the birth of Apollo and Artemis differ from version to version, but the core of the story always remains essentially the same: Hera's antipathy — Leto's wandering — delivery on a barren island.

c. There has been a great deal of speculation as to who the Hyperboreans were — whether wholly mythic or based in some degree on fact. It is clear that even the ancients weren't sure what the answer to this question was.

d. There are many versions of Apollo's conquest of Delphi. In one version he kills Python because she had, before his birth, harrassed Leto. In other versions there seems to be some confusion between Python and Typhon, another serpent. What is clear is that Apollo took over an already established sacred spot and that he took it over from an earth goddess, probably Gaia or Themis. Archeological evidence confirms that the site was originally sacred to an earth goddess. The change from female to male is a process we have seen before − cf. the discussion of Hera.[1]

e. In classical times Delphi was the most important oracle in Greece. It was neutral ground − i.e., it belonged to no political unit − and was open to people from all city states and countries. Through a *pythia,* or a woman priestess, and a priest of Apollo, the will of Zeus was communicated to men. Delphi had tremendous impact over the centuries in influencing decisions about war, colonization, and politics. Delphi was also the site of the Pythian Games, one of the four major athletic contests in ancient Greece. The games were said to be started as a memorial to Python.

f. One of Apollo's most important functions was in removing or purifying pollution brought about by blood guilt. In historic times he seems to stand for a civilizing process here. Where blood guilt originally required vengeance from kin, in later times the process became a legal one that could be settled by the Areopagus. Aeschylus' final play in the Orestes Trilogy, *The Eumenides,* clearly shows this change.

g. In some versions of the story of Asclepius' raising of the dead, Hades complained to Zeus that, if Asclepius continued, his domain would be threatened. In other versions the final outrage came when Asclepius was said to have taken payment for raising the dead.

h. In some myths about Asclepius, Apollo removed him to the heavens as a star after he had been destroyed by Zeus. While Asclepius was clearly a mortal in Homer, he later took on the characteristics of a god. His most important sanctuary was at Epidaurus where archeologists have uncovered hundreds of testimonials to wonderful cures that took place there. The Romans embraced him as the god of healing in the third century B.C., perverting his name to Asculepius.

i. Apollo was not "god of the sun." While some ancient and medieval philosophers seemed to make a metaphorical association between Apollo's brilliance and the sun, there is little or no basis in ancient mythological sources for making this association.

1. See page 13, note (a) and page 11, note (b).

Artemis (Diana)

Artemis, Apollo's twin sister, was first and foremost the virgin huntress who roamed through sacred groves and forests accompanied by a band of nymphs, her devoted companions. But she was more than that, and often her attributes are apparently contradictory. Even in her most common guise, these contradictions begin to emerge. While she was devoted to the young of both animals and humans, she was also the patroness of hunting and took particular delight in hunting deer. While she was a fanatic virgin, she was also a patroness of childbirth. While the woods were her home, she was also a watcher of harbors. Often gentle, she could also be remarkably cruel, as we will see in the stories of Actaeon and Callisto.

The daughter of Zeus and Leto, she was born with Apollo on Delos as we have already seen.[1] As a child she asked her father to allow her to remain a maiden, to give her arrows and a bow, and to give her nymphs as her companions, requests that Zeus happily granted. In addition, she sought out the finest hounds to join her in the hunt. Of her followers, nymphs and mortals alike, she demanded a vow of absolute chastity. Hippolytus, in Euripides' play of that name, says that the chastity demanded by Artemis is more than something learned or something abstained from but is in the very heart of the follower.

The nymph Britomartis on Crete was one of Artemis' favorite companions. When King Minos happened to see the beautiful nymph one day, he fell madly in love with her and was determined to have her. The nymph fled in groves and under bushes while for nine months Minos searched for her. Finally he found her at the top of a cliff from which there was no escape. Rather than break her vow of chastity, however, Britomartis threw herself from the cliff into the sea, where she was caught in a fisherman's net and saved. In some versions her flight from Minos does not end there, but Minos follows her to Aegina. There she successfully foils him and becomes worshipped by the people of Aegina as Aphaia.

Another of Artemis' favorites was **Callisto,** daughter of Lycaon, king of Arcadia. She too had sworn an oath of chastity. When Zeus happened to see her one day, he was taken by her beauty but particularly by her vigor. She was not one of those girls who sit at home preening themselves and weaving and spinning; she was an active girl, a warrior and a huntress. Zeus was determined to have her and he devised a strategy. Turning himself into a likeness of Artemis, he approached the girl as she was returning from a successful hunt.

1. See page 19.

ARTEMIS AND ACTAEON. Attic Red-Figured vase by the Pan Painter 5th
Century B.C. Actaeon has seen Artemis bathing and is now being punished;
his dogs, driven mad by the goddess, are in the process of devouring him.
Though most versions of the myth say that he was first turned into a stag,
this artist has not chosen to represent this. Artemis, as a patron of the wild,
wears a fawn skin over her shoulders. *Courtesy, Museum of Fine Arts, Boston.*

When she showed the disguised god her catch, he kissed her and then hugged her. But there was something unmaidenly about the embrace, and as he continued to hold her she began to realize that this was not Artemis but that she was being deceived. She struggled to free herself, but Zeus had his will. Disgraced, Callisto tried to hide the fact from Artemis, but several months later, when they were returning from a particularly tiring hunt, Artemis suggested that they bathe. The girl demurred, but Artemis insisted, and when the nymphs stripped off Callisto's clothes, it was clear what had happened. In fact, she was nearly ready to deliver a son, Arcas, the future king of Arcadia. The furious Artemis would listen to no explanation and banned Callisto forever from her company. Hera, jealous that her husband would still find the girl attractive after she had delivered Arcas, turned her into a bear. According to some versions of the story, Hera then convinced Artemis to shoot the bear.

Artemis could be remarkably cruel and unfeeling. While she was gentle to males who devoted themselves wholly to her, she was vicious with those who crossed her, even if the crossing was unintentional. **Actaeon,** the son of Autone and Aristaeus of Thebes, had been raised by the Centaur Chiron to be a hunter. One day, returning from a hunt, he lost his way and, hot and tired, came upon a large cave from which he could hear the bubbling of a stream. Unfortunately, Artemis had chosen that cave as a place to bathe with her nymphs. When he entered the cave, not knowing that there was anyone inside, his eyes fell on the naked goddess. The nymphs tried to hide her with their bodies, but she was so much taller than they were that her naked body showed clearly above them. Outraged, Artemis threw water in the boy's face and turned him into a stag. Then, still angry, she drove his pack of fifty hounds mad so that they attacked their transformed master and devoured him. When another goddess might merely have blinded a mortal who saw her flesh, Artemis destroyed him.

a. Artemis was probably the least "naturalized" of the Olympians. She was probably a pre-Hellenic fertility goddess, an origin that would explain some of the contradictions in her attributes. One of her major temples was at Ephesus, where she was worshipped as a many-breasted deity with clear fertility implications.

b. A later version of the Callisto story tells that Zeus continued to love the girl even after she had been turned into a bear. When one day her son Arcas was out hunting — for he had inherited his mother's interest in the sport — and was about the kill the bear, not realizing that it was his mother, Zeus protected the animal by changing both it and Arcas into neighboring constellations. She, of course, became Ursa Major, the Big Bear.

27

Hermes (Mercury)

Of all the Olympians, Hermes is the most appealing. He alone had a sparkling sense of humor. He did not need to laugh at anyone, as did some of his uncles and cousins; he simply enjoyed laughing. Unlike his more serious brother Apollo, he was amoral. He was a liar and a trickster; yet he was always cheerful, courteous, and kind. He was the patron of traders, but he was also the patron of thieves. He was the guide to travelers, but now and again he took glee in leading them astray. He was the god of luck, but luck goes both ways.

In classical art he usually appears as a late adolescent, somewhat younger and less muscular than his brother Apollo. Often he wears a *petasos,* or broad hat, and carries the *caduceus,* or herald's staff entwined by a male and a female snake. In later art he wears *talaria,* or winged sandals. His beauty is less mature than Apollo's and he was, as such, the patron of young men.

Hermes' mother was the nymph Maia, one of the seven Pleiades, daughters of Atlas and Pleione. Zeus, for once successful in his attempt to elude Hera's jealousy, met with Maia at night in a deep cave on Mount Cyllene in Arcadia. There, safe from the eyes of mortals and immortals alike, they took their pleasure and there, after the tenth month of pregnancy, Maia delivered Hermes.

As precocious as, if not more so than, his brother Apollo, Hermes left his cradle on the day he was born. At the mouth of the cave he found a tortoise and, delighted with his discovery, he took it back into his chamber where he cut off its limbs and scooped out its entrails. From the empty shell he created the seven stringed lyre and immediately sang a song of his own begetting. Then, hungry and looking for a laugh, he wandered from the cave.

Before long he came upon the cattle of his brother Apollo. Selecting fifty cows and leaving the bull behind, the child drove his herd backwards to the sea; furthermore, he created strange shoes for himself so that he couldn't be followed. He then drove the herd, still backwards, to the mouth of the river Alphaeus near Pylos. On the way he passed an old man to whom he promised great blessings if he would keep quiet about what he had seen. Corralling most of the cattle, Hermes chose two which he wrestled to the ground, breaking their necks. Then he cut them up into twelve equal pieces, invented the kindling of fire, and roasted the meat as a sacrifice to the twelve Olympians. But, when he was about to eat, he realized that he couldn't. He was one of the twelve; he was foolishly sacrificing to himself, and the gods never eat meat sacrificed to them; they only savor the smell.

28

At dawn Hermes returned to his cave and jumped into his cradle, assuming the role of a proper baby. But his mother knew all and warned him that his brother would be furious. He practiced his eloquence on her and concluded by warning that, if Apollo gave him a hard time, he would spare no effort in making his life miserable.

Meanwhile, Apollo, having discovered the loss of his cattle, started searching. When he came upon the old man, he asked whether he had seen anything unusual. The old man told everything, and Apollo realized who the culprit was. But because of the confused tracks, he still didn't know where his cattle were. Furious, he went to Maia's cave and searched it from top to bottom while Hermes lay in his cradle acting like a baby. Finally Apollo confronted the child who, again with marvellous eloquence, argued that he couldn't have stolen the cattle because he didn't even know what a cow was. "After all, I'm only a baby." Apollo threatened the child with eternity in Tartarus, and they finally decided to go to father Zeus for arbitration.

Zeus found the whole situation amusing and was particularly tickled by his youngest son's wit and ingenuity; but finally he ordered that Hermes return the cattle. The child had no choice but to obey. When the two brothers arrived at the spot where the herd was hidden, the older one tried to bind the younger one with reeds, but the bindings kept falling off and instantly sprouting in the ground. Then Hermes began to play his lyre, and Apollo was enchanted by the instrument. He had never heard anything like it before. Under the influence of this new music the brothers were reconciled, and Hermes gave Apollo the lyre as a gift. In return, Apollo gave Hermes his shepherd's crook and made him keeper of herds.

Once back on Olympus, Hermes promised never to steal anything from Apollo again and, in return, Apollo gave him his staff, which was to become the caduceus and symbol of Hermes. In addition, he gave the young god some rights to divination, though he warned him not to infringe on his own oracular rights. Zeus made his young son lord of lions and boars and dogs and flocks, and in addition he appointed him messenger to Hades. This final role was to become one of his most important ones — *Hermes psychopompus* (Guide of Souls). He was the god who gently summoned the dying to Hades.

In addition to being Hades' messenger, Hermes took on the general function of messenger of the gods. His primary responsibility was to carry out the will of his father. One story in particular illustrates this function clearly. Zeus had fallen in love with the mortal Io, daughter of the first king of Argos. When Hera found out about the affair. Zeus turned Io into a cow to protect her, but in response Hera made the cow sacred to herself and placed Argus, the hundred-eyed, to be her guardian. At the request of Zeus, Hermes went to free Io. To do this he had to dispatch Argus, which he did by lulling him to sleep and then smashing him with a boulder. Thus Hermes is often referred to as the "slayer of Argus."

Hermes never married and, relative to some of his peers, he had few love affairs. One of his important trysts, however, was with Aphrodite, who bore him a son, **Hermaphroditus**. As his name implies, the child inherited characteristics of both the mother and the father, especially their beauty. For protection, he was sent to a cave on Mount Ida where he was brought up by Naiads, nymphs of the area. When he was fifteen, Hermaphroditus left Ida to see the world. He traveled extensively and one day, in the land of the Carians, he came to a beautiful pool, surrounded by green grass.

The pool was the home of the nymph Salmacis. She of all the nymphs was not a follower of Artemis. She didn't hunt, but rather spent her time grooming herself and bathing. When she saw the beautiful boy, she was instantly overcome by a desire to have him. She presented herself to him and suggested that they make love — but poor Hermaphroditus didn't even know what love was and could only stand and blush. When Salmacis made advances, he was shocked and warned her that he would leave if she didn't stop. The nymph withdrew but hid behind a bush to watch. Hermaphroditus, convinced that she was gone, decided to bathe and when he took off his clothes, Salmacis went wild with passion and jumped into the pool after him. She embraced him and wouldn't let go, no matter how much he struggled. When he kept resisting, she prayed to the gods that they might be as one, and in answer their bodies were united. They became one body with a dual (male/female) nature.

Hermes' one other significant child was **Pan**, who was born to him by the daughter of Dryopes. When the child was born, the nurse was horrified at his goat feet and horns, and she discarded him. Hermes, however, was delighted by his son and brought him to Olympus where all the gods received him happily. Dionysus was particularly pleased by the child's nature. The child was named Pan, the Greek word for "all," because all the gods had accepted him.

a. Hermes clearly went through many transformations on the way to becoming the Olympian we know. While he is definitely associated with primitive Arcadia, we don't know how he got there. We do know that he was from an early time associated with human fertility and with animals, but whether he is a native of Arcadia or was brought there by travelers is a moot point.

30

b. While statues of Hermes usually represent him as a beautiful young male, the god was also represented in other ways. The earliest symbol of the god was either a pile of stones or a stone phallus. Even in fifth century Athens, the epitome of Greek refinement, he was represented in front of houses and public buildings by a *herme* — a stone column with an archaic head on the top and an erect phallus in the center of the column. These herms were considered important and sacred objects.

c. There seem to have been many Pans. Hesiod knows a Pan before the birth of Hermes, and in later times he became a type and there were multiple "Pans."

d. During the Hellenistic Period, Hermaphroditus became a favorite subject in sculpture. He is usually represented sleeping, with female hips, but with the rest of his body primarily male.

e. An extremely perceptive reader will have noticed a contradiction here in how Apollo got his lyre. In the section on "Apollo" he was said to get it at birth.[1] Here he got it from Hermes.

Athena (Minerva)

Athena, daughter of Zeus, was equal to her father in wisdom. Always loyal to him, she was the child he loved most and by giving her his aegis, he shared his authority with her. Athena was self-sufficient and despised the amorous attentions of men. With her sister Artemis and her aunt Hestia, she was one of three immortals who could resist the power of Aphrodite. Her wisdom, both practical and abstract, was her most outstanding strength. While she provided technical knowledge about spinning and weaving, taming horses, and sculpture, she was also conceived by writers and philosophers as the embodiment of wisdom itself — the idea of wisdom.

Though she would be a brilliant warrior when necessary, she preferred to settle issues through councils and, as passion interferes with reasoned decision making, she abhorred it. She was profoundly concerned with the plight of mankind, if not with that of individual men, and the city as an assembly of mortals living peacefully together was her focus.

In classical art, Athena usually appears as a beautiful but stern young woman. She is usually armed with a crested helmet, a shield with a gorgon's head on it, and a long spear in one hand. Sometimes she wears the aegis over her shoulders. Sometimes she also holds a spindle in one hand. The spear and the spindle represent two distinct aspects of her nature. On the one hand she is "the

1. See page 20-21.

Mighty" (*Sthenias*), "the Champion" (*Promachos*) and "the Warlike" (*Areia*); on the other hand she is goddess of the city (*Polias*), of council (*Bulaia*), and of handicrafts (*Ergane*). She vastly preferred peace and only resorted to war when it was necessary to restore peace. Consequently, she was an arch-foe of Ares, who reveled in war for its own sake. She was one of the most moral and righteous of the Olympians.

Athena had a unique birth. Having swallowed the pregnant Metis after being warned that her offspring would take his place as lord of heaven, Zeus gave birth to Athena through his head. When she was full term, Zeus summoned Hephaistus who, with his axe, split the Thunderer's skull. Out of the crack leaped Athena, fully armed in flashing gold, shouting mightily and shaking her spear. Olympus shook as she emerged; Ouranos and Gaia trembled before her; the sea churned and foamed; an awe-struck Helios stopped his chariot in midcourse when he saw her.

Two of Helios' mortal sons, at the prompting of their father, climbed to the highest point on the island of Rhodes to offer the new goddess her first sacrifice. When they got to the site of the sacrifice, they realized that in their haste to be the first, they had forgotten one thing — the fire with which to burn the offerings. Zeus, recognizing their problem and their good intentions, brought a yellow cloud over them that rained down gold. Athena later rewarded them with the gift of art: from that point on their sculptures would be life-like. This gift was passed on, and Rhodes became a center of sculpture in the ancient world.

Athena was sent to Triton for her upbringing. Triton's daughter **Pallas** and the young goddess became closest of friends and spent much time together practicing the art of war. One day, however, they quarreled and began to fight with their weapons in earnest. Zeus observed what was happening and at one point, when Pallas was about to strike a dangerous blow, he dropped down his aegis in front of her. Startled, the mortal girl looked up and, taking advantage of the pause, Athena struck her with a staggering blow. When Pallas died of her wound, Athena was overcome by grief at the loss of her friend and carved a likeness of the girl out of wood. She wrapped her aegis around it, set it up by Zeus, and paid homage to it, calling it the Palladium.[1] Later, in a moment of anger, Zeus threw it from Olympus. It landed in Asia Minor where Ilus found it, and taking it as a sign from Zeus, founded Ilium (Troy).

Athena taught women to spin and weave and was herself a master of those arts. One mortal, **Arachne**, a girl from a humble

1. See illustration, page 133.

BIRTH OF ATHENA. Attic Black-Figured Vase, 6th Century B.C. Athena, fully armed, bursts from Zeus' head. Zeus, sitting on his throne, holds thunderbolts in his right hand — it is always intriguing to note how people, who have no idea what thunder and lightning are, visualize a thunderbolt. With his left hand Zeus reaches out to Eileithyia, goddess of childbirth. Behind Zeus, Apollo can be identified by his lyre — in Attic Black-Figured vase painting he is usually bearded, as he is here. To the far left, Hermes can be identified by his winged sandals. To the far right, Ares, soon to become Athena's arch-rival, can be identified by his armor. *Courtesy, Museum of Fine Arts, Boston.*

background in Lydia, gained a wide reputation for her proficiency in the art. Unwisely she went so far as to brag to her friends that she could out-weave and out-embroider even Athena. Surely Athena couldn't let such hybris pass unnoticed, so she came to Arachne disguised as an old woman and advised her that such boasting was foolish and could only get her into trouble. When Arachne would not listen, Athena revealed herself in her true form and took on the challenge. The two went at it at their respective looms. For the subject of her piece, the goddess chose dignified representations of the gods, including the contest between herself and Poseidon for the patronage of Athens.[1] Arachne chose as her subject the various amorous crimes of the gods — rapes and seductions. When they were finished, Athena could find no flaw in the mortal's weaving, but she was outraged at the girl's success and even more so at the subject of her piece; consequently, she struck her again and again on the head. Humiliated, Arachne hanged herself in disgrace. Athena, however, had afterthoughts and taking pity on the girl turned her into a spider so that she might continue to weave.

If Athena was the embodiment of wisdom, she was also the embodiment of virginity. She never once seems to have had an amorous feeling. One of her constant companions was the nymph Charicle, and on one occasion when the two were bathing in a pool, Charicle's son **Tiresias,** a young hunter, came to the pool for a drink, unaware of their presence. His eyes fell on the body of the naked goddess and in anger she blinded him. Charicle, deeply upset at what had happened to her son, pleaded with the goddess, asking that she reconsider her action. But Athena said she had no choice. It is divine law that a mortal may not look on the naked body of a goddess without her consent. As a favor to her friend, however, Athena granted Tiresias the gifts of prophecy and divination, promising him a long life and guaranteeing that he would be able to retain these powers in the next life.

There is another version of how Tiresias lost his sight and gained his powers of prophecy. Having seen snakes copulating and having wounded them, he was turned from a man into a woman. Observing them again several years later, he was turned back into a man. Thus, having experienced both roles, he was called by Hera and Zeus to settle a dispute. Their question was, who gets more pleasure out of sex, the man or the woman. When he answered that a woman gets ten times the pleasure, Hera blinded him — but Zeus gave him the art of soothsaying.

The closest Athena came to actually having an offspring was with Hephaistus, the craftsman of the gods. Once, when he felt that he had lost the affection of his wife, Aphrodite, Athena happened to come to him for some armor. Passion replaced the hurt in his heart, and he tried to persuade Athena to accept his love. When she rejected him and fled, he pursued her, hopping clumsily after her in his lame-

1. See page 15.

ness. He finally managed to catch her, but she continued to resist. In the frenzy of the struggle, he could stand it no longer and his seed spilled onto her thigh. Thoroughly disgusted, Athena wiped it from her thigh with a piece of wool and threw it onto the ground. From Hephaistus' seed **Erichthonius** was conceived, and when he came full term, Gaia gave him to Athena who accepted him as her child.

Later on, Athena put Erichthonius into a chest and gave him to the three daughters of Cecrops — Aglaurus, Herse, and Pandrosus — but warned them that they must not look into the chest. Naturally they did look and, seeing either a child encircled by two snakes or a child that was half snake, they went mad and jumped to their deaths from the Acropolis. Erichthonius went on to become an early king of Athens.

a. Athena was probably something quite different before she evolved into the virgin protectress of civilized life. Many scholars agree that she was originally a pre-Hellenic divinity associated with the Mycenean warrior aristocracy. Her warrior attributes seem to stretch far back in time. There is no agreement as to whether she was always a virgin.

b. In early representations, Athena's virginity and maidenly qualities are stressed. During the fifth century, however, when Athens had assumed a major role in the leadership of Greece, she became more matronly and certainly more aggressive.

c. There are several versions of how Athena managed to get out of her father's head. In some she springs without the help of anyone, in others Hephaistus helps, and in still others either Prometheus or Hermes does the honors.

d. The Triton who is the father of Pallas seems to be a different Triton from the one we've seen as the son of Poseidon and Amphitrite. He may be the personification of a lake and river on the Libyan coast of the Mediterranean.

e. Athena is often called *Pallas*. The story told above is one explanation for this epithet, though it is by no means the only one. In some accounts a winged Pallas is called Athena's father. In others, this Pallas, or another giant named Pallas, tries to violate Athena and she kills him. In still others, Pallas is the son of Pandion, king of Athens and founder of the family of the Pallantidae.

f. Athena is frequently called *Glaukopis*. The translation of this word is difficult and not at all consistent. Sometimes it is rendered "bright-eyed," sometimes "grey-eyed," sometimes as "owl-eyed." The owl, incidentally, was the bird sacred to her.

g. Athena is also called *Tritogenia*. The truth is, no one really knows what this word means, though there is much confident speculation on the subject.

Hephaistus (Vulcan)

The one god on Olympus who did not represent physical perfection was Hephaistus. His feet crippled from birth, he provided the Olympians with a kind of comic relief, for they used to laugh at him as he hobbled from place to place. But he made up for his physical defects with his skill as a craftsman. You will recall that it was Hephaistus who built the houses and palaces on Olympus, who provided armor for the gods, and who assisted at the birth of Athena. He was a gruff, kindly god, whose hearty goodness made him stand out from most of his vain relatives.

Hephaistus' mother was Hera, and he didn't have a father. Furious at Zeus for creating Athena on his own, Hera planned a counter-miracle, and she conceived Hephaistus on her own. But the child she bore was weak and crippled. Humiliated by what she had produced, she threw the child from Olympus. Fortunately he landed in the sea and the sea nymph Thetis took him in and kept him for nine years. During those years he learned and perfected his art, and when, at one point, Hera saw an example of his jewelry, she called him back.

Being now reinstated on Olympus, Hephaistus and his mother were reconciled. On one occasion he tried to intervene in a quarrel between Zeus and his mother, who was being hung from Olympus with anvils on her feet. In a rage Zeus picked him up, and again he was thrown from the sacred mountain, this time landing half-dead on Lemnos, where he was taken in and cared for by the local inhabitants.

Once he did seek revenge for the unkindness so often done to him. His mother had again banished him from Olympus. As an apparent gift, he sent a throne to her, but when she sat on it, she stuck fast and was unable to get up. No one could figure out how to free her from the throne; the gods, therefore, finally sent Ares to Hephaistus as a messenger. When he returned, unsuccessful, Dionysus went, and by getting the smith drunk, he managed to bring him back on a donkey, surrounded by a boisterous collection of satyrs. Still angry, Hephaistus refused to free Hera until he was promised that he could have Aphrodite as his wife. Zeus agreed, but he also required that Hephaistus provide him with many splendid gifts. Needless to say, Aphrodite was not enthusiastic at the prospect of such a husband, and their relationship was never a stable one.

a. Hephaistus probably came to Greece from the East, where he had been a fire god, associated with volcanic activity. His association with Lemnos, once a volcanic island, suggests this past. He was, however, thoroughly Hellenized as the craftsman of the gods.

36

b. Though Aphrodite is usually seen as his wife, sometimes he is said to be the husband of Aglaea, the youngest of the Graces. Sometimes his wife is Charis.

c. Usually Hephaistus is said to have been born with deformed feet, though in some variations he is crippled as a result of his fall from Olympus when thrown by Zeus.

d. Homer definitely put Hephaistus on Olympus, as did most of the Greek writers. Later authors, including Vergil and Callimachus, put the forge underground and the Romans called him Vulcan.

e. Some later authors make the Cyclops helpers of Hephaistus.

Aphrodite (Venus)

Aphrodite was the Olympian who, at one time or another, actively affected the life of almost everyone. She was the goddess of love. Spring, with its fresh blossoms, was her favorite season, and the blooming rose was her flower. She was the rapture of a passionate embrace and she could cast a spell over a mortal or a god, making him forget all obligations and duties as he reveled in his love. Yet there was another side to this goddess. With that rapture and obliviousness to the rest of the world can come terror and destruction. Though lovers may be happy together, ultimately they have to face others who may not understand their love. Worse yet, one may fall in love with another who will not or cannot respond. The dramatist Euripides catches this horror of love most vividly in his tragedies *Hippolytus* and *Medea*. The love Aphrodite provokes is a powerful yearning for another; she cares nothing about the marriage rites or the marriage bed, and she cares nothing about the consequences of the passion.

Aphrodite, you will recall,[1] was born from the foam created by the action of the sea on Ouranos' severed members. First the breezes carried her to the island of Cythera and then on to Cyprus where, as she stepped ashore, new grass grew up beneath her feet. Both islands became sacred to her, and she is often called Cytherea and Cyprogenes. The Horae welcomed and dressed the newly arrived goddess and took her to Olympus where the gods were overwhelmed by her beauty. Later the Charities became her companions and danced with her, anointed her with oil and wove garments for her. She always retained some connection with the sea, and sailors often prayed to her for safe voyages.

All mortals and immortals alike, with the exception of

1. See page 2.

Athena, Artemis, and Hestia, were subject to her power, and no surer pain could come than by resisting her or mocking her. When the mortal Hippolytus refused to show her proper respect, she caused his stepmother, Phaedra, to fall in love with him, leading to the destruction of both.[1] When Myrrha, the mother of Adonis, neglected to honor her, she inflamed her with lust for her own father. Even Zeus was subject to her power. Once, however, he tired of her machinations and decided to teach her a lesson so that she would no longer be able to mock and laugh as she toyed with the loves of the gods. Very simply, Zeus arranged for Aphrodite to fall in love with a mortal.

The mortal Zeus chose was the Trojan youth Anchises. Aphrodite found him tending sheep on Mount Ida in Asia and was instantly aroused by his beauty. She planned her attack and, once all his fellow shepherds had gone off with their flocks, she appeared at the door of his house. Anchises had never seen such a beautiful woman and questioned whether or not she was a goddess. But she claimed to be a mortal and even gave her genealogy. One thing led to another, and rather quickly at that, so that very soon Aphrodite had satisfied her craving. After their lovemaking, Anchises fell asleep, but Aphrodite, reassuming all her godly glory, woke him. Terrified, the mortal begged the goddess not to destroy him for having slept with her — as we know,[2] and as Anchises knew, divine law prohibits a mortal from seeing the flesh of a goddess without her consent — but the consent was there, and Aphrodite comforted her lover. Nonetheless, she was ashamed for having lusted after a mortal, and she warned him that if he ever told another of his success with her, he would be destroyed by a thunderbolt from Zeus. The offspring of this union was the Trojan hero, Aeneas.

As we have said, the marriage bed was not sacred to Aphrodite. In fact, though she was married to Hephaistus, the craftsman of the gods, her marriage vows seemed to have little effect upon her actions. Her most serious extra-marital affair was with Ares, god of war. On one famous occasion she was caught, though she didn't seem to learn a lesson from the confrontation.

Whenever Hephaistus left his home for the night, Ares would come and make love to Aphrodite. Once they overslept and Helios, as he passed over, saw them and reported what he had seen to Hephaistus. Outraged, Hephaistus planned a trap. Using all his skill, he crafted a mesh of invisible but unbreakable chains, and he hung it over his bed. Then, telling his wife that he was going away for a few days to visit his friends the Lemnians, he left the house. True to

1. See page 204. 2. See page 34.

form, Ares soon arrived and took Aphrodite to bed. Hephaistus, having been clued again by Helios, quietly returned and dropped his net on the lovers. They were caught — in fact, the net was so effective that they couldn't move even a limb; therefore, they had to lie there paralyzed in the midst of lovemaking, visible to anyone who wanted to see them. Hephaistus raged and called the gods to see the couple — the goddesses, out of modesty, stayed home — and he demanded that Zeus return all of the gifts he had had to give in order to get Aphrodite as his wife. The rest of the gods found the whole situation vastly amusing. Finally, through the intervention of Poseidon, who promised that Ares would give proper atonement, Hephaistus lifted the net. Harmonia was said to be the offspring of Ares and Aphrodite, as were Deimos (Terror) and Phobos (Fear).

Extreme vanity was another of Aphrodite's characteristics, though among the goddesses this was not a unique trait. When Eris (Strife) was angry at not having been invited to the wedding of Peleus and Thetis, she decided to get revenge by staging a contest. Thus she offered a golden apple as a prize for the most beautiful of the goddesses. Hera, Aphrodite, and Athena were in the running, and Zeus made Paris, the son of the Trojan king Priam, the judge. Each goddess tried to bribe him: Hera with the offer of dominion over all men, Athena with victory in war, and Aphrodite with the hand of the most beautiful mortal, who at that time was Helen, wife of Menelaus of Sparta. He chose the last, claimed his reward, and thus brought about the great war between Greece and Troy.

In classical times, Eros was often seen as a companion of Aphrodite. The myths of his origin form a web of inconsistencies. As we have already seen,[1] he was involved in creation and appeared there as a direct descendant of Chaos. At other times he is called the child of Erebus and Night. Still other traditions say that he is the son of Aphrodite by Ares, or sometimes by Zeus, or even by Hermes. He doesn't actually appear as her companion, however, until quite late in both literature and art.

In the early stories of Eros, he was a force rather than a god. When he first took on anthropomorphic characteristics, he was envisioned as a male adolescent, usually quite athletic, and as such he was seen as the patron of young male beauty. As he changed from a force to a god, his power changed from impersonal to personal. Where, as a force, he had caused the primal union of opposites, as a god he provoked the desire in humans for one another. In fact, the word "eros" appears as a common noun in ancient Greek, indicating a highly charged emotional tie between humans.

1. See page 1.

EROS AS AN ADOLESCENT. Attic White Ground Vase by Douris, 5th Century B.C. *Courtesy, The Cleveland Museum of Art, Purchase, Leonard C. Hanna, Jr. Bequest.*

By the fourth century, Eros had turned into a child in art, and in both literature and art he was always associated with Aphrodite. The chubby winged baby that we know from Renaissance painting didn't appear until that time. At no time were there temples to Eros or cults in which he was worshipped.

a. Aphrodite came to Greece from the East where she was the goddess of fertility and love of the Babylonians and of other Near Eastern cultures. By classical times, however, she had taken on wholly Greek characteristics.

b. While the most common story of the birth of Aphrodite is the one recounted here, she is sometimes called the daughter of Zeus and Dione. Such birth makes her more firmly an Olympian, but there are no existing myths that deal with that union.

c. Some myths have Aphrodite married to Ares. Who her husband was, however, had little to do with her actions, as we have seen.

d. Early representation of Aphrodite in art shows her as a comely, fully dressed woman. Only later was she shown as naked, the most famous representation being the statue by Praxiteles at Cnidos, of which several Roman copies exist.

e. Sometimes Aphrodite is called *Pandemos,* meaning "of all people" — at other times she is called *Ourania,* meaning "heavenly." Plato, in the *Symposium,* makes these two names into a distinction between physical and spiritual love. This distinction, which has passed down in literature and thought, is Plato's invention and has no mythological basis.

f. One of the most important sanctuaries of Aphrodite in the ancient world was in Corinth. There, temple harlots gave their bodies to the goddess, and lovemaking was seen there as a sacred activity. When St. Paul wrote of the immorality of the Corinthians, perhaps he knew of this old tradition.

g. Most of the men associated with Aphrodite were not viewed by the ancients as particularly masculine. Rather, a man who spent too much time courting women was seen as effeminate. In Euripides' *Bacchae,* the stranger who visits Thebes is taunted by Pentheus: "I assume you don't wrestle. Your hair's too long and your skin's too good; you must keep out of the sun so that at night you can hunt Aphrodite with your beauty."

EROS AS A CHILD. Hellenistic bronze statue, *Courtesy, Metropolitan Museum of Art, New York, Rogers Fund, 1943.*

41

Ares (Mars)

Ares was one of the least significant gods in the lives of the Greeks, and there is very little mythology associated with him. Zeus summed up Ares quite concisely when he said to him, "You enjoy quarrels and fights and I hate you more than any of the gods on Olympus." Of the Olympians, he was the only legitimate son of Zeus and Hera, but he was liked by virtually no one. Sometimes known as "the Butcher" he was the god of war and fighting and, unlike Athena, he reveled in violence. He is the embodiment of the bully. He comes on tough, but he whines and cries miserably when he loses or gets hurt.

We have already seen an account of Ares' affair with Aphrodite.[1] His children by her were said to be Harmonia, Phobos (Fear) and Deimos (Terror). In some traditions they were also said to have produced Eros and Anteros. In other traditions he was also said to have had an affair with Cyrene, who bore him Diomedes, a later king of Thrace.

Dionysus (Liber)

Dionysus, sometimes called Bacchus, was the youngest of the Olympians, joining the family long after the twelve had established themselves in their houses and palaces on Olympus. According to some traditions, he became the thirteenth Olympian; according to another, Hestia relinquished her place to him. Whatever the case, he was not received enthusiastically, and much of the mythology of Dionysus deals with his struggle for acceptance by gods and mortals alike.

He differed from the other Olympians in one important way — where they distanced themselves from mortals, except for occasional amorous exploits, Dionysus joined with mortals in their revels. Where they wanted mortals to remember their mortality — Dionysus wanted to free them from that realization and to become one with him. He was the mad god, the god of the vine and of wine, and those who worshipped him joined in wild, often drunken dances and songs, accompanied by frantic music from flutes and cymbals, tambourines and drums.

To those who accepted him and joined with him, Dionysus brought joy; to those who resisted him and scorned him, he brought

1. See page 38.

MAENAD. Roman copy of a late 5th Century Greek relief. While in literature maenads are usually portrayed in a wild or frenzied state, in art they are often represented in an ecstatic, trance-like state. Note that the maenad is holding a thyrsus, the sacred staff of Dionysus. *Courtesy, Metropolitan Museum of Art, New York, Fletcher Fund, 1935.*

destruction through madness. To the Olympians he was the enemy of dignity and moderation and manliness. To mortals he was a paradox best embodied in wine. At first the wine drinker feels happy, relaxed, and freed from cares. The more he drinks, the freer he feels, as many of his inhibitions fall. But ultimately if he continues to drink, he may become violent or morose, finally losing consciousness in drunken "madness." Like Dionysus, wine can be beneficial and it can be destructive. He was a god in whom opposites coexisted.

In ancient vase painting, Dionysus usually appears as a bearded figure, dressed in a long womanly gown. In later paintings this stereotype changes to that of a beardless, rather effeminate youth. In sculpture he often appears in the latter form, and at times, when only a head remains, one has difficulty telling whether it is the head of a man or of a woman. His sexuality, in mythology, is ambiguous.

DIONYSUS WITH A SATYR. Attic Red-Figured Cup by Makron, 5th Century B.C. A satyr with an athletic build, a horse's tail and goat-like ears reaches out with a wine jug to fill Dionysus' cup. Dionysus, though bearded, wears woman-like clothes. His head wreathed with leaves, he reaches out to a vine. *Courtesy, Museum of Fine Arts, Boston.*

Though few amorous adventures are attributed to him, he was sometimes depicted as a bull or a goat, two unquestionably virile forms. This combination of virility and effeminacy is another example of the coexistence of opposites.

In literature and in painting, Dionysus is usually surrounded by a unique troupe of followers. The female members of the troupe are usually called **maenads** or *lenai* or *bassarides*; the males are usu-

44

ally called **satyrs** or *sileni*. The females are literally madwomen who, in trancelike states, dance an ecstatic dance to the god. Sometimes they are associated with Dionysus' nurses, sometimes they are simply seen as devotees of the god; but always they are his votaries. They are always fully clothed and often they wear fawn skins over their shoulders and carry snakes or have them in their hair or draped over their bodies. At least one member of the troupe — sometimes Dionysus himself — carries a *thyrsus*, a long staff topped with a pine cone. The thyrsus is a symbol associated exclusively with Dionysus.

The satyrs are distinctly male. They are almost always depicted as naked and often as being sexually aroused. While they are predominantly human, they always have some animal characteristics. Sometimes they have a horse's tail, sometimes pointed ears, sometimes hooves instead of feet. They spend most of their time drinking and in the undiscriminating search for sexual release. As they appear in art, sileni are simply older satyrs. While satyrs get jubilant and raucous when they drink, sileni usually get sloppily drunk and need others to care for them.

In classical mythology, Dionysus was the son of **Semele**, daughter of king Cadmus of Thebes, and Zeus. When Hera learned that Semele was pregnant by Zeus, she went to the mortal, disguised as an old woman, and tricked her into destroying herself. Zeus, in the process of seducing Semele, had promised her that he would honor any request she made of him. Thus Hera in disguise convinced the girl to ask Zeus to appear to her in all his divine glory, just as he had appeared to Hera when he was courting her. When the girl made her request, Zeus tried to persuade her not to ask that, but he had made a promise, and when she persisted he had no choice but to honor the request. Thus he appeared in blinding splendor and she was destroyed by his thunderbolts. But Zeus took the child from her womb and sewed it into his own thigh, where it reached full term and, like Athena, was thus male-born.

Once the child was born from his thigh, Zeus entrusted it to Hermes who took it to Ino, another of Cadmus' daughters, and her husband Athamas, instructing them to rear the child as a girl so that Hera would not discover it. But wise Hera was not fooled by the ploy, and though Hermes had already removed the child to the care of the Nymphs of Nysa, she punished the mortal couple by driving them mad. Athamas, in a god-inspired frenzy, killed his son Learchus and then pursued Ino and their other son Melicertes. Trapped at the top of a cliff, holding her son, the mad Athamas fast approaching, Ino jumped into the sea. Fortunately, Poseidon knew what had happened and took pity on her, making both Ino and her son immortal and changing their names to Leucothea and Palaemon.

Dionysus spent the rest of his childhood with the Nymphs of Nysa having no contact whatsoever with males. Later, according to some traditions, he spent time with the old, rather effeminate satyr **Silenus**, who was his tutor. But Hera was not through with the young god. Of all her jealous rages, the one against Dionysus lasted longest, and again and again she sought ways to punish him. This time she afflicted him with temporary insanity and sent him wandering to the corners of the earth.

So Dionysus wandered with his troupe of women from Lydia and Phrygia across Persia, through Arabia, and up the coast of Asia Minor, finally to Greece. In some later accounts he even went to India in his wanderings. Everywhere he went during his mad journey he established his new cult, particularly affecting the women of cities and towns. They would follow him, raving, into the hills and there dance his sacred dance with him, abandoning all strictures of society. Many men, particularly rulers, saw this god as the enemy of order and even of civilization, and as he moved into Greece, Dionysus met greater and greater resistance.

As he came through Macedonia into Thrace, he met **Lycurgus**, king of the Edones, who was the first to persecute him. Unwilling to accept this effeminate, disruptive young god, Lycurgus chased Dionysus and his nurses, savagely beating them with an ox goad. Terrified by this violent resistance, Dionysus fled into the sea where he found comfort from Thetis. There, in her motherly arms, he quivered and trembled and hid. Mortals are always unwise to challenge a god, even a young and tender one. In retaliation, Dionysus drove Lycurgus mad. Imagining that he was cutting down a vine, sacred to Dionysus, Lycurgus attacked his son with an axe, cutting off his limbs. When he recovered his senses, he repented, but he had his son's blood on his hands, and a curse of barrenness came upon his land. Through an oracle, his people learned that the only way to remove the curse would be to kill Lycurgus, and thus he was put to death.

The next resistance Dionysus met was in Thebes where his cousin **Pentheus** ruled, having inherited the throne from Cadmus. Dionysus was for two reasons particularly anxious to have his worship established in Thebes. First, it was his mother's home and one of his birthplaces. Secondly, his mother's sisters, after his mother had been destroyed, had spread a vicious rumor. They said that Semele had been pregnant by a soldier rather than by Zeus. The Zeus story, they said, was a fabrication she had created with her father to hide the disgrace from the family. They said that she had been killed because Zeus was angry at her brazen lie. Thus, Dionysus wanted to prove his divinity, clear his mother's name, and punish his aunts.

When Dionysus arrived in Thebes with his troupe, he drove the women mad, and they followed him into the hills to dance and revel with him. This is the focus of Euripides' play, the *Bacchae*. Pentheus tried to punish Dionysus, claiming that he was an imposter, an enemy of the sacred marriage vows, and a disrupter of all sense of order. But Dionysus quickly gained the upper hand and persuaded Pentheus to come up into the mountains with him to watch the women in their revels. Under the spell of the god, Pentheus went along, but when the women saw him they attacked him, tearing him to pieces. His own mother, Agave, Semele's sister, was the leader of the pack and under the spell of Dionysus, she thought she was tearing a lion to pieces. Triumphantly she returned to Thebes, carrying her son's head. Gradually, as she regained her senses, she realized what she had done.

The women of Argos, daughters of Proetus, were another group who resisted the power of Dionysus. They too were driven mad and roamed in mountains. The seer Melampus promised Proetus that he would cure the women if the king would grant him sovereignty over one third of his realm. Proetus refused, feeling that the price was too high. But when the madness of the women became even more extreme, he gave in. Melampus, with a group of young men, hounded the women, chasing them with a frenzied dance across the country. One dropped and died of exhaustion, but the others were cured and the seer collected his fee. The daughters of Minyas in Orchomenos were still another group who resisted Dionysus and profaned his festival by spinning and weaving during it. They too were punished. According to one tradition, they were turned into bats.

Another event that indicates the power of the god took place when he was a youth. Standing on a bluff overlooking the sea, he was seen by pirates on a ship passing by. Because of his purple robes, his rich dark hair, and his astounding young beauty, they assumed that he was the son of a king and took him captive in order to ransom him. They tried to tie his hands, but the bonds kept falling off and the youth only sat and smiled at their efforts. He didn't resist, he didn't speak — he just smiled. As the ship sailed off with him, wine streamed through the bilges and ran across the deck, and a heavenly fragrance rose up from it. The helmsman, realizing that their captive must be a god, warned the crew, but they paid no attention to him. Later, vines sprouted out of the mast and great clusters of grapes hung down over the sails. At this, the crew realized their mistake, but it was too late. The young god turned himself into a lion and created a ferocious bear midships. The terrified crew abandoned ship, jumping overboard, and they were turned into dolphins. The helmsman, however, because of his wisdom, was saved.

Finally, Dionysus brought the vine to Attica. There he taught the mortal Icarius how to cultivate the vine and how to make wine from grapes. Wanting to share this gift with other men, Icarius invited a group of shepherds to join him one evening, and he gave them wine to drink. They were enchanted by the new drink and drank great quantities of it unmixed with water. But as they drank, they felt new and frightening things happening to them and, convinced that he had bewitched them, they killed Icarius. By the light of day, when they had slept off the effects of the wine, they realized what they had done and buried Icarius. Later, his daughter Erigone, with the help of his dog, searched for her father and when she found him and discovered what had happened, she hanged herself.

In spite of all this resistance, Dionysus became accepted in Attica and ultimately was to become the patron of tragic drama at his festivals in Athens during the classical period. Furthermore, in spite of being one of the most complex of the Greek gods, he is the one of them who lived longest as a powerful force in the lives and minds of men.

Though Dionysus had no children who are important in Greek mythology, he did marry Ariadne, the daughter of King Minos of Crete. After Theseus had abandoned her on Naxos, Dionysus took her to be his wife, but this story will be dealt with in more detail when we come to Theseus.

Dionysus was always devoted to his mother, Semele, and, having rescued her from Hades, ultimately established her as a divinity in his cult.

a. Though Dionysus is a latecomer to the Olympian family, there is convincing evidence that he was known even to the Minoans in the second millennium B.C. How he arrived in Greece is a matter of considerable scholarly debate, but the East-West route mentioned in the story — the same one described by Euripides in the *Bacchae* — seems to have some authenticity to it. The resistance described in many of the stories about the god may indicate actual historical processes.

b. In later times, Dionysus was incorporated into the Orphic tradition. There, another birth story was told in which he was the son of Zeus and Persephone and was called **Zagreus**. Destroyed by the Titans, his heart was rescued by Athena and eaten by Zeus, which allowed the father of the gods to recreate him through Semele. In the form of Zagreus, he was included in the Eleusinian mysteries.[1]

c. The worship of Bacchus, another name for Dionysus, was transformed into a "mystery religion" in its own right and was the most democratic of the religions in the Greek world. Freemen, women, and slaves alike could participate in the mysteries, which seem to have offered the promise of some sort of immortality. The mysteries were adopted by the Romans and continued, even when banned by the Roman Senate, into the second century A.D. At Pompei there are some superb wall paintings depicting stages of initiation into the Bacchic mysteries.

d. Satyrs developed independent of Dionysus and often appear in art alone or with other deities. As creatures embodying the primal, unrestrained forces of nature, however, it was natural that they should accompany Dionysus. As with many minor forces in mythology, the sileni were at times plural, and at other times the name was used to indicate one Silenus.

e. Homer clearly knew of Dionysus, but he did not include him as an important divinity. This is natural: Homer was writing of an aristocratic-warrior society, a society in which Dionysus and what he represented could have no part. Homer includes the Lycurgus story, where Dionysus appears as a coward. His version differs from the one told here only in the conclusion: according to Homer, Zeus blinded Lycurgus as a punishment for challenging a god.

f. Dionysus was said to have been challenged by the hero Perseus and even to have been killed by him. In Delphi, the sanctuary shared by Apollo and Dionysus, there was said to be the grave of Dionysus. Yearly he was resurrected, a trait common in nature divinities.

1. See page 18, note (b).

CHAPTER III

MONSTERS AND REBELLIONS

The Giants

You will recall[1] that when drops of Cronos' blood fell upon the earth, both the Furies and a race of giants were conceived. These giants were insurpassable in size and stature; they were terrifying to look at; they had thick hair on their heads and faces, and they had snakes for feet. It is generally believed that Mother Earth, being angry at Zeus for his treatment of her sons, the Titans, stirred these giants against the Olympians. At any rate, they kept on throwing boulders and blazing trees at the abodes of the god.

It had been prophesied that the gods themselves would not be able to destroy these giants. Only with the help of a mortal man could they get rid of these menaces. But the Earth, too, had heard of this prophecy. Accordingly, she looked for some herb to keep the giants safe from a mortal. Zeus, in order to thwart her hunt, ordered the Dawn and the Moon and the Sun to stop giving forth any light, and he himself went down to earth and with Athena's assistance found the herb for himself. He then requested assistance from Heracles, the mightiest of the heroes, and there was a terrific battle. The gods did not have an easy time of it — Hera, in fact, almost got raped by the giant Porphyrion — but they fought splendidly. Athena grabbed Enceladus and dashed the island of Sicily upon him; then later she stripped off the skin of Pallas and used it as a shield for herself. Heracles killed many giants with his arrows after the gods had struck them. Between the efforts of the gods and Heracles, all the giants were vanquished.

Typhon

After Zeus had driven the Titans from the sky, Mother Earth mated with Tartarus and bore the monstrous Typhon. A hundred serpent heads grew from his shoulders; fire flashed from the eyes under his eyebrows and blazed from his heads. Half man and half monster,

1. See page 2.

he was the most gigantic living thing ever to be seen on the face of the earth. He was taller than a mountain; his head met up with the stars. He had wings all over his body, his eyes shot fire, and his face was full of matted hair. He had snakes for feet, fire for a tongue. The sounds his heads made were usually unintelligible, for now he would speak the way a god might speak, now he would make sounds like those of a bull or a lion or a young dog, and now he would make some hissing or whizzing or whooshing sound.

He once rushed up to the heavens. Some sources say that the gods, seeing him, were struck with such terror that they fled into Egypt. Pursued by the monster even to that place, they went into hiding and disguised themselves: Zeus as a ram, Apollo as a raven, Dionysus as a goat, Artemis as a cat, Hera as a cow, Aphrodite as a fish, Hermes as an ibis, Ares as a bear.

Coming to his senses, however, Zeus stood his ground. He hurled thunderbolts at the giant and, getting as close to the beast as he could, struck Typhon with his sickle. Then, finding the monster to be wounded, he pounced upon him. But Typhon held the god with his serpent-like coils, got the sickle from Zeus, and cut off certain muscles in his hands and feet. He then, having dragged the helpless god to a cave, hid those muscles. He entrusted a female dragon named Delphyne to watch over this precious booty. Hermes, however, managed to sneak into the cave, stole the muscles back, and returned them to Zeus who now, having gained back his strength and might, dashed thunderbolts down upon Typhon. Typhon fled all over the world, and eventually got into the area of Sicily where Zeus threw Mount Etna upon him. Even to this day it is said that fire from this mountain comes from Typhon.

Other sources, however, are kinder to the immortal gods. They say that Zeus took immediate action. As soon as he was aware of Typhon, he thundered mightily and dreadfully, and the whole world — the earth and the sky and the ocean and Tartarus itself — resounded. The vast Olympus shook under his feet and the earth groaned with pain. And there was unbearable heat, both from Zeus' lightning and from Typhon's fire; the whole earth and the whole sky and the whole sea boiled. Enormous waves billowed about the beaches. There were earthquakes, and even Hades and the Titans locked in Tartarus trembled as they felt the shocks of this violence. Then Zeus let forth his wrath, took his weapons — his lightning and his thunderbolts — and having sprung upon the beast, he smashed him from Olympus and enveloped each and every one of his awful heads with fire. Thus maimed, the monster fell and the earth again

51

groaned. And as he fell the flames from the fiend hit mountain glens and burnt and melted the earth. Then, being distressed, Zeus dashed Typhon into Tartarus.

From Typhon come the winds, not the usual ones, but rather the unpredictable and violent ones, the ones that are so dangerous and unwelcome to sailors and so destructive to farmers. For the former, falling upon the sea, scatter ships and sink seamen, nor do they bring any good to men. The others, similarly, as they flit over the fields of the earth, undo the hard work of men. Typhon has bequeathed to us the typhoons of the world.

The sons of Aloeus

There was a woman named Iphimedia, the wife of a man named Aloeus. But she fell in love with Poseidon and she often would go down to the shore and, taking the waters in her hands, let them drop into her lap. Poseidon responded, and she gave birth to two sons, **Otus** and **Ephialtes.** They were beautiful children but they grew at an enormous rate: by the time they were nine years old, their chests measured nine cubits and they were nine fathoms high, and it is thought that they grew at a commensurate rate — i.e., a fathom, or six feet, taller each year and a cubit, or about two feet, broader.

Whether out of youthful defiance or out of sheer perversity of nature, they attempted several outrages. They kidnapped Ares, tied him up with powerful bonds, and kept him locked up for thirteen months in a bronze barrel. He almost perished there, but Hermes finally rescued him.

They also decided that they would take over Olympus. They took two mountains, Mount Pelion and Mount Ossa, and heaped one on top of the other so that they could get up to Olympus. Then they threatened to wreak all sorts of disturbances on earth by putting mountains in the sea and by turning what was land into seas.

Furthermore, each of them began lusting after an immortal: Otus went after Artemis and Ephialtes after Hera. A grand chase began. Artemis changed herself into a deer, and the brothers, becoming distracted from their goals, desired to show off their marksmanship and went after the deer. The deer ran between them, each let loose his arrow, and each killed the other.

They were sent down to Tartarus. There, they were tied to a column with bonds of snakes.

a. The Typhon story presents a motif common to many cultures: the dragon slayer. Compare Beowulf and Grendel in Anglo-Saxon mythology, Marduk and the monsters in Babylonian mythology, Sigurd and Fafnir in Norse mythology, and St. George and the dragon in Christian folklore. Everything about the dragon represents excess: its size, its violence, its attempts to disrupt and challenge the ordered world, its solitariness, its irrationality.

b. All three of these stories present a confrontation between order and disorder: disorder threatens order, order must be temporarily suspended, disorder is met on its own terms and vanquished, and order is reinstated.

c. These three stories add to the development of the Olympians. The gods have now been tested — much in the same way that the dynasties of Ouranos and Cronos were tested — they have met the test, and they have established themselves as supreme forces.

d. The giant Pallas that Athena subdued in this chapter should be distinguished from the Pallas who was her companion as a girl.[1]

e. We have already seen, in our discussion of Poseidon,[2] that some of the Olympians themselves once attempted a rebellion against Zeus. What happened was that several of the gods, among whom were Hera and Poseidon, plotted to subdue Zeus. The loyal Thetis, however, summoned Briareus, one of the hundred-handed creatures who had helped Zeus in the battle against the Titans. Briareus so intimidated the would-be usurpers that they quivered and yielded. As always, Zeus triumphed.

1. See page 32 and page 35, note (e).
2. See page 15.

CHAPTER IV

THE CREATION OF MAN

The world is now settled. Not only has warfare ceased but the broad divisions of order from chaos have been effected. The earth is not just a flat mass but a full-bodied creation possessed of seas, rivers and oceans, mountains, hills, valleys and plains, forests and deserts, night and day, heat and cold, rain, snow and wind, clouds, lightning and thunder, sun, moon, and stars and varying degrees of intensity and magnitudes of all these attributes.

How animal life came upon the earth is unclear. Ancient sources do not say much about the subject and, when they do, they are vague and invariably contradict each other. There is no generally accepted theory, no *Genesis* to guide us in our queries. But one strain does assume a certain prominence, a strain attributing the creation of life to **Prometheus**, the Titan, son of Iapetus and ally of Zeus in his battle against the forces of Cronos.[1]

Some sources say that the gods themselves created the living creatures on the earth. Others say that Prometheus, while he was wandering upon the earth, would pick up pieces of clay; being by nature curious and imaginative, he would mold these pieces into various shapes. Thus came about the many varied forms of animal life that inhabit the earth.

Accompanying Prometheus in his wanderings was his dull brother **Epimetheus**. Epimetheus prevailed upon Prometheus to let him endow each form of life with some special attribute. Consequently, as Prometheus would create a new species, Epimetheus would give it something unique. To some species he assigned strength without speed; to others swiftness without much strength; to some he gave natural armor for protection; to those that were small he gave wings. Every creature had some attribute by which it might protect itself and survive. Then, after he had endowed them with the ability to avoid destruction, he equipped them against the weather and seasons: some got thick hides, others got feathers, others got a covering of hair — enough to protect each from heat and cold.

Now, among Prometheus' creations was man, and Prometheus favored him above all the others. But at first these new crea-

1. See page 5.

tures were very sorry figures indeed. One of the problems was that Epimetheus, whose name means "hindsight" or "afterthought" just as Prometheus' means "foresight," by this time had given away all his gifts; there was nothing left for man. Consequently, Prometheus gave man just a dash of each quality that had been given to the other creatures. Furthermore, Athena, being impressed with this new type of creature, is said to have breathed a higher spirit into man.

But man still wasn't much. He had sight but no vision; he merely drifted aimlessly, confused and ignorant. He had no skills, no crafts, but rather lived underground like an ant or burrowed in some cave. Men quickly perished from sickness and disease. Man had no understanding of the seasons and he merely existed from one moment to another, ingloriously and senselessly, without mind, reason, or dignity. Zeus looked at these creatures, paltry and helpless, groveling about purposelessly and had little use for them. He looked upon them with utmost contempt and, in fact, entertained the notion of summarily annihilating the race and of replacing it with a new one.

But man had a champion in the son of Iapetus who would not accept Zeus' contempt. Already men differed from beasts in that, while the beasts always had to look toward the earth as they stood on their four feet, man at least could look directly at the sky. And so Prometheus set to work to improve this race. He taught these creatures the knowledge of the stars, the use of numbers and the science of computation, the alphabet, the art of writing, and the development of mind and memory. He taught them how to use the other animals to serve them and do their heavy labor for them. He gave them the knowledge of sailing and of farming. And he taught them how to care for themselves, how to use balms and drugs in order to ward off and cure sickness. Furthermore, he taught them the art of divination and augury, how to interpret dreams and how to determine both favorable and unfavorable omens from birds.

If man had hitherto lived in darkness, he was now living in light; if he had been living in ignorance, he was now living in insight and knowledge; if he had been helpless, he could now fend for himself. He was no longer just a helpless creature of a day. All sorts of arts and skills and comforts came to mankind from Prometheus.

Seeing this improvement, Zeus apparently mellowed in his feelings toward man. He apparently even allowed Prometheus to borrow fire for man's use; and when man would use it for sacrifices of burnt offerings to the gods, Zeus was even more kindly disposed toward Prometheus' creation.

But one day Prometheus got it into his mind to test Zeus' powers. He invited the son of Cronos to a feast, the main course being a luscious ox. Then he cut up the ox in preparation for his guest; he took the best cuts of meat and fat and wrapped them up in the mangy hide of the animal; similarly he took the bones and other inedible parts and wrapped them in a slim covering of lovely meat. Then he offered Zeus his pick.

"Son of Iapetus," exclaimed Zeus, "well known among important people, how unfairly and unequally have you divided the portions."

"Zeus, most powerful and greatest of the immortal gods, have no concern. Take whatever portion pleases you," replied the crafty Prometheus.

And so Zeus did choose. But he knew what Prometheus was doing. Nonetheless, he went along with Prometheus' ruse and chose the seemingly best portion for himself. Then, pretending surprise and indignation when he saw that his portion was all bone, he raged.

"You will meet my wrath, son of Iapetus," flared forth Zeus. And indeed Zeus did take action. He decided to punish Prometheus through his favorite creature, man, and hence he removed from man the privilege of borrowing fire.

Needless to say, Prometheus was not about to accept this action. Consequently, one day he sneaked up to the source of heavenly fire, the Sun, or perhaps it was Hephaistus' forge, and in a fennel stalk he stole a portion of this fire, and took it down to mankind. When Zeus became aware of this theft, his wrath flared:

"Son of Iapetus, clever and resourceful above all others, you are proud for having deceived me and stolen the fire. Know, however, that a terrible punishment will come upon you and upon all your mortals. I will give a bane to them that will seem a source of delight but will actually forevermore be a source of trouble."

And with these words Zeus laughed and immediately acted upon his words. He had Hephaistus mold a new shape; Athena gave it fine clothes and the ability to weave and sew; Aphrodite made it alluring and seductive and gave it grace and charm; Apollo gave it the power of song; and Hermes gave it a fast tongue for sweet talk and persuasion and a disposition inclined toward deception and trickery. Thus woman was created. And she was called **Pandora,** All-Gifts, because everyone dwelling upon Olympus gave her a gift, a gift designed to lead man into mischief, misery, suffering, and woe.

Then, when he had brought this snare to perfection, Father Zeus sent the messenger Hermes to take her to Epimetheus, that careless and thoughtless brother of Prometheus. After Zeus' stern words and prediction, Prometheus had warned his brother never to accept a gift from Olympian Zeus and had advised him that, if any gift were offered, he should send it back immediately lest it turn out to be a source of trouble to mankind. But Epimetheus forgot the warning, perhaps being the first to be inveigled by Pandora's charms.

Now, the race of man had been living on the earth free from care and troubles and labor and sickness. In fact, in such a way began the shared life of Epimetheus and Pandora. But in their house was a container — a box or a chest or a jug of some sort — carefully sealed and removed from conspicuous sight. But so inconspicuous was it that it kept on attracting Pandora's attention. Some say that Hermes had delivered this container as part of Pandora's dowry and that Zeus had carefully filled it with all kinds of horrors. Others say that Prometheus himself had stored in it all the unfavorable attributes from the creation days, attributes that he neither wanted to give to his creatures nor wanted to be at large in the world. At any rate, whether it was from Prometheus or from Zeus, Epimetheus had been distinctly warned to leave the container alone and never, under any circumstances, open it. But Pandora's curiosity was stronger than Epimetheus' warnings. One day when her husband was away, she opened the container, and out flew all the terrible things: sickness, old age, hatred, jealousy, greed, spite, envy, lust, ill will, deception, falsehood, and a host of others — all the qualities that lead man to pain, sorrow, and unhappiness. Since that time the earth and the sea have been full of unpleasantness; in the day and in the night unwanted illnesses visit men, silently bringing their evils wherever they go and to whomever they happen upon.

Pandora did manage to reseal the container, but only one quality could she save: hope. Hope alone remained behind.

Meanwhile, Zeus had not forgotten about Prometheus. He ordered Hephaistus to take Prometheus to Mount Caucasus in the East and to pin him to the mountain. He was bound in this deserted place, deprived of the sound and the sight of man, always wishing for the sun when the cold night chilled him and always wishing for the night when the hot sun baked him, bound in an upright position, unable to sleep, unable to bend his knees. Here he was fettered for many years, thirty thousand years according to one source. Each day an eagle would lunge upon him and gnaw at his liver, which would in turn grow back each night. And so was Prometheus punished for stealing the fire until much later when he was released by Heracles.

a. Lovers of consistency will be terribly frustrated by the details in this set of stories. Plato, for instance, says that Prometheus stole the fire in order to compensate for Epimetheus' careless squandering of gifts; he also says that it was the gods themselves that created man. Hesiod, either himself or via some interpolator, says that Zeus was aware of Prometheus' deception at the banquet from the beginning; other sources suggest that Zeus took Prometheus in good faith and was genuinely irate when he found his portion of bones. Regardless, the problems enter: if the former is accepted, then one wonders whether Zeus had an ulterior motive; did he want to punish mankind? Did he go along with Prometheus' scheme just to have some excuse to punish man? If the latter is accepted, then Zeus isn't as clever as he is supposed to be.

Aeschylus says that early man was wracked by ignorance and sickness; Hesiod says that early man lived a life totally free from care and any sort of malady. Furthermore there is little clue to time sequence, as the stories in the next chapter will illustrate, for another group of stories will describe the first race of men to have been living under Cronos' reign and will say that the gods created the first two races of men and Zeus the second two, never mentioning Prometheus' involvement in creation.

b. Even the story of Pandora has veiled ambiguities. Just how is one to interpret the fact that hope was the only quality that did not escape? Does the story suggest that, while all evils of the world were let loose, hope was not? that hope still remains locked up in Pandora's box? Or does it suggest that hope is there in Pandora's box ready for us whenever we should need it; that merely our knowing that it exists is sufficient?

c. Certainly the student of comparative mythology will find a great deal of material in the Prometheus story: the creation of man from Earth (clay or dust); the delayed creation of woman; an Edenic state of existence interrupted by woman, unwittingly seductive and alluring and captivating but whose only real weakness is her curiosity. There is the motif of the taboo, the forbidden object, the violation of the taboo, and the consequences to mortals: the loss of this Edenic existence and its replacement by toil and pain and sorrow. And there is the notion of the god-benefactor, the greater-than-human being who devotes his entire energy to the improvement of man's lot and who is in turn cruelly punished for his energies.

d. There is a very important side note to the Prometheus story which may help explain why Zeus was so eager to get him out of the way: Zeus, as you will recall from a previous chapter,[1] led a promiscuous life. Furthermore, it had been prophesied that some day he would sire a son who would surpass him in power and might. When you put these two details together, Zeus had quite a bit to be concerned about, especially since he did not know the name of the woman who was destined to bear that son. Prometheus' mother, Themis, had told her son the secret of who that woman was to be; hence, part of Prometheus' torture was due to his unwillingness to reveal the secret to Zeus.

1. See page 10.

e. The story of Prometheus is rich in symbolic and figurative implications. While Aeschylus, in his *Prometheus Bound*, does indeed embellish the old story, he does not distort the significance of Prometheus as a defiance against arbitrary might and authority, as a representation of basic human ingenuity, perhaps excessive ingenuity, and as a figurative way of accounting for the instinct in man that drives him to improve himself socially, morally, technologically, artistically, and culturally.

f. Remarkable similarity, up to a point, can be found between Prometheus and the Norse god Loki: both are characterized by ingenuity and resourcefulness; both stole something that brought about disastrous consequences (cf. Andvari's ring and the consequences of the curse upon it); both found disfavor with the head god and both were bound for an immense period of time. But, whereas Prometheus is regarded as a positive force, Loki becomes more and more a sinister and destructive force.

g. When Zeus selected the bones for himself, a tradition was established among mortals. From that time on, mortals, when they sacrificed to the gods, assumed that the gods did not like the taste of meat and hence gave them only the savor of meat and not the meat itself.

The pre-Homeric world was envisioned to be a flat circle, surrounded by the Ocean, from which all other bodies of water had their source. Libya is the name for Africa. There are many entrances to the Underworld, but the two most common were at Taenarum, where Heracles entered, and near the Cimmereans, where Odysseus entered.

60

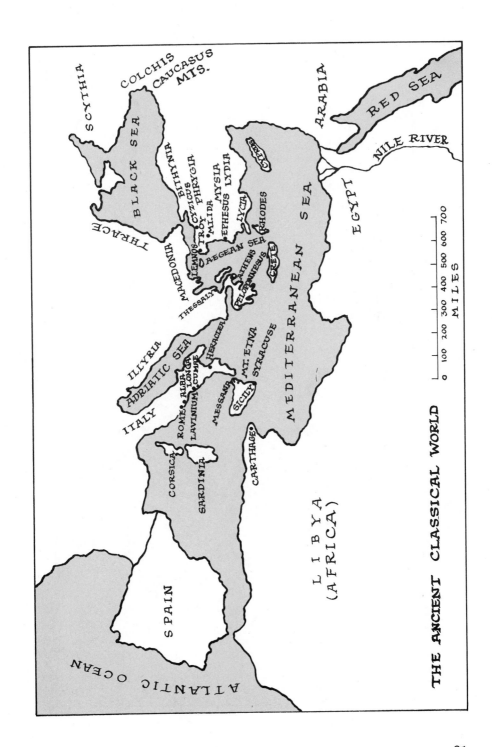

THE ANCIENT CLASSICAL WORLD

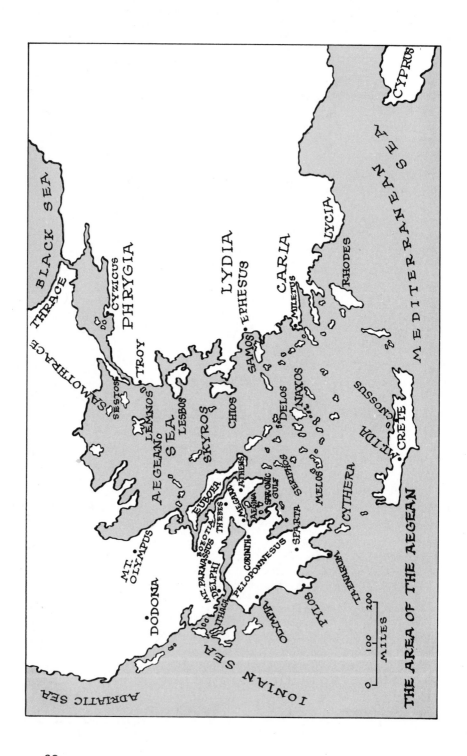

THE AREA OF THE AEGEAN

BLACK SEA

THRACE

SAMOTHRACE

CYZICUS

PHRYGIA

SESTOS

TROY

LEMNOS

AEGEAN SEA

LYDIA

EPHESUS

SAMOS

CARIA

MILETUS

LYCIA

RHODES

MEDITERRANEAN SEA

CYPRUS

SKYROS

CHIOS

LESBOS

DELOS

NAXOS

SERIPHOS

MELOS

CYTHERA

CNOSSUS

IDA

CRETE

MT. OLYMPUS

DODONA

MT. PARNASSUS

DELPHI

ITHACA

BOEOTIA

EUBOEA

THEBES

MEGARA

ATHENS

AEGINA

SARONIC GULF

CORINTH

PELOPONNESUS

SPARTA

EUROTAS

OLYMPIA

PYLOS

TAENARUM

IONIAN SEA

ADRIATIC SEA

MILES

0   100   200

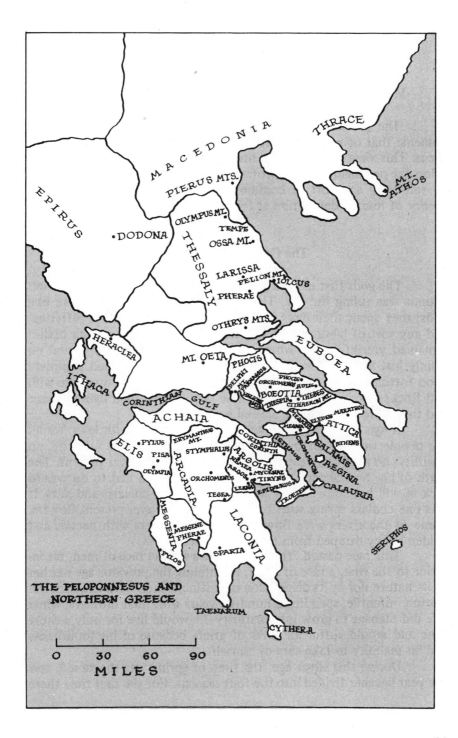

THE PELOPONNESUS AND
NORTHERN GREECE

0   30   60   90
MILES

CHAPTER V

MYTHS OF DETERIORATION AND DESTRUCTION

The previous chapter described one theory of human development: that of gradual improvement through the efforts of Prometheus. This view is primarily a literary one, used by Aeschylus to develop the personality of his protagonist Prometheus but not necessarily reflecting any sort of common belief. Far more common is the theory of human devolution as told by Hesiod and imitated by Ovid.

The Great Ages of Man

The gods first made a golden race of clear-speaking men when Cronos was ruling the sky. The people of this race used to live like gods; they spent their days free from care, distress, misery, suffering, and any sort of labor. There was no old age, but rather their bodies remained youthful and, when they did die, they merely passed on calmly just as if they were gently falling asleep. They had complete good fortune; crops and fruit bountifully grew of their own free will, and flocks were in abundance. These people lived their lives in peace and they were loved by the blessed gods.

It was indeed a **golden age**. There was no need for laws, for all the people were by instinct honest and just. There was no strife, no hostility, no need for weapons, and tranquillity was ever present. The earth of her own accord gave her bounty: all men had to do was to pick at will her strawberries and blueberries and cherries and nuts. It was one endless spring with balmy breezes and ever-present flowers. Some of the rivers were flowing with milk, others with nectar, and golden honey dripped from the verdant trees.

This race passed. Then there was a second race of men, far inferior to the first, a race of silver, resembling the previous age neither in its nature nor in its disposition or instincts. Men were childish, immature, infantile, spending a hundred years with their mothers; when one did manage to grow into maturity, he would live for only a short time and would suffer all sorts of griefs because of his foolishness and his inability to take care of himself.

During this **silver age**, the time of spring was shortened, and the year became divided into the four seasons. For the first time there

64

was heavy heat and discomforting cold. For the first time people lived in shelters: caves or twigs and shrubs bound with bark. And then for the first time did people have to sow the land and till the soil and harness beasts to the plow.

These men were reckless and foolish and vain and arrogant. Furthermore, they were not willing to honor the gods. Eventually the earth engulfed this generation. Then Father Zeus formed a third race, a **race of bronze**, not at all like the age of silver. This was the age of the sword and the spear, of war and violence and insult and outrage. Men had hardened spirits, no sensitivity, no concern for one another; no longer did they feed on the fruits of the land but ate the flesh of animals. They were enormously strong: mighty arms grew from their broad shoulders. They fought with bronze weapons, lived in bronze houses, worked the soil with bronze tools. They died ingloriously, often subdued by each other's hands, plunging into the dark and dank domain of icy Hades. But as coarse and brutish and callous as they were, at least they were not impious.

The earth eventually engulfed this race, too. Then Zeus, the son of Cronos, created a fourth race, one much more honorable and noble, a god-like **race of heroes** who are often called demi-gods. But war brought about their demise also, some before the seven gates of Thebes, fighting the forces of King Cadmus, others before the walls of Troy in behalf of Helen. Yes, death took these heroes, but Father Zeus gave them a place of their own, apart from mortal men, at the very end of the earth. Cronos rules them. They live free from care on the Islands of the Blessed, a calm and happy life, and three times a year does fertile land bear them fruit as sweet as honey.

And now the present age! If only I could have died before or have been born afterward (quoth Hesiod)! Any age would be better than this one. This is indeed the **iron age**. This is an age of corrupt men, men who day and night suffer wretchedness and toil. Soon after birth they age and decay. Everyone is at odds with everyone else: father and son, son and parent, guest and host, companion and companion, brother and brother. People are rude and harsh and critical toward their parents and heedless of the gods. The aged parents have to endure disrespect and ingratitude. Cities sack cities, and violence is the order of the day. Trust, goodness, justice are gone; callousness, arrogance, evildoing are the only respected qualities. There is no justice, there is no sense of shame, there is no decorum and propriety. The wicked injure the good with all sorts of slander and perjury and arrant lies. Envy, malice, and spite are triumphant while virtue and honor and prudence and justice have fled, abandoning the world of men. Nothing but wretchedness is left; the earth is now drenched with slaughter, disloyalty, plunder, and rapine, war and violence, and the absence of all that is good. And we have not yet seen the worst!

a. Just about every era that has ever existed has had its critics who see their present age as hopeless and corrupt, especially when contrasted with the ages of the past, which are always seen as much better and always idealized. But you can't go home again and you can't recapture the past.

b. Here too is the motif both of paradise lost and innocence lost. Man has moved from the world of innocence, a one-dimensional world, into the world of experience, a much fuller world. He can never regain the idyllic existence that he once had. Man has fallen. Compare the similarities in *Genesis*.

c. The actual horror of the details cited in the description of the Iron Age becomes even more prominent when you realize that the following are examples of crimes that brought particular vengeance from the gods: doing harm to a person seeking your protection; doing harm to a guest or to a host; secretly seducing someone else's wife; harming orphan children; being disrespectful to the gods. The worst, however, is being rude to your parents, especially aged parents.

d. You have to read two different approaches to creation, the literary approach as depicted in the Prometheus story and the mythological account depicting a gradual deterioration in the different ages of man. There is still a third approach to the phenomenon, a philosophical approach as illustrated by Plato in his *Timaeus* and Lucretius in the fifth book of his *De Rerum Natura*. Lucretius depicts man as having improved in sophistication and technology; attendant, however, to these improvements are excessive luxury, ambition, competition, warfare, unhappiness, and ennui. He also takes a distinctly anti-religious view in his creation of the world. Plato's work is complex and sophisticated and borrows from the philosopher Pythagoras. He speaks of a god who, focusing upon the four Pythagorean fundamental elements of fire, air, water, and earth and relying heavily upon Pythagorean numerical, mathematical, and geometrical relationships, merely organized preexisting inchoate conditions.

e. There is not necessarily any causal or chronological connection between the stories in this chapter and those in the previous chapter. Hence, the reader should not be puzzled when he sees humans living under the reign of Cronos and when he sees Cronos holding sway over a golden age.

Zeus' anger and the story of Lycaon

The earth was indeed teeming with corrupt creatures. When Zeus looked at them from his seat on lofty Olympus, he sighed in despair. The more he observed, the sadder and angrier he became. Consequently, he summoned all the gods to an assembly. When they all took their respective seats in his marble assembly hall, Zeus took his own seat, holding his ivory scepter, and shook his head — that nod which shakes the land and the seas and the stars. For it is this awe-inspiring nod that symbolizes the decrees and decisions of Zeus — and spoke:

"I have always been a caring leader. When the giants started their assaults against us, I took action. But as awful as they were, they were nothing compared to what we're dealing with now. Now there is even a greater menace: the race of humans. They must go; they must be destroyed. There is no use in trying to improve them; they are too far gone; they're like an ugly blotch or a disease or an infection that must be cut out and removed before it spreads and poisons the healthy parts.

"In fact, let me tell you a story. I had been getting reports about what was happening on earth for quite a while; therefore, I decided to go down and to see for myself whether these rumors were accurate or not. I took the shape of a human and went on a tour. Well, let me tell you, to mention all the details of the abominations I saw would take an immense tale. Let me just say this: the rumors were understatements, not exaggerations.

"On one of my visits I arrived in Arcadia at the house of King Lycaon. I gave the sign that I was a god, as is my usual practice, and the people began to pray. But Lycaon jeered them, sneering at their piety. He decided to find out by a test whether I was in fact a god. At first he entertained the notion of killing me in my sleep. But that idea wasn't good enough. So he devised another one, much more sensational. Taking a hostage — a hostage, mind you! — he slit his throat, threw some of his limbs into boiling water and roasted the other limbs. These limbs he served to me for breakfast. Can you imagine! Have you ever heard of such sacrilege and such impiety! Well, I promptly dashed his house with lightning. He became so terrified that he ran off with a cry of horror; even now he cannot speak but rather bays . . . or rather howls . . . vainly trying to speak. His rabid mouth foams and those passions of his so quick for human carnage now yearn for cattle. His clothes changed to shaggy hair, his arms became another set of legs, and now in the shape of a wolf he quite resembles his former self; he still has the same grey hair, the same look of ferocity in his face, the same lurid eyes, and the same semblance of savagery.

"So, as you can see, the race of men deserves extinction."

The Flood

Hearing this story, many of the gods hailed Zeus' words with enthusiasm. Others, however, were somewhat apprehensive: what will it be like without mortals? Who will offer us sacrifices? Are you going to allow the wild animals simply to plunder everything on earth?

But Zeus allayed their fears, promising a much better race.

He was now resolved. But just as he was about to send his lightning over the face of the globe, he realized that the sky might itself accidentally catch fire from the intensity of such widespread flames. So he devised a new method: he decided to destroy the race of men with waves and to send down storms from the whole sky. There was a crash, and down the dense rains came. Everywhere a person went there were downpours from the sky and there was no let-up. Plants fell, crops were destroyed; in vain was the year-long labor of the farmer.

But Zeus was not contented with his own havoc from the skies. He enlisted the aid of his brother Poseidon, who called together all his rivers: "Let loose all your force," he enjoined them; "break all your bounds, disregard your shores and your banks; let there be no distinction between land and sea." And so did they obey. Poseidon struck the earth with his trident. Waters rushed through the open plains and they tore away the shrubs and the crops and the animals and the men and the houses . . . whatever they met they took with them. If anything was able to resist one onslaught of water, there was soon another one, mightier, to which there was no resistance. And now there was no distinction between land and sea, for everything was sea. While one man would try to seek safety on some hill, another one would sit in some makeshift boat and use oars where just a while ago he had been using his hoe. Some men sailed over their crops or over some submerged hut; others snatched fish as they sat at the top of tall elm trees. The Nereids, nymphs of the water, swimming under water admired forest groves and cities and buildings while dolphins played among the tops of trees. Wolves swam among sheep, the lion floated with the tiger, the birds hunted long for some place to land but eventually their fatigued wings gave way and they fell into the sea. Here and there a stray mountain top became an island in the sea. Almost everyone died; most of those who did manage to find some shelter starved.

Deucalion and Pyrrha

Almost everyone perished in this flood. But there was one couple, Deucalion, a son of Prometheus, and his wife Pyrrha, who survived. Warned about the oncoming flood by Prometheus, Deucalion and Pyrrha secured a boat and provisions and sailed for nine days and nine nights through the tempestuous deluge. They sought land, and eventually found one of the few tracts of land untouched by the sea. It was the peak of Mount Parnassus in the land of Phocis, or rather what had been the land of Phocis. They disembarked from their boat upon this craggy mountain top. There were no people more honorable and god-fearing than Deucalion and Pyrrha and as soon as they landed, they prayed, prayed to the nymphs of the area and to Themis, a goddess of Justice, who had sway over the shrines of Parnassus.

Now, when Zeus saw that the only people to survive the flood were such honorable people, innocent, and were even then praying to the gods, he mellowed. He scattered the clouds, calmed the skies, and stopped the downpour; then he asked Poseidon to bring his end under control. Poseidon obeyed. He ordered his son Triton to sound his trumpet to signal the return of all the waters while he himself put aside his trident and calmed the seas. Gradually the shores of the seas began to reappear, the rivers went back to their beds, hills and valleys could be seen once more.

Deucalion looked around and saw nothing but havoc and emptiness, heard nothing but silence, and he wept. "My wife, we are the only survivors on the earth; all the others have perished. Are we to be the last people on earth? For we are old and have not the power to renew life." And so they prayed.

Themis heard their prayers and she was touched by their piety and their modesty and their sincerity. And she spoke to them in the form of an oracle.

"Depart from here," she said, "and cover your heads; loosen your clothes and then cast behind you the bones of your mother."

The two of them were dumbfounded. What did this cryptic message mean? They bandied speculations of one sort and another when finally Deucalion struck on the following: "The oracle is often ambiguous. Bones of our mother! Indeed! Our common mother is the earth, the mother of us all. And her bones, of course, are the rocks of the earth."

And so the two of them obeyed the words of the oracle, gathering stones and throwing them over their shoulders. As soon

69

as they hit the ground, the stones began to lose their hardness and to assume a distinct shape. The stones that Deucalion threw became men and the ones Pyrrha threw became women. And thus the race of man, a hardier race, was renewed.

Philemon and Baucis

Zeus would occasionally seek some new diversion from his Olympian palace. And so he would from time to time come down to earth and see what there was to see. One day Hermes accompanied him, both of them having assumed mortal shape, and they called at dozens of houses, seeking a place to rest for the night. But they were welcomed nowhere; doors were peremptorily closed. Finally they tried one very small, modest house. The tenants, an elderly couple, warmly greeted them. Philemon and his wife Baucis had been living there ever since their marriage many decades before, and their life was as simple now as it had been when they began living together. The husband immediately insisted that the two travelers sit down and rest for a bit, while his wife promptly started the fire and began preparing a meal. Meanwhile the four of them chatted, and the hosts did everything they could to keep the guests from being restless or bored or uncomfortable. There was warmth and hospitality and cordiality.

After the meal was served — a meal of fruit, cherries marinated in wine, lettuce, cheese, radishes, eggs, wine, nuts, dates, figs, plums, apples, grapes, and golden honey — the four of them continued with their conversation. But Philemon and Baucis soon realized that, in spite of the fact that the four of them were helping themselves from the goblet of wine in the center of the table, the goblet was remaining full. They were apprehensive, then frightened; they immediately prayed to the gods in heaven. Fearing that this phenomenon might have something to do with the simple meal they had prepared for their guests, they excused themselves to add their goose to the menu, a goose that they had been saving to serve as a sacrifice to the gods. It was all they had. But the goose eluded them, for they being old were slow, and it ran right up to Zeus and Hermes. The two gods, impressed with the goodness of Philemon and Baucis, revealed themselves. "We are gods and this neighborhood of yours will pay for its impiety. But you two will be spared. Now let us leave; follow us, and take refuge on the hills."

They obeyed. Supported by their walking sticks, they

70

reached the top of a high hill. But as they looked down, all they could see was a swamp; nothing remained of what they once knew except their own house. And while they were amazed at what they were seeing and were wondering at what had happened to all their neighbors, they saw their own house, that small hut, being changed into a temple. Columns replaced wooden beams, the straw thatching became golden, the ground became marble, the doors became filled with embossed carvings, and even the roof became gold.

"Now tell us, worthy people, what would you like for yourselves?" inquired Zeus. The two mortals conferred and they made two requests. "Let us be your priests and care for one of your temples, and let us die together; we have lived together for a long time; may we also never have to see the other's tomb."

They were granted their requests. They became keepers of the temple that had once been their home. And when the time for their death came, each beheld the other becoming leafy limbs of trees, intertwined, with just one trunk. And so, as they had lived together, they died together and are still united. You can still see that tree; and not far from it you can still see a murky swamp, a fen that was once a land where people lived.

a. The parallels between the flood of Zeus and the flood in the *Old Testament* are obvious, even to the point of having a common Noah.

b. A fairly common theme in mythology is that of the metamorphosis or change. Often the metamorphosis embodies a sort of poetic justice. Hence, Odysseus' men, when they visit Circe in Book X of the *Odyssey*, are changed into pigs, which is symbolically entirely appropriate because they have been acting like pigs, leading their lives with only swinish creature comforts in mind. Similarly Lycaon, having been ravenous and bestial, is turned into a wolf. And similarly, Philemon and Baucis, who lived a noble and harmonious life, find dignity and oneness in their death.

c. One of the most common strains in the myths of degeneration is that of violated hospitality. We saw this strain cited as one of the great condemnations of the Iron Age. Lycaon not only insults his guest, who just happens to be Zeus, but also kills an innocent hostage, someone sent to him in good faith. Lycaon's breach of hospitality is really the catalyst for Zeus' destroying of the whole world. That is how seriously the Greeks regarded the guest-host relationship.

d. Of course, the Philemon/Baucis story explains the importance of the guest-host relationship. After all, a stranger just might turn out to be a god. Furthermore, there were no hotels, no guest houses. When a Greek traveled, he depended upon the good will of people to shelter and feed him. It was not a privilege, it was a right, an expectation. Throughout the *Odyssey* appear examples of the guest-host relationship and the high value which the Greeks placed upon it.

e. There is a school of thought which compares the story of Philemon and Baucis with the story of Abraham and Lot in the cities of Sodom and Gomorrah. It is far-fetched but nonetheless curious. One might even be reminded of the story in Norse mythology where Odin rewards the hospitality of an aged couple by protecting their son Rogner from the giant Skrymsli, a totally coincidental similarity but one that again illustrates the motif of rewarded hospitality.

f. In spite of the fact that these stories are all collected within one chapter, there is not necessarily any chronological connection among them. They are merely separate stories, each sufficient unto itself, and the only connection is a thematic one.

g. For another variation of the Deucalion/Pyrrha story, see the story of Cadmus. The idea of men springing from rocks also is similar to the idea of men springing from the teeth of a dragon in the adventures of Jason and his quest for the golden fleece. Again, it is the earth that gives birth to new creatures.

h. Regarding the end of the Deucalion/Pyrrha story, some sources try to force a connection between the Greek word for stone (*laas*) and the word for people (*laos*). Although it is an attractive connection, the two words are not related.

i. Deucalion, the son of Prometheus, had a son named Hellen. Hellen gave his name to the *Hellenes,* and four of his descendants gave their names to the great divisions of the Greeks: The Acheans, Dorians, Ionians, and Aeoleans. The following table lists some of the major names in the genealogy.

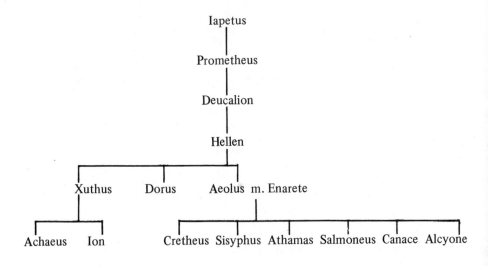

CHAPTER VI

HADES AND THE UNDERWORLD

Hades (Pluto)

Just as Zeus ruled the skies and Poseidon the seas, so Hades ruled the Underworld. The name Hades means "not able to be seen," for Hades comes upon men unaware. He had a helmet, a gift from the Cyclops, that made him invisible. He might have been unwelcome but he was not evil or satanic. He was merely a representation of all those mysterious forces that await people after death and of those unknown forces that occur beneath the Earth. Since the area under the Earth was his and since that is where resources and metals and gems are found, he eventually became associated with the Greek word for wealth (*ploutos*) and emerged in Roman mythology as Pluto. Although Hades was a very powerful figure, he was not one of the Olympian gods, for he rarely ever left the Underworld, but like Poseidon and the other gods, he was subject to Zeus.

He governed the Underworld with his wife Persephone, who visited him for several months out of every year and whose story has already been told.[1] She had little love for him and never became a real wife to him, but she did become an effective queen and she took on more and more of a role as Queen of the Underworld, sometimes even deciding who should or should not be able to enter her domain.

Although one often hears the Underworld referred to as Hades, such a reference is inappropriate. The House of Hades or some such equivalent is the proper phraseology.

The Underworld

The concept of the Underworld both as an actual geographical location and as a projection of what happens to people after they die was not a fixed one. It varied from historical period to historical period and from people to people within the different historical periods. There was no one fixed view of the Underworld; rather there were different and often contradictory views of what the Underworld was

1. See page 16-17.

like. Only some of the bolder differences are included here, for there are enough features that do seem fairly constant to provide a reasonably full picture.

One of the best accounts of the Underworld comes from Hesiod, writing in the eighth century but often reflecting long-standing traditional views. His account is more imaginative than lucid, and we have already seen part of it in the description of Zeus' banishment of the Titans:

> Dark and murky Tartarus is as far beneath the earth as the earth is beneath the sky. It would take nine full days for an anvil to fall from the sky to the earth, similarly another nine full days to fall from the earth to Tartarus. There is a bronze fence around the place and there are three layers of darkness. The highest part of the area is like a neck, and it is here that one enters from the earth; here at the neck are the roots of the earth and the sea. The descent from the top to the bottom is so enormous that it would take a year, and you, while descending, would be constantly buffeted by one whirlwind and another.

> One of the first places you would see as you left the earth would be the high-ceilinged palace of Hades and Persephone. A dreadful and ruthless dog guards the entrance: he is very nice to you when you enter but if you try to go out, he pounces upon you and tears you apart. He has fifty heads and an incredibly loud voice. There too is the River Styx, daughter of Tethys and Oceanus, with her freezing-cold water. One-tenth of the waters of Oceanus comprises the Styx. The lowest part extends indefinitely into Chaos and it is here that the Titans have been confined.

Hesiod's account is actually much fuller than the two paragraphs just presented, but those paragraphs give a bit of the flavor.

Entrance to the Underworld came through death, although under very special circumstances it was possible for a mortal while still alive to visit. When you died, Hermes would come for you and would usher you to the land below. He would lead you to the River Styx, which served as the official boundary between the land of the living and the land of the dead. One tradition had some living person put a coin in your mouth just after you died so that you would be able to give that coin to **Charon,** the ferryman of the Styx, as his fare. If you didn't have the fare, you would wander forever along the banks of the river, never finding any rest. Charon is an old man, the son of Erebus, disheveled, rather dirty; his clothes are shabby; he is usually either cynical or cantankerous. His small boat is in constant need of repair.

Before you are ushered by Hermes, however, it is absolutely essential that you receive proper burial. In an emergency, burial may

74

CHARON IN HIS BOAT. Red Figured Vase with a white ground, attributed to the Sabouroff Painter, 5th Century B.C. Charon, the ferryman of the River Styx, is waiting for a passenger. The arm and wand to the right belong to Hermes Psychopompus, who is leading the soul of a recently dead man to Charon. *Courtesy, Metropolitan Museum of Art, New York, Rogers Fund, 1921.*

simply mean that some living person sprinkle a bit of earth upon you. If you came upon a corpse, you were expected to give it at least a symbolic burial by sprinkling three handfuls of earth upon it; otherwise you yourself would be accursed. In some localities and during some historical periods, proper burial could mean cremation, and myths allude frequently to the funeral pyre, a pile of wood on

75

which a corpse was placed for burning. An unburied spirit could not enter the Underworld; Charon would not take him across the Styx. The spirit would wander forever over the earth, always restive, and this was considered one of the worst things that could possibly happen.

Once you get across the Styx, you go by the dog **Cerberus**. Some writers say that he has a hundred heads, others say he has only fifty, and still others say he has only three. Regardless, he pays you little mind as you enter but will destroy you if you try to leave. He has the tail of a serpent, his back is covered with the heads of snakes, and each of his mouths can produce a thunderously deafening roar. As you pass Cerberus, you have entered into the domain of Hades, often described as an enormous palace which extends very deep down. You meet three judges: Minos, Aeacus, and Rhadamanthus. Minos was the son of Zeus and Europa and in life had been a king of Crete; Rhadamanthus, his brother, had been particularly just in life; Aeacus, son of Zeus and Aegina, ruled in life over the Myrmidons and was the grandfather of the warrior Achilles. Whether each of the three had his own sphere of influence in the Underworld is a moot point; almost every author who writes about the three judges assigns to each a different domain. There is absolutely no consistency whatsoever. For instance, while some authors say that Rhadamanthus' domain is the Elysian Fields, Plato says that he judges the dead from Asia, while Vergil claims that he judges the souls of those who had been evil in life.

At any rate, you are judged. Unless you have done something absolutely dreadful — such as disrespecting your parents, violating the guest/host relationship, or defying the gods — you spend your existence as a ghost or shade, merely a shadowy, insubstantial representation of your former self; it is an empty, sterile, numb existence characterized by neither pleasure nor pain, by neither excitement nor depression, by neither joy nor sorrow: it is characterized only by nothingness.

When you enter this part of the Underworld, you often drink of the River **Lethe** in order to forget everything from your past: oblivion makes the unending tedium less oppressive. This part of the Underworld is sometimes referred to as Erebus, sometimes as the Domain of Hades, sometimes merely as the Underworld.

Those who committed serious sins in their lives go to the Land of the Damned, often referred to as Tartarus. Here the sinners are punished for eternity, and the nature of their punishment is usually centered upon some type of perpetual frustration. Very rarely does the notion of actual physical pain and suffering enter into the concept of the Underworld, at least in the early periods of history.

Finally there are the Islands of the Blessed, Elysium or the **Elysian Fields.** You will recall[1] that here is where the heroes from Hesiod's fourth great age went. Other writers add to that description saying that there are wonderful ocean breezes and golden flowers, some on the land and others actually in the water. They say that life there is very carefree; there is neither snow nor winter nor even a quick rainstorm, and the ocean is always sending gentle breezes to refresh the inhabitants.

The relationship among the various parts of the Underworld is inconsistent as is the actual topography. Whereas the early view was that most of the souls went to that state of limbo that was sometimes called Erebus, sometimes Asphodel, and sometimes merely referred to as the Underworld and that only the egregiously wicked and the favored of the gods suffered punishment or experienced bliss in Elysium, gradually such distinctions became even more blurred, and there was somewhat of a movement into the belief that one's lot in the Underworld reflected one's life on earth. Punishment and bliss became much less exclusive.

The following represents a digest of some of the other important names associated with the Underworld:

There were five rivers: the Styx or the hateful river, the Lethe or the river of forgetfulness, the Acheron or the river of distress, the Cocytus or the river of lament and wailing, and the Phlegethon (Pyriphlegethon) or the river of blazing fire. The Styx and the Acheron were sometimes each referred to as the one that Charon must usher a spirit across.

The **Styx** herself was the daughter of the Titans Tethys and Oceanus and her offspring were Cratos (Strength or Power), Bia (Violence or Force), Nike (Victory), and Zelos (Jealousy). Her waters were supposedly very cold and she completely surrounded the Underworld. The River, furthermore, was the river of oaths. Since she had assisted Zeus and his party in their battle of the Titans, she was rewarded by being assigned as the witness of the most sacred oaths. If a god were to take a false oath over the Styx, he would be breathless for a year, as if in a trance; then for the next nine years he would not be able to mix with the other gods.

The inhabitants of the Underworld were sometimes called "shades," "souls," "spirits," "shadows," "ghosts" (the word has nothing to do with our conception of creatures that haunt), and in Roman literature *manes.*

1. See page 65.

In addition to Hades and Persephone, there were a few other powers associated with the Underworld. There were the Three Furies or Erinyes who were described in Chapter I: Alecto, Tisiphone, and Megaera. There was Thanatos, one of the sons of Night, who was merely a personification of Death. And there was Hypnos, another son of Night, who was a personification of Sleep.

One of the most enigmatic and elusive of all the divinities is **Hecate**. Great granddaughter of the Titans Coeus and Phoebe and granddaughter of Leto, she was related to Artemis and Apollo. She was often identified with the moon — not, however, as a goddess of light but rather of darkness. She represented what a person does or what happens to a person by moonlight or darkness.

She was originally a kindly but powerful earth goddess, a patron, for instance, of statesmen, warriors, athletes, sailors, horsemen, flocks, and children. If people sacrificed to her, they could gain much honor; and if she heard this prayer kindly, she could secure them much wealth, for she had the power. But as she gave, so did she also withhold or even take away, and she appears quite arbitrary about whom she supported and whom she scorned. Hence, she could represent both fertility and deprivation.

She was the one who was aware of the abduction of Persephone from the earth into the Underworld by Hades. In fact, after Persephone was rescued, she and Persephone embraced, and, it would appear, the two of them became quite close. That association may contribute to Hecate's eventually becoming a goddess primarily associated with the Underworld, for in later literature and art she definitely becomes a force of the occult, of black magic, sorcery, witches, spells, rites, incantations, and mysteries. It is primarily in this capacity as a sorceress/witch/magician that she has come down to us in western literature.

Here is a description of how she appeared when summoned by the proper rite:

> The dreadful goddess arose from the most remote part of the Underworld and around her on the oak branches horrible snakes were twining; there was a flash of countless torches, and the dogs of hell howled all around her. The meadows shook as she walked, and the nymphs that haunt swamps and rivers screamed.

Hecate was the patron of the sorceress Medea. She was also reputed to have been the mother of that bane to sailors, Scylla.

A few figures managed to enter the Underworld and leave it:

Odysseus, to consult with Tiresias, the blind prophet, about his return back to Ithaca.

78

Heracles, when he went to kidnap Cerberus.

Theseus, when he tried to kidnap Persephone for his friend Pirithous.

Aeneas, when he went to see his father Anchises.

Orpheus, when he went to reclaim his wife, Eurydice.

Persephone, during her yearly stay with Hades.

Alcestis, when she gave her life for her husband's and was either rescued by Heracles or rejected by Persephone.

Adonis, when he was entrusted to Persephone as a baby.

Dionysus, who went to rescue his mother, Semele.

Psyche, when she was fulfilling her chores for Aphrodite.

Finally, no description of the Underworld would be complete without a mention of some of the famous sinners and their punishments:

Tantalus was a son of Zeus and there are various accounts of his crime. a) Reveling too much in his prosperity and becoming too proud, he wished to test the cleverness of the gods. Consequently, he invited them to a banquet and, having cut up his son Pelops, served Pelops' limbs to the gods. b) He stole nectar and ambrosia from the gods and offered them to his companions. c) He divulged personal details about the gods. d) He lied under oath, denying that he knew anything about Zeus' dog, which had, in fact, been stolen by Pandareus and entrusted to Tantalus. His punishment is described by Homer:

> Tantalus suffers terrible pains as he stands in a pond. He is thirsty, but just as he lowers his head to drink, the water lowers. Tall trees overhang him, trees teeming with juicy fruit of apples and pears and figs and olives; but just as he lifts himself to grab one, the wind whisks them away.

Another tradition states that he perpetually has a rock ready to fall upon his head and exists in a state of constant apprehension. Euripides even claims that he is suspended in mid-air.

Sisyphus was the son of Aeolus and founder of Corinth. When Zeus, having lusted after Aegina, took her away, Sisyphus told her father Asopus that Zeus had abducted her. For this betrayal of Zeus, he was sent to the Underworld: he must push an enormous stone up a steep hill; just as he is about to reach the top, either he stumbles or the rock shifts balance, for the rock rolls back down the hill.

Sisyphus comes down to us as one of the shrewdest, craftiest, and most dishonest of all mortals. One story tells that when Death came to claim Sisyphus, he slipped strong bonds upon him and held him prisoner; consequently, no one was able to die. Naturally this hit Ares the hardest; therefore, he personally came and freed Death. Then, before Sisyphus died, he left instructions with his wife that he not be buried. Through his wiles he then persuaded Persephone that he should not be in the realm of Hades since he had not received proper burial. Persephone fell for his line and allowed him to go back up to Earth, and Hermes himself had to force him back into the Underworld. In life he was a notorious thief; he was also famed for his greediness, fraud, and propensity to cheat. He can be imagined as the archetypal con artist. It is even said that he raped Anticleia before she married Laertes and thus was the actual father of Odysseus.

Ixion represents one of the worst sinners of all. He first killed his father-in-law so that he would not have to fulfill his promise of a fine bridal gift. Zeus, however, pardoned him, for Zeus had had an affair with Ixion's wife, Dia, and had even fathered a son, Pirithous, later to be the companion of Theseus. Zeus allowed Ixion to dine with the Olympians, and in the process Ixion fell in love with Hera. Hera became indignant, but Zeus was amused. He decided to test the intensity of Ixion's passion and made a model of Hera out of a cloud. Ixion's passion was indeed as intense as had been suspected. He slept with this mock-Hera, not knowing it was a counterfeit, and went back to earth, where he boasted of having made a conquest of the goddess. It was for his boasting that he was punished. He was tied to a wheel — some say that it was constantly on fire — that never stopped spinning. Meanwhile, that counterfeit of Hera that he had spent the night with gave birth to Centaurus. Centaurus, in turn, indeed his father's son, in union with a horse, fathered the Centaurs, a species of creatures that were half man, half horse.

Tityus, the giant son of Gaia, has already been alluded to in the description of Apollo.[1] For his sin of trying to rape Leto, the giant was stretched out over nine acres of ground while two vultures sitting on either side of him pecked at his liver.

There were fifty **daughters of Danaus**, King of Argos. His brother, Aegyptus, King of Egypt, who had fifty sons, visited Danaus one day, asked for a reconciliation, and suggested that his own fifty sons marry Danaus' fifty daughters. Danaus was suspicious. He, therefore, devised a plan. He instructed his daughters to marry as Aegyptus had suggested and then to kill their respective husbands. The pairings were determined by lot; then there was a marriage feast, and that night the daughters of King Danaus stabbed their husbands as they slept . . . all except Hypermnestra, who had fallen in love with hers.

1. See page 20.

For their impiety in killing their husbands, the forty-nine guilty daughters were required to fill a large container with water. The container, however, was full of holes, and no matter how hard they tried — or are still trying — they could not fill it.

Pirithous was the son of Zeus and Ixion's wife, Dia, and eventually he became a close friend of Theseus. The two of them had gone down to the Underworld to try to secure Persephone as a bride for Pirithous. But Hades had caught them and fixed them to the slab of stone on which they were sitting: they and the stone became one. Eventually, however, Theseus was released by Heracles, but Heracles could not save Pirithous; when he tried to lift Pirithous, there was an earthquake, and he sank back into the earth.

CHAPTER VII

MYTHS OF DEATH AND RESURRECTION

The story of Orpheus

Orpheus was the son of Calliope, one of the nine Muses, the goddesses of inspiration. He grew up in Thrace where, trained by Apollo, he learned the use of the lyre and the art of song, and by the time he was a young man, he was as fine a musician as anyone who had ever lived. All nature responded to his song: the winds would stop rustling, the beasts would stop whatever they were doing, even the leaves of the trees would turn their attention to Orpheus when he came by.

While still a young man, he joined Jason on his quest for the Golden Fleece. People say that he would charm the firmest rocks on the hillsides, that the rivers would follow him, and that even the wild oaks of the forest marched in file to the shores of Thrace. While aboard the *Argo,* Orpheus' lyre would inspire the crew in its rowing just as it might inspire a group of youths to dance in honor of Apollo. His music stopped quarrels, and even after he finished a song, people would still be absolutely silent and intent, so charming and captivating was his music. At another time when the Argonauts were in danger of being harmed by the Sirens, Orpheus sang so splendidly that he outdid the Sirens' song, thereby allowing his shipmates to stay on course. And at another time when the Argonauts were suffering from thirst, Orpheus prevailed upon the Hesperides to find water for them. Throughout his adventure with the Argonauts, he showed good judgment and the ability to charm man, beast, nature, and gods.

After the adventure with Jason, Orpheus returned home and fell in love with a maiden called Eurydice. Soon after they were married, Eurydice, while running through a field, was bitten by a snake and died. Orpheus wept; the whole world heard his sorrow.

Orpheus' grief was so great that he resolved to go down to the Underworld in order to get her back. He came to Hades and to Persephone, for she happened to be with him at this time, and said,

"Sir, let me speak with complete candor. I have come here not to visit Tartarus nor to inflict any sort of harm on those whom you host here. I have come for my wife. She died in the prime of

82

her life. I tried to endure her loss, but Love was too strong. Sir, you know yourself of the powers of Love. Look at what you went through to gain this young lady," and he pointed to Persephone. "Sir, I beg of you: give back life to Eurydice. We will both join you here when old age comes upon us. Meanwhile, may I prevail upon you for this one boon?"

The effect that this song — for he did not speak the words above but rather sang them — had upon the creatures of the Underworld was astonishing. Tantalus stopped going after his drink of water, Ixion's wheel stopped spinning, the vultures stopped pecking at Tityus, Sisyphus' rock remained stationary, and even the heartless Furies began to weep. Cerberus became distracted from his watch, and all the spirits of the Underworld gathered in full force to hear his beautiful music. Even Hades himself was moved, and he summoned Eurydice. She was still limping from her snake bite. The two greeted each other eagerly. Eurydice would be allowed to rejoin her husband, but he would have to lead her out of the Underworld and under no condition must he set his eyes upon her until they were both securely back on earth.

Forward and upward did they go on a steep, gloomy, and murky path; each was silent. Finally he reached the surface. Desperate to see her, wondering whether she was really still behind him, he turned, and immediately she fell back into the hands of Hades. No words of complaint or indignation on her part; just one sincere "goodbye." And the two were forevermore separated from enjoying together the fruits of the earth.

A hill was nearby and on that hill a wide, open, verdant plain. There was no shade whatsoever in this place. There Orpheus went; he sat down and began to sing. Immediately a refreshing shade came to the place. An oak tree joined him as did poplars and delicate lime trees, beech trees, laurels, willows, evergreens and an assortment of other kinds.

They say that he wept constantly for seven months, that his tears often mixed with his songs, and that his songs soothed even the wildest animals. The trees of the woods, the beasts of the forest, even the rocks followed him. He now avoided women completely even though several women had desired him and had grieved when spurned by him, and he is said to have been the first to encourage men to give their affections to youths.

One day a group of Thracian women, dressed only in the skins of animals, saw him from the top of a hill. One of them, tossing her head and giving her hair to the winds, gave out a cry: "There he is, there he is! There is the one who has snubbed us, ignored us, disdained our company for so long a time." She threw a stone, but it lodged at his feet, subdued by his music. The women got more and more aroused. All moderation, all discretion, all judgment left and dreadful madness ran rampant. All their weapons would have become harmless, tamed by his song, except that these women began making such a noise, stamping their feet, playing their drums and tambourines, clapping their hands, yelling, and chanting that they drowned out Orpheus' voice. He was hit and fell over.

At first the women grabbed several of the birds and snakes and wild beasts that had succumbed to Orpheus' music and they tore these creatures apart with their hands in an even greater rage. And then they pounced upon the poet himself; some threw stones, others threw pieces of dirt, others threw sticks. Then they mutilated him, tearing him limb from limb, many of them using harrows, rakes, and spades from nearby farms. They scattered his limbs all over. The head and the lyre fell into the River Hebrus; from there they floated to the sea and to the shores of Lesbos. A vicious serpent attacked the head as it was floating to this new shore, but Apollo drove out the beast. The Muses gathered the rest of his limbs and buried them at the foot of Mount Olympus, and even now the nightingales that perch upon his grave sing more sweetly and more grandly than any other nightingales.

Meanwhile, the spirit of the dead Orpheus descended to Tartarus. Here he found his wife; the two of them embraced; once again they walked hand in hand; oftentimes he would lead her in their walks; but no more did he have to worry about turning around.

The women tried to wash their hands of Orpheus' blood; but as often as they tried to dip their hands into the river, the more underground it went, not wanting to defile its waters with the blood from their hands.

Aphrodite and Adonis

Cinyras, King of Cyprus, a place sacred to Aphrodite, had a daughter named Myrrha who was courted by the finest suitors in the land. But she ignored Aphrodite, a goddess never to be spurned, and the goddess punished her by planting in her a passion for her father which, as hard as she tried to resist, overwhelmed her. Through the wiles of her nurse, she managed to spend several nights with him, he never knowing who it was that he was embracing until one fateful evening when he brought in a light. Horrified when he recognized that his companion was his daughter, he grabbed a spear to kill her, but she, young and lithe, escaped him and ran off into the woods. Repentant she prayed to whatever god would hear her: "Oh gods, if any of you have mercy on those who repent, pity me now. I have done wrong, I know that, and I am deserving of punishment. It is right that I mix with neither the living nor the dead, so foul a deed have I committed. Therefore, disguise me, so that no one may recognize me in my shame."

A compassionate deity heard her prayer — perhaps it was Aphrodite — and she was changed into a tree, the myrrh tree, and, though she lost all recognition of her former self, she still sheds tears, tears of frankincense.

A child, however, was conceived in that union between Myrrha and Cinyras, and Aphrodite helped his birth, a splendidly beautiful boy. His name was Adonis. Moved by his beauty and concerned for his safety, Aphrodite concealed the boy in a chest and entrusted him to Persephone, the Queen of the Underworld, for safekeeping. Persephone, however, opened the chest, and when she beheld the boy, she too fell in love with him. A dispute arose between the two goddesses, and Zeus was asked to arbitrate. He decided that the boy should spend a third of the year with one of the goddesses, another third with the other, and the final third by himself. But when Adonis relinquished his own four months to Aphrodite, Persephone became jealous. She, in turn, filled Ares with jealousy, for Ares was always eager for Aphrodite's favors.

Ares, now, was not about to take second place to a paltry human being. He went to Artemis and prevailed upon her to assist him in his revenge.

Adonis used to spend much of his time in the forests, often hunting. On one of these occasions, he came across a boar. He shot at the boar but only wounded it. The animal, overcome by pain and rage, counter-attacked his assailant and gored him in the groin. Some say that this boar had been sent by Artemis; others say that the boar was the disguised Ares; still others suggest that neither Artemis nor Ares had any part in the deed. At any rate, the beautiful Adonis was dead.

Aphrodite heard his dying groans and went to him, but it was too late. She kissed him. The mountains, the rivers, and the flowers wept with her. But Persephone had had her revenge; the fair Adonis is with her still, and she will never have to share him.

Aphrodite then sprinkled the blood from his wound with nectar and in a short time flowers sprang up, flowers the same color as blood, the flower called the "anemone" or "wind flower," because it blossoms only when the wind blows but is so fragile that it often falls from those very winds.

Aphrodite then summoned that boar which had so meanly deprived her of her beloved Adonis. But the boar pleaded with her:

"Cytherea, I swear to you that I did not want to wound him, but when I saw him I was so taken by his beauty that I sought merely to kiss him. That was my only intention; little did I realize the force of my kiss."

Aphrodite was moved by his words and she understood what he was saying and she pitied him.

Alcestis

Admetus was King of Pherae in Thessaly. It was he, you will recall[1], that Apollo served during those years in which he was punished for his wanton slaying of the Cyclops in revenge for Zeus' killing of Asclepius. Both Apollo and Admetus got along well; Apollo assumed his role as servant with grace, and Admetus was a sensitive and kind master.

Now, Admetus fell in love with a young maiden named Alcestis, the daughter of Pelias. Alcestis was courted from wide and far; therefore, her father, to settle the rivalries for her hand, decided that only he who could team together a lion and a boar to a chariot would win her. Admetus with Apollo's assistance performed the feat and hence won the object of his love. They were married. But Admetus, in the impetuousness of his marriage rites, omitted to offer sacrifice to Artemis, the patron of young girls and a goddess never to be disregarded. The goddess' indignation was aroused; that night, when Admetus went to the bedroom, he found the room filled with snakes. Apollo got him quickly to appease the goddess, and all was well for a while.

But their happiness was short lived. Apollo, wanting to repay the kindness of his host, went to the Fates to learn about Admetus' destiny. What he learned, however, was not what he expected. Lachesis had already apportioned Admetus' thread of life, and Atropos was just about to cut the thread. In an instant, the god left and returned, bringing with him this time some wine; with his usual grace and

1. See page 22.

86

charm he prevailed upon them to drink. While they were high and their defenses were down, Apollo cajoled them into making a little deal: they would leave Admetus' life-thread alone if he could find another person who would voluntarily offer his life in place of Admetus'. Admetus, upon hearing of this bargain from Apollo, immediately set out to find someone to take his place. He asked his parents; they refused, relishing every breath of life that they were entitled to: "We may not have a very long time here among the living," remarked his father, "but every minute of life is sweet!" Quite a quarrel ensued between father and son, but neither side yielded. In fact, Admetus could find no one to volunteer his life for him . . . no one except Alcestis, his wife, who out of love for her husband and out of concern lest their children be fatherless, volunteered herself. Death came and claimed the loyal Alcestis.

All of Thessaly joined with Admetus in mourning. Manes of horses were ordered to be sheared, there was to be no music in Pherae for a year; the males were all to shave their heads, and everyone was to wear black clothing.

Now just at this time, Heracles appeared in Pherae. He was in the midst of one of his labors and was seeking a brief respite. He called on Admetus' house. He immediately sensed that something was wrong, but could get no straight answer. In fact, Admetus equivocated, hemmed and hawed, doing everything he could not to tell Heracles that the household was in mourning. Heracles even suggested that he might go elsewhere, but Admetus would hear none of this, so keenly did he feel his responsibilities as a host. In fact, to prevent any stain upon his hospitality, he had Heracles put in a room which faced the outside of the palace so that his guest might not hear the sounds of mourning from within the house.

Heracles stayed and took full advantage of Admetus' hospitality. He bumbled around to an almost comic extent. The servants of the house complained about his rowdiness. He drank too much, shouted for more, garlanded himself with ivy and myrtle, and sang boisterously. When he observed their sullen looks, he tried to cajole them. "Life is too short to pout. No one knows whether he'll be alive tomorrow or not. Therefore, take this advice from me: enjoy today; enjoy the present. Be happy, drink, and above all give Aphrodite her due."

The servants claimed that it was no time for merriment and then proceeded to tell Heracles about the story of Alcestis. Heracles listened, amazed as he realized the true extent of Admetus' hospitality. Then he decided that he had to reward such cordiality. "I will go out and find the Lord of the Dead," decided Heracles; "he's probably right now near the tomb of his latest conquest. I'll sneak up on him and catch him off guard and latch on to him with such a hold that he'll not be able to move. Nor will he ever get free until he gives up the girl to me." And that is exactly what he did; he challenged Death and he won. Alcestis was returned to the world of the living.

a. Apollodorus, telling the story of Alcestis, has two important variations from the version told here. First of all, he claims that Admetus, after he had soothed the indignant Artemis on that first night of his marriage, apparently was so effective that it was she then who granted him the privilege of being able to find a substitute when it was to be the time for his death. Of course, she was in part influenced by the charms of her brother Apollo. Secondly, he states that when Alcestis died, Persephone would not admit her into the Underworld, apparently feeling that the circumstances of her death were improper. But Apollodorus does also recognize the other version, i.e., the subduing of Hades by Heracles.

b.The Alcestis story is somewhat unique in Greek mythology, for it is one of the few stories that stress positive aspects of human relationships: Alcestis' love for and devotion to her husband, shown by her willingness to sacrifice herself for him; Admetus' loyalty to her, shown by his sincere mourning; Admetus' exceptional hospitality, shown by his insistence upon making Heracles welcome while concealing his own sorrow; and Heracles' sense of appreciation to his host and his innate fearlessness, shown by his immediate willingness to tackle Death itself.

c. In considering myths of death and rebirth, one should not forget the Egyptian Phoenix. The Phoenix was a remarkably beautiful bird. Its wings were a blend of red and gold, and in stature it was like an eagle. According to tradition, the bird exists, gradually aging, for five hundred years. Then he is consumed by fire and from his own ashes rises anew, reborn and revitalized.

Neither should one forget the Demeter-Persephone story,[1] a clear example of death and rebirth. The story of Persephone offers a good illustration of the aetiological type of myth. Crops, plant life, and all life from the earth start to wane when Persephone goes to visit Hades each year, and they all begin to revive when she returns four months later. But not only does the myth offer an explanation for the cycle of plants. It also gives some hope to men. Perhaps death does not demand the finality that it may seem to demand.

d. The story of Orpheus stresses his brilliance as a poet and musician. Several poems allegedly written by him formed the basis for a mystery religion known as **Orphism**. As in all mystery religions — such as the Eleusinian Mysteries already referred to[2] — details of the cult were kept secret from all but the initiated. One of the central tenets of the cult

1. See page 16-17.

2. See page 18, note (b).

was the promise of some sort of life after death. A unique aspect of the cult was its emphasis upon sin. repentance, and asceticism. The central god of Orphism was Zagreus,[1] who was identified with Dionysus, and Orpheus was his prophet. From the alleged writings of Orpheus sprang a mythology with many eccentric details — a mythology quite different from the traditional body of myths.

e. In examining the motif of death and rebirth, one should not forget the stories, already told, of the births of Athena, Dionysus, and Asclepius. Remember, too, that Asclepius was said to have revived the dead and himself to have been revived from the dead by Apollo.

f. There is remarkable similarity between the Greek fertility myths — especially those of Orpheus, of Demeter and Persephone, and of Zagreus, that Orphic counterpart of Dionysus — and the Isis-Osiris story in Egyptian mythology. Like Orpheus, Osiris was a civilizing force throughout the world; like Orpheus, he was torn apart and pieced back together — this motif, curiously, seems to be a common one in mythologies: see, for instance, the same idea in the Finnish story of Lemminkeinen in the *Kalevala,* the national epic of Finland — in fact, he actually died and was resurrected twice. In this capacity of being reborn, he is quite similar to Persephone; whereas Persephone represents the death and return of crops, Osiris represents the flooding and withdrawal of the waters of the Nile, the river that fertilizes the crops. After his final death, Osiris was sent to the Underworld and made a god of the dead. His wife, Isis, mourned and hunted for him in much the same way that Demeter hunted for Persephone; both Demeter and Isis were divinities of vegetation, especially the idea of rebirth that vegetation predicates. Just as Demeter effected the resurrection of Persephone and just as Isis twice effected the rebirth of Osiris, so both Isis and Demeter yearly effect the rebirth of crops. Like Demeter, Isis taught the use of land for crops; like Demeter, Isis developed a very important cult associated with herself; like Demeter, Isis bathed a baby of a foreign queen in flames in order to insure immortality; and in both cases the mothers interfered. For a fuller account of the Isis-Osiris story, see Plutarch's essay, *On Isis and Osiris.* This essay also cites many parallels between the motifs just cited and Zagreus, the Orphic Dionysus.

g. One might also note the similarity between the stories of Demeter/ Persephone and of Orpheus and the Christian ritual celebrated during Lent and Easter.

1.   See page 48, note (b).

CHAPTER VIII

MYTHS OF THE FALL

The story of Orion

In spite of the fact that he was a giant, Orion was an exceptionally handsome man, the son of Poseidon and Euryale. Living in Boeotia, he had ample opportunity to indulge his interests in hunting, and he became a very mighty hunter. He was known also as a hero, for he had built several works through his great strength and his love of glory. He made a harbor on Sicily, for instance, and he was partially responsible for turning Sicily from a peninsula into an island. His powers were such that he is said even to have been able to walk the sea.

He first married a woman named Side, but she claimed she was more beautiful than Hera and was thrown into the Underworld. Then he went to the land of Chios where he fell in love with Merope, the daughter of Dionysus' son Oenopion. He asked the father for her hand, and he consented providing that Orion would clean the island of all its wild beasts. Orion agreed. When Oenopion kept on stalling the time for the marriage, Orion became frustrated and once, in a moment of intoxication, tried to rape Merope. He was unsuccessful, but he aroused the spite of Oenopion. The King enlisted the assistance of a few satyrs who got Orion so drunk that he fell asleep, and Oenopion put out his eyes.

Hearing that the rays of the rising sun had restorative powers, he went east. Then, he tuned his ear to the sound of Hephaistus' workmen, the Cyclops on the island of Lemnos, and the god there gave him one of his apprentices as a guide, a young fellow named Cedalion. They got to the sunrise, Orion looked directly up, and he was cured.

But he now had revenge on his mind. Oenopion would pay for his crime! The King, however, was in hiding: Hephaistus and Poseidon had made him a chamber under the ground. Meanwhile, as Orion hunted for Oenopion, Eos, the Dawn, saw him and fell in love with him, for it was her fate constantly to fall in love with handsome young men. This was a punishment from Aphrodite, who had never forgiven Eos for sleeping with Ares.

How Orion met his end is told differently by different people. Some say that when the gods saw the relationship between Orion and Eos, they prevailed upon Artemis to kill the hunter. Others say that Artemis killed him when he challenged her at discus throwing. Still others say that he tried to rape her and was instantly put in his place. A fourth account claims that he boasted that there was no animal he couldn't conquer. The Earth was indignant at such a claim and sent a scorpion; Orion destroyed the scorpion but did not survive its sting. It is said that Asclepius brought Orion back to life; but the two of them were smitten by Zeus' thunderbolt, and Orion entered the sky as a constellation, and even now, when the Scorpion arises in the East, Orion flees in the West. Finally, a fifth account claims that Orion had ingratiated himself much too closely with Artemis; both would hunt and run through the woods all day. Apollo, wondering whether his twin sister would be led astray by this powerful and handsome creature, tricked her into firing her arrow at an object in the sea; it turned out to be Orion, and he was slain. The last account claims that Orion fell in love with the Pleiades and chased them night and day for several years. When Zeus saw the frustration of both parties, he lifted them both into the sky. Though the accounts of Orion's fall differ, they each indicate that he had gone too far.

The story of Phaeton

The palace of Helios, the Sun, was a lofty one. There were stately columns with gold, double doors of silver, and ceilings of ivory. There were even splendid engravings done by Hephaistus himself.

One day a youth approached this palace. He seemed confused, dazzled by all the splendor; he had to cover his eyes when he approached Helios so dazzling was his appearance. The youth was Phaeton, a son of Helios, who had been living with his mother but who now was eager to announce himself to his father. He had heard that he was Helios' son and now wanted some proof.

Helios was charmed by the youth and he offered to give him any gift that he wanted as proof of his birth. He confirmed this promise with an oath from the waters of the River Styx. Scarcely had he taken this oath when the boy asked to steer his horse-drawn chariot for just one day. Helios hesitated. "I know that I have promised you anything," he replied, "but that is not a good idea at all.

What you're asking for is fraught with danger. Such a trip takes too much skill and experience. Please, ask for something else. Guiding that chariot is the job for immortals, not mortals. Even Zeus would not attempt such a venture, and even I have moments that make me shudder. The ascent up from the East is steep; the middle of the route is extraordinarily high, and I am often apprehensive as I look down; the descent is very risky; there are other bodies in the heavens that have to be avoided: there is the bull-like Taurus, the claws of Scorpion, the arrows of Sagittarius, just to name a few of the hazards. No, son, do not make this request. Look around at the many wonders of the world; select anything else that pleases you, but I beg you not to persist in your first wish: you are asking me to lead you to your death."

But Phaeton would hear none of his cautions, and Helios was held to his promise. The boy was led to the chariot with its golden axles and silver spokes, all studded with gems. The father anointed him with a balm so that he would not be burned by the blazing heat and then gave him a final bit of advice: "Use the whip very sparingly and keep a firm hold on the bridle. Make sure that you maintain full control, for the horses are eager to go their own way. Follow the path that has been made from my journeys, and keep a middle route; otherwise you will set fire either to the heavens or to the earth."

He tried once more to dissuade the headstrong boy but his pleas were in vain. Phaeton jumped into the chariot, eager to be about his journey. Helios' four horses began the ascent, but they sensed that something was different. The chariot was lighter; the reins lacked their usual authority. And they took advantage of their new freedom, rushing off the path and following their own desires. The boy was alarmed; he didn't know what to do; he had no control; he tried the reins but lacked the strength to bring the horses back on route. Only then did he realize the wisdom of his father's words. He was carried about like a leaf in the wind or like a raft on a raging sea.

Meanwhile the ice of the North began to melt; the Moon wondered what her brother's horses were doing lower than her own; the clouds began to sent forth steam; the Earth began to blaze; grass, trees, bushes all burned up; cities were consumed by fire, forests and mountains burned out of control; there were earthquakes and even Tartarus saw light; deserts sprang up out of the ocean; mountains turned into islands. Even Atlas, supporting the heavens, suffered and was about to release his hold on the world.

Zeus watched the holocaust and realized that, if he did nothing, everyone would perish. Having neither clouds nor rain with which to soothe the suffering from the heat, he took one of his thunderbolts and hurled it at the charioteer. The horses were startled and broke from their harnesses; the chariot was scattered in pieces throughout the heavens; and Phaeton, now dead, hurled through the skies like a shooting star, and fell into the River Eridaunus.

The banks of that river swarmed with those who mourned the young Phaeton. The river overflowed with their tears. His sisters mourned so intensely that they became trees overlooking the water and his friend, Cycnus, also in mourning, became a swan. Even now, the swan avoids the heat and chooses instead to swim in the cool waters of lakes and pools.

Meanwhile, Apollo retrieved the horses and Zeus restored most of the parched areas of the earth. And when Hephaistus had built Helios a new chariot, it was never again out of the god's hands.

Niobe

The gods had indeed been very kind to Niobe. She was the daughter of Tantalus, a powerful king in Asia Minor; she had power, wealth, and beauty; and she was the mother of seven sons and seven daughters. It was these children that gave her the most pleasure, and she took immense pride in them.

One day Mantho, the daughter of the blind prophet Tiresias, summoned all the women to offer a sacrifice to Leto, the mother of Apollo and Artemis. When Mantho said that she had been inspired by the goddess to make this request, all the women immediately prepared their sacrifices. But Niobe strutted in their midst with no intention of heeding Mantho's words. "Leto! Who is she! Why are you bothering to worship her? Have you ever seen her? Better you should worship me! Tantalus was my father, the only mortal to eat at the table of the gods. Taygete, one of the Pleiades, was my mother. Atlas, who carries the heavens on his shoulders, was one of my grandfathers and Zeus himself the other. Zeus is also my father-in-law, for he fathered my husband Amphion. I have wealth; I have beauty; I have power; I have the noblest of ancestries; and I have fourteen magnificent children. Now look at Leto: the daughter of some obscure Titan named Coeus, the mother of only two children; furthermore, when she wanted to give birth to them, Hera sent the serpent, Python, after her. Compare her to me. I am the one you should be worshipping, not Leto."

Meanwhile, Leto had been listening to these words, and she was outraged. She summoned her twin children and told them of the abuses she had just heard. Apollo dashed down to earth where Niobe's boys were out on horses hunting. One by one Apollo destroyed these children with his arrows.

When her husband, Amphion, heard of this calamity, he stabbed himself, unable to endure his grief. Niobe, however, drenched with tears, cursed Leto. Hearing her new insults, Artemis then took her arrows to Niobe's daughters. One by one they fell dead before their mother. Niobe, now childless, now a widow, sat down and continued to weep. She found her way to the top of Mount Sipylus in Boeotia and there she was turned into a stone, a stone that even now sheds tears.

Salmoneus

Salmoneus founded the city of Salmone in Elis. There he became tyrannical, overbearing, proud, much too taken with himself. He began to compare himself to Zeus. He stopped all worship of Zeus in his land and ordered that he be worshipped instead. He drove a horse-drawn chariot and smashed cymbals together, beat upon deep, hollow kettles and threw lighted torches pretending that he was issuing forth thunder and lightning. Zeus let him have his way for a while, and when the god had had enough, he sent one of his real bolts, struck Salmoneus head-on, and destroyed the city.

Bellerophon

Bellerophon was the grandson of King Sisyphus of Corinth, that craftiest, cleverest, and sneakiest of all men whom Zeus condemned to eternal frustration in Tartarus. When Bellerophon was a young man, he accidentally killed his brother; consequently, he was exiled from Corinth and he had to seek purification. He came to King Proetus, whose palace was at Tiryns. Proetus accordingly purified him and allowed him to spend time with him as a guest. But during that time, Proetus' wife developed a passion for Bellerophon. She pressed him and pressed him for an alliance, but Bellerophon would not violate Proetus' hospitality. Finally, when the wife realized that she would get nowhere with the young man, she slandered him to her husband. She said that he had tried to seduce her.

Proetus was outraged, and vengeance reeked in his blood. But he did not dare to kill someone whom he had just purified and someone who was his guest. Therefore, he decided to have the youth disposed of by someone else. He asked Bellerophon to deliver a letter to his father-in-law, King Iobates of Lycia. In that letter, he directed Iobates to kill Bellerophon, saying that the young man had violently insulted his daughter.

When Iobates read the letter, he was mystified. Not only was the letter cryptic but here was what appeared to be a fine and honorable young man. Now, he too did not want blood on his hands; therefore, he sent Bellerophon off on a mission to rid the land of a terrible monster called the **Chimaera**. This beast had the head of a lion, the mid-part of a goat, and the tail of a serpent; it breathed fire, was as large as a dragon, and it was now devastating the countryside killing both man and beast. Since it had the strength of three creatures, it was too mighty for any mortal warrior, and Iobates suspected that Bellerophon would fall, as had many before him, to the ravages of the beast.

When Bellerophon saw the creature, he despaired. But Athena came to his aid. She showed him how to tame the wild Pegasus, the winged horse, offspring of Medusa and Poseidon. He soared up into the sky, descended upon the beast from above, and slew the monster. Iobates then had him vanquish the Solymi, a warlike and violent tribe of mountain dwellers; he even had him subdue the Amazons, that aggressive and warlike race of women, who were encroaching upon Lycia.

After Bellerophon had accomplished these feats, Iobates was impressed. He could not believe that such a person could have done what Proetus had suggested. Therefore, he showed Bellerophon the letter. Bellerophon realized that both Iobates and Proetus had been deceived, deduced that Proetus' wife had fabricated the whole story out of revenge, and then explained it all to Iobates. He, hearing Bellerophon's story, made him heir to the throne of Lycia and gave him one of his daughters in marriage.

But little by little, Bellerophon became headstrong. He would ride Pegasus through the skies; in fact, he turned his eyes toward the heavens and tried to ride up to join the gods. Pegasus, some say pricked by Zeus, threw the prince and he fell to the earth. He did not die but he was severely maimed, and he spent the rest of his days lame, friendless, and scorned by gods and men.

All humans have their *moira*, their lot, fate, destiny or, to look at the word from another angle, that which is their due. To try to get more than what one was entitled to was one of the most serious of sins. This was the sin of hybris. The word can be translated as "pride," "arrogance," or "recklessness." Taking too much for granted or not giving the gods their due, or reveling in too much prosperity are all examples of hybris. Being so self-assured that one celebrates one's victory in a fight before one actually fights might be an example of hybris; so would Niobe's boast that she was greater than Leto because she had seven times as many children and because she was of royal blood whereas Leto was a nobody. Many of the protagonists in Greek tragedy commit hybris; they take a position that may be defensible enough, but they take it to extremes; they go too far; they become blinded by self-righteousness, and they become dogmatic and sanctimonious. Those actions are also examples of hybris. When a person forgets that he is a human, with human limitations, and acts like a god or plays the role of a god, then he also commits hybris. The key word in understanding the concept of hybris is *excessiveness,* excessiveness in almost any aspect of life.

Hybris was usually promptly punished, and the agent of such punishment was often thought to be **Nemesis.** She was said to have been a daughter of Night. She might be described as a control or a curb or a regulator over excess. She was sometimes thought of as "divine anger" or "divine indignation" and she was the personification of Retribution. If a person became too prosperous, Nemesis would probably take some of that prosperity. After all, too much prosperity might arouse the jealousy of the gods; but if a person boasts in his prosperity, then he is not only arousing their jealousy but also challenging them, and such challenges are usually met.

Besides hybris and Nemesis, there is a third concept: that of **Ate.** The concept of Ate is not a fixed one. Sometimes she is regarded, like Nemesis, as a retributive force, a punisher, or an avenging agent. Sometimes she is regarded as that impulse that prompts a person to commit hybris — i.e., recklessness or blind folly. Finally she is sometimes regarded as the consequence of that recklessness or folly — i.e., the suffering or misery that a person must endure. In that capacity she is a nasty and spiteful creature who sneers and laughs at people in their misery.

CHAPTER IX

ABSTRACT DIVINITIES

The ancients acknowledged a number of divinities who were not active in the way that the Olympian gods and goddesses were active but rather served as forces of refinement, culture, inspiration, civilization, orderliness, or control. The Furies, Nemesis, and Ate helped to keep man in his place; the Moirae constantly reminded man that he was mortal; Tyche reminded man that he must take nothing in his life for granted; Themis assured man that there was a rightness to his world even though that rightness might sometimes seem confusing; the Horae reminded man that there was an order over his physical world; the Graces encouraged man to be festive; and the Muses inspired man, allowing him to rise above mere banality and to transcend the commonplace.

Themis was a daughter of Gaia and Ouranos and hence one of the Titanesses. Zeus consorted with her and the union produced those civilizing forces known as the Horae and those sobering forces known as the Moirae. Themis was not so much an actual goddess as she was a divine force representing tradition, precedent, custom and practice, natural rightness and order, that which is intrinsically right as opposed to man-made law. Her throne was near Zeus' and she was highly regarded on Olympus. She originally had an oracle at Delphi but later relinquished it to Apollo; nevertheless, she did retain her gift of prophecy. It was she who prophesied that the Nereid Thetis would have a son more powerful than his father. Aeschylus' Prometheus claimed to have had Themis as his mother. Themis was also the one who allegedly was present when Deucalion and Pyrrha disembarked on Mount Parnassus and she was the one who advised them on how to re-people the earth.[1] Eventually her sway expanded and she came to represent not only rightness but justice and law as well.

The Muses were goddesses of inspiration. After the battle with the Titans, Zeus went to the Titaness Mnemosyne on Mount Pieria and slept with her for nine nights. She gave birth to nine daughters, the Muses. The immortals loved the Muses because they used to tell of the mighty deeds of the gods and goddesses of lofty Olympus. They spent a lot of time on Mount Olympus, where they were always welcome, and they were famous for bringing wherever

1. See page 69.

they went a feeling of forgetfulness of evils, worries, and cares. But they were happiest either on Mount Helicon or on Mount Parnassus.

Helicon was a marvelous place in Boeotia. There were two fountains, Aganippe and Hippocrene, which inspired those who drank from them. There were also many varieties of plants that had restorative and medicinal powers. There were wild strawberries that grew sweeter than in any other place, and the soil was very fertile. There were all sorts of verdant trees and there were even plants that tempered the poison of snakes. Eventually this place became a favorite haunt of Apollo, who shared with the Muses an interest in music, poetry, song, and culture in general.

Mount Parnassus was another favorite of theirs. This mountain was in Phocis, and it was a place also sacred to Dionysus and Pan and again Apollo, perhaps because it was so close to Delphi. Like the springs on Helicon, the Castalia on Parnassus provided inspiration.

Although at first there was disagreement as to just who the Muses were, it is now generally agreed that the following comprise the nine:

1. Calliope, the Muse of epic poetry
2. Clio, the Muse of history
3. Euterpe, the Muse of lyric poetry and flute playing
4. Thalia, the Muse of comedy
5. Melpomene, the Muse of tragedy
6. Terpsichore, the Muse of the dance
7. Erato, the Muse of love and erotic poetry
8. Polyhymnia, the Muse of lofty and sacred poetry and hymns and of geometry
9. Urania, the Muse of astronomy

The Muses were benevolent deities but they had their limits. King Pierus, for instance, had nine daughters who boasted that they were superior to the Muses. There was a contest; the Muses won and banished the King's daughters, turning them into magpies, a bird that chatters and yammers all day, whose voice is shrill and raucous, and who is either ignored or scorned. From that time on the Muses were sometimes called the *Pierides*.

On another occasion Thramyris, a very handsome and talented young man, challenged the Muses. The terms were that if he won the contest, he would sleep with each of them; if he lost, they could do with him as they pleased. He lost. They blinded him and took away his ability to sing.

It was the Muses who gave the Sphinx her famous riddle, and

it was they who deprived the Sirens of their wings and feathers when the Sirens challenged the nine sisters to a singing contest. The Muses allegedly made crowns for themselves from these feathers.

The **Graces** or **Charities** were born from the union of Zeus and the Titaness Eurynome. There were three of them: Aglaea (Splendor, Festivity), Euphrosyne (Cheerfulness, Merriment), and Thalia (Bountifulness, Bloom). As can be seen from their names, the Charities were divinities of festivity and happiness. "They bring happiness to god and man," remarks one poet. They effected an atmosphere that made men gentle, kind, and refined. They could make a person seem glorious and noble. By the aid of the Graces, all things that were pleasant and able to bring cheer could come to mortals, and even the gods invited them when it was the occasion for dancing or feasting. In short, they were forces which brought a feeling of civilized, healthy, and wholesome happiness, a happiness that often comes from fellowship and social commingling. They, however, had nothing to do with pleasure, particularly those pleasures that we can achieve from gratifying our passions, instincts, or senses. Rather, it was a refined, pure, high-minded happiness, and usually in the background were the virtues of charm, refinement, control, moderation, sobriety, and always good taste.

The Charities are often depicted as inspirations for song, and indeed they shared this function with the Muses with whom they were frequent companions. They are also often associated, as might be expected, with Apollo and especially Aphrodite. They were the ones who would help Aphrodite prepare herself, washing her, anointing her with ambrosial oil, and dressing her. They would help her become more charming, elegant, and beautiful, but they would never accompany her in her seductions.

The **Horae** were sometimes called the Hours; actually they were the Seasons. In general they represented an orderly unit of time. They were born from Zeus and Themis, and they inherited their basic attribute from their mother: that of order. All of their functions predicated orderliness. In Homer they guarded the gates of heaven. They regulated the seasons of the year, and they were often depicted as dancing in measured, orderly rhythm and, in doing so, as leading out one season and leading in another. Hence, their dance was a figurative way of representing the passage of time. They were often pictured as garlanded "rich in flowers." As representing the seasons, they had a concern with agriculture, especially since crops are fostered by the seasons. Originally associated with the growth of crops, they gradually became associated with the growth of children.

Again, it was orderly growth, gradual and natural growth. Finally, since they regulated the seasons, they also assumed the attributes of weather in general.

They were the ones who accompanied Persephone each year in her stay with Hades; they brought back Adonis from the Underworld; they adorned Pandora with the flowers of spring in her debut on Earth; they were said to have been the nurses of Hera; they met Aphrodite when she emerged from the sea at Cyprus and adorned her with all sorts of fineries.

The number of Horae varied; sometimes there were two, sometimes four, sometimes nine, ten, or eleven. The generally accepted number is three: Eunomia, or Order; Dike, or Justice; and Irene, or Peace. One can see how, from being divinities of natural order, they gradually became divinities of human order as represented by their names. In their function of adding tasteful adornment to man or god, they were often associated with the Charities, and some writers do not seem to make much of a distinction between the two groups.

The **Moirae, Fates**, or **Parcae** have already been mentioned.[1] They were generally thought to be the daughters of Night, although sometimes Zeus and Themis were cited as their parents. The word *moira* itself means "lot," "share," "destiny," and it is often used to refer to one's allotment or share in life. In the plural, *moirae*, the word usually refers to the three Fates; they are often pictured as very old crones, slow, but inexorably steady. Their function as agents of fate is often depicted allegorically: Clotho, the Spinner, spins a piece of thread for each person, and that thread is the life thread. Lachesis, the Measurer, assigns to people just how much thread each is to have. Atropos, the Inflexible or Inevitable, is the one who cuts that thread and consequently brings death to mortals. The Moirae knew the future but only rarely could they be prevailed upon to reveal that future. They also moved in the same circles as the Furies or Erinyes, and they sometimes commissioned the Furies when vengeance was in order. They often sat near Zeus and he was the only god that they would obey. The most notable exception occurred when they revealed to Apollo the fate of Admetus and were cajoled by him to allow Admetus to present a substitute when it was time for his death. But, as we have seen,[2] Apollo had gotten them drunk.

Finally there is **Tyche**, in Latin **Fortuna**, a daughter of Oceanus and Tethys. She did not assume a position of much importance

1. See page 3, note (4).
2. See page 87.

until quite late in Greek culture. At first she was merely an abstraction of good or bad luck, not at all thought of as either a goddess or even a divine force: merely a word denoting accident or chance. Around the fourth century B.C., however, Tyche took on a much more distinct form and cult, and as Fortuna she became prominent in Roman thought. From the fourth century on, Tyche gradually began to assume some of the functions that had been held by Zeus and the Moirae. As the orthodox attitudes toward the traditional gods began to wane, some of the Olympians' attributes merged into Tyche. In Hellenistic times, for instance, temples were built to Tyche as they had been to Zeus. Her cult concerned itself with the regulation and outcome of events, and it was that aspect of Zeus and the Moirae that she absorbed.

CHAPTER X

POWERFUL FORCES

Gaia

Gaia (Gaea, Ge, Gae) was the Earth, the Mother Earth, who gives birth to everything that grows and lives. She has been mentioned in the "Creation" chapter; in the story of creation she was the first clearly defined body. She was often called "deep-bosomed" and was usually considered the mother of everyone. A Homeric hymn lauds her as feeding all things that inhabit the earth and dwell in the sea and fly in the air, "and from thee come people, who have children, and it is up to you whether life is given or taken away." Defined so clearly as a fertility and reproductive force, Gaia was naturally identified with Demeter, and there were cults of her all over Greece, but especially in Eleusis. She is said to have had the first oracle at Delphi, later giving way to Themis and then to Apollo.

She had innumerable offspring, as cited in the creation chapter, most of which served to make her more attractive and interesting: the ocean, the starry heavens, and the mountains. And when one considers her grandchildren, she can easily be seen as the great mother of everything.

One of her offspring is particularly interesting, **Antaeus,** her son by Poseidon. Having had poor luck with her most recent sons, the giants Typhon, Tityus, and Briareus, she decided to move the site of birth for this new child from the north country to Libya, and there indeed did she give birth to her fourth giant. Antaeus grew up in a cave in Libya, where he fed on lions. Unlike his brothers, he did not challenge the gods or lust after goddesses; rather, he took a fancy to travelers. Whenever one would pass his cave, he would insist that there be a wrestling match. Of course, he would always win and kill his opponent. Then he would use their skulls to roof the temple of Poseidon.

He was aided, furthermore, by his mother. Whenever a limb of his would become tired, all he would have to do was to have that limb touch the earth and it would immediately renew its strength. With this strength, he could wear down all opposition; and so he did for several years.

102

One of his challenges was the hero Heracles, who happened to be passing through Libya. Of course Heracles had to accept the challenge. He took off his skin from the lion of Nemea, Antaeus took off his skin from the lion of Libya. Heracles covered himself with oil, Antaeus with sand. Wrestlers usually sprinkled sand over themselves after they had put on oil, but in this case it was added protection: the sand, after all, was from the earth.

The fight was a rough one; each felt that he had found his match. At first, Heracles was careful not to wear himself out, thinking that he would be able to conserve his own strength while tiring Antaeus. This strategy didn't work. Then he would lift Antaeus up with all his might and dash him upon the ground. The contact with the Earth only made Antaeus twice as strong and he would rebound totally invigorated. Heracles stood amazed at such stamina; he couldn't believe what was happening. This happened over and over again; in fact, Antaeus would not even wait to be thrown. He would fall of his own accord to the ground and arise more powerful. Meanwhile Heracles was getting weary. Eventually, however, he realized what was happening. From that point, he was determined that Antaeus would not touch the ground. He got the giant into a stranglehold, lifted him off the ground, squeezed him with all his strength while Antaeus, unable to make any contact with the earth, got weaker and weaker, until finally he died.

Pan

Pan, a son of Hermes, was a favorite among the gods; in fact, one source of his name is that he was a delight to all the gods. He had the feet of a goat, two horns on his forehead, loved noise and dancing, was hairy, dirty, lusty, ugly, and disheveled; yet, in his own way he was a charming creature. He was particularly fond of shepherds and was their special protector; in a general sense he was a divinity of the country, of sheep, goats, and other grazing flocks, of forests, valleys, hills, and glens. He loved to sing; in fact, it is said that he sometimes surpassed even the birds with his songs; and when the mountain or forest nymphs would join him, the sound was overwhelming. He loved to nap in the afternoon, and woe be to anyone who disturbed Pan's rest. He would create such a ruckus that an intruder would be terrified, and from the result of such intrusions comes the word panic. He pursued many nymphs with his amorous advances and even had his way with a few. His favorite haunt was Arcadia, an area that became known for the rustic life. Indeed Pan was a rustic god, simple and earthy, extroverted and fun-loving, coarse, smelly, but generally winsome.

Once in these chilly mountains of Arcadia lived a Naiad — a water nymph — called **Syrinx**. Syrinx was particularly devoted to Artemis; in fact, to such an extent did she emulate that goddess that the only difference obvious to the eye was that Artemis had a golden bow while Syrinx had a wooden one; even so, she was often thought to be the goddess herself. Naturally, being a devotee of Artemis, she had no interest in amorous pursuits, and she had often escaped both lusty satyrs and other local deities who frequented the woods and fields.

One day Pan saw her returning from the hills. As soon as he saw her, his goatlike nature took over and he lusted after the girl. She fled over the pathless ground until she came to the banks of the River Ladon. Unable to cross, she prayed to her sister nymphs for protection. They saw her in her distress and assisted her. Quickly she became joined with the many reeds that teemed along the banks of the river. When Pan got to the area, realizing that Syrinx had been changed, he grabbed a handful of those reeds hoping to get a hold on the girl, but there was no chance. He sat sighing; but as he sat, wind by chance blew into the hollow reeds that he held and created a sound not unlike Pan's own sighs. Enchanted by these new sounds, he decided to preserve them. Consequently, he took the reeds, joined them together, fastened them with a base of wax, and kept them forever with him. Even now they are known as the Pipes of Pan.

Rhea and Cybele

Rhea was originally a Titaness who, together with Cronos, bore the first six important gods: Hestia, Demeter, Hera, Hades, Poseidon, and Zeus. After this initial burst of energy, she does not appear as a major force in mythology except for an occasional cameo appearance. For instance, she was the one who served as messenger from Zeus to Demeter when Zeus had resolved the controversy over Persephone.

From even a cursory glance at the two phases of the creation story told in Chapter I, one can see the parallels between the Gaia-Ouranos phase and the Rhea-Cronos phase. The two stories are remarkably similar, and there was indeed an identification between Rhea and Gaia. Whereas, however, Gaia seems to be almost an imper-

PAN. Hellenistic bronze statuette. Though his torso is
distinctly human, his head and his legs are goat-like.
In his right hand he holds the pipes of Pan. Note
particularly the impishness of his expression suggested by his eyes and mouth. *Courtesy, Museum of
Fine Arts, Boston.*

sonal and primarily benevolent force, Rhea becomes a very personal and active force, especially in Crete, where she had left the baby Zeus with the nymphs and Curetes in order to escape detection by Cronos.

She somehow became associated with Cybele, a divinity from Phrygia in Asia Minor, whose function in Phrygia seems to have been quite similar to Rhea's in Crete. The process of absorption of identities probably occurred when the Greeks began settling in Asia Minor, an absorption that was stimulated by the similarities between the two divinities: both were mother goddesses; both represented fertility and sexual energy; both had enthusiastic and boisterous attendants, Rhea having her Curetes and Cybele her Corybantes. The matter becomes even more complicated when the Romans picked up the cult, for they merged Rhea and Cybele into their *Magna Mater,* a concept originally associated with Gaia.

Eventually the influence of Dionysus became prevalent in Asia Minor, an influence which, with its emphasis upon the orgiastic and ritualistic, amalgamated with the Rhea/Cybele cult. Perhaps the best introduction to the cult is the story of Attis.

Once Zeus spilled his seed on the earth and the offspring was a being that was both male and female; its name was Agdistis or Cybele. The gods, however, not being pleased with such a creature, divested the being of its masculine organs and buried them; on this spot grew an almond tree. Nana, a daughter of the River Sangarius, then placed one of the fruits of this tree in her bosom, and this resulted in the birth of **Attis.** Attis was nurtured by a goat and he grew into a young man of remarkable beauty, such beauty that Cybele fell in love with him. She bound the youth to herself as priest of her shrine and got from him a pledge of complete fidelity and chastity. Devoted to her, he promised what she requested and vowed that, if he should ever be false to her, that act would be his last. But in the course of events, he fell in love with a nymph named Sagaritis and he broke his pledge to Cybele. When she discovered his infidelity, she first killed the nymph and then drove him mad: the combination of his breach of loyalty to Cybele and the loss of his Sagaritis so distracted him that he ran in a frenzy to the top of Mount Ida and in his fury took a sharp stone and castrated himself. Cybele then regretted that she had filled the youth with such madness and consequently prevailed upon Zeus never to allow Attis' body to decay. Some say that violets arose from his blood, others that Cybele changed him into a pine tree.

Worship of Cybele was wild. She was said to be crowned and

106

to drive a chariot yoked with lions and usually to have a whip with which she struck both her lions and her followers. Her priests, the Corybantes or Galli, were often eunuchs, having impetuously mutilated themselves in her service, most likely from the precedent of Attis. Everyone in her company played the drums or cymbals or tambourines or horns or musical pipes; their music was wild and primitive. They carried weapons wherever they went to terrify the uninitiated. Wherever they went they danced and often shed their blood from self-mutilation. The maenads wildly shook their heads and their hair crowned with ivy, and they shouted or cried chants to the Mother. Cybele's entourage thus wandered all day in hysterical abandonment, singing and dancing, and at night they collapsed.

Priapus

At one point, Aphrodite had had a very short affair with either Hermes or Dionysus. Hera, when she learned of it, was annoyed at Aphrodite's disgraceful conduct, and when the time came for Aphrodite to give birth to the fruit of her union, Hera caused the result to be comically — some would say grotesquely — deformed: some say it was a quasi-man with a huge and erect phallus; others say it was just a phallus shaped like a man . . . or perhaps a man shaped like a phallus. At any rate, his mother not wanting to have anything to do with him, Priapus was raised among the shepherds.

Priapus was really little more than a symbol of fertility and of energetic potency. He became associated with Pan, with Dionysus, and even with Hermes, and through these associations it is not difficult to see why he was considered a patron of the vine, of agriculture, especially flocks and goats, and of local gardens. Like the herm,[1] images of Priapus could be found as a good luck charm in front of private homes. Eventually he became little more than a ribald joke, and one could find little Priapi decorating the tops of cakes.

Priapus has almost no role in mythology; he is primarily a symbol or a force. While his name appears frequently in Hellenistic erotic poetry and in both Greek and Roman art and sculpture, there are not many actual stories concerning him, and two of the most famous are essentially the same. The first concerns his pursuit of the nymph Lotis; he sneaks up on her as she is sleeping but just as he is about to make his move, Silenus' ass brays, the nymph wakes up,

1. See page 31, note (b).   107

pushes the ruddy Priapus aside, and everyone laughs. The second story is almost identical:

Cybele invited the gods to a party; she also invited the satyrs and nymphs; Silenus, although not invited, showed up. There was a grand time. Everyone had his fill of wine and food. That night, some of the gods continued to drink, others wandered around Mount Ida, others tried to get some sleep, and still others cavorted with each other. Hestia, ever proper Aunt Hestia, was sleeping very calmly. Meanwhile, Priapus was off chasing nymphs and goddesses. Suddenly he spotted Hestia; no one knows whether he thought she was some nymph or whether he knew she was a goddess; it makes no difference: lust filled him. On tiptoe, one step at a time, he inched up toward her. He was just about to pounce upon her when Silenus' donkey brayed and woke up the goddess. She shrieked, he darted off, foiled in his attempts, and the rest of the gathering laughed as he had been caught not in, but ready for, the act.

Aristaeus

Aristaeus was the son of Apollo and Cyrene. Apollo carried Cyrene off from Thessaly and took her to Libya. There he made her a nymph and he gave their son to Chiron, the Centaur, to be brought up. When Aristaeus came of age, the Muses taught him the art of healing and they put him in charge of their sheep, apparently teaching him all about the skills of shepherding. Eventually Aristaeus became an agricultural deity, a patron god of farmers, particularly in Thessaly, for he somehow managed to get back to his mother's home. He was said to have been the inventor of beekeeping techniques and the discoverer of honey and olive growing. It seems that wherever he went, he was a force for the good, and indeed he traveled extensively throughout the Greek communities. By his marriage with Autonoe, a daughter of Cadmus, he was the father of Actaeon.[1]

His involvement with bees forms a famous story in classical literature. He was in keen despair because, for some strange reason, no bees would come near his honeycombs. Having consulted with his mother, he was advised to seek Proteus, that elusive seer of the future who lived in the sea and would evade giving any prophecies by changing himself into all sorts of shapes. Aristaeus bound him and pinned him down and finally got him to speak. Proteus told him that

1. See page 27.

the bees were avoiding Aristaeus because Eurydice's companions, nymphs who used to dance and pick flowers with her, had put a blight on the bees. They were angry with Aristaeus, for it was he from whom Eurydice was running on that day when she stepped on that fateful snake[1] — Aristaeus in his travels had seen her and had fallen in love with her. Proteus then told Aristaeus to supplicate those nymphs. Apparently he was successful, for, following Proteus' advice, he set out the carcass of a slaughtered ox; from its decaying corpse arose a swarm of new bees.

1. See page 82.

AURORA IN HER CHARIOT.
Graeco-Roman gem. *Courtesy, Museum of Fine Arts, Boston.*

CHAPTER XI

POWERS OF THE SKY, EARTH, AND SEA

Eos (Aurora). Daughter of the Titans Hyperion and Theia, Eos was the Dawn. She is often described as "the rosy-fingered" dawn, since the first light of the morning is a mellow, flesh-colored shade of pink; some of her other epithets are "early-born," "beautifully throned," "with saffron colored veil." Sometimes she was pictured as driving a chariot across the sky yoked with swift-footed horses; hence she was at times equated with the day itself. With Astraeus she bore the four winds, the Morning Star (Lucifer), the Evening Star (Hesperus), and the other bright stars that adorn the heavens; with Tithonus she bore the handsome Memnon, King of the Ethiopians and a warrior with Priam in the Trojan War, killed by Achilles.

When **Memnon** was killed, Eos mourned to such an extent that the usual crimson colors of the morning turned grey and pallid. She fell before the knees of Zeus. "I realize," she said, "that I am inferior to all the other goddesses; I know I have fewer temples than anyone else; yet, I am a goddess. I come to you not for altars and temples and sacrifices, but merely for my son Memnon. Grant him some honor. Think of how much I do for you each day as I push back the night and I fill the heavens with light; then perhaps you will hear my plea." Zeus heard her prayer and from the ashes of Memnon's funeral pyre came birds. Meanwhile Eos still weeps for her son, and her tears can be seen all over the world as dew drops.

On another occasion Eos took Orion to be with her. But the other gods were indignant and hence Artemis slew the young man. There are, however, other versions of the Orion story.[1]

The story of Eos' marriage with Tithonus is legendary. She secured from Zeus immortality for Tithonus but neglected to include the request for eternal youth, and Tithonus was to the ancients what Methuselah is to us. The story is mentioned again in the story of the Trojan House.[2]

The Winds. There were four winds, sons of Eos and Astraeus and therefore brothers of Hesperus, of the Morning Star, and of the other stars in the heavens. Eurus was the East Wind; Notus (Auster) the South Wind; Boreas (Aquilo) the North Wind; and Zephyrus (Favonius) the West Wind.

1. See page 90. 2. See page 160.

ACHILLES SLAYS MEMNON. Attic Red-Figured Vase, 5th Century B.C. Achilles has just slain Memnon, who falls into the arms of his mother, Eos. Athena, wearing her helmet and her aegis, encourages Achilles. Just as Aphrodite favored the Trojans, Athena favored the Greeks in the Trojan War. *Courtesy, Museum of Fine Arts, Boston.*

Boreas once fell in love with some horses of King Erichthonius, son of Dardanus, founder of Troy. These horses by Boreas had twelve offspring, horses of incredible speed. On another occasion, having carried off Orithyia, daughter of the Athenian King Erechtheus as she was playing by the bank of a river, he fathered Zetes and Calais, who later became Argonauts and who make frequent brief appearances in mythology.

Zephyrus, who eventually became a gentle and steady wind, also had his share of affairs. He was said to have lived with Iris, the Rainbow, at the Western pole of the ocean. He once fell in love with a nymph named Chloris, married her, gave her the gift of enjoying perpetual spring, and made her a patron of flowers. It is even said that Zephyrus, in love with Hyacinth and jealous of Apollo's successes with the boy, turned the discus that Hyacinth threw and caused it to kill the youth.

Nymphs. Always eager to assign forms of life to the various forces of nature, the ancients figuratively attributed the rustling of trees, grass, crops, the sounds and movements of the winds, streams, and rivers, and other such forces to the movements of the nymphs. The nymphs were divinities who were benevolent, beautiful, and usu-

111

ally harmless, and they seemed to spend much of their time fleeing from or involved in amorous pursuits. There are several types of nymphs:

a. Nymphs of the trees, such as the Meliads, who frequented the ash tree; the Dryads and Hamadryads, whose favorite was the oak but who inhabited stately trees in general; and the Melids, who inhabited fruit trees.

b. Nymphs of the mountains, such as Oreads

c. Nymphs of the forests and glens

d. Nymphs of the waters, such as Naiads, the fresh water nymphs; the Nereids, the sea nymphs, especially of the Mediterranean — there were supposedly fifty Nereids, daughters of Nereus and Doris — and the Oceanids, Ocean Nymphs, the three thousand daughters of Oceanus and Tethys.

In addition there were dozens of other smaller categories, nymphs of countless other trees, of specific rivers and lakes, specific mountains, and of geographical areas.

Because of their connection with fields, woods, mountains, and rivers, they were often associated with fertility gods, such as Pan and Hermes (fields and flocks), Dionysus (vegetation), and Artemis (wild animals).

The nymphs played secondary roles in much of mythology, constantly singing and dancing, or fleeing. The Meliads were the ones who brought up the baby Zeus on Crete; the Dryads were the ones who deprived Aristaeus of his bees when their companion, Eurydice, died; and the Nereids helped to guide the ship *Argo*. The nymphs had innumerable offspring by both men and gods.

Homer, through Aphrodite, offers a fine description of nymphs, specifically Oreads, but the description could apply to Dryads as well:

> The deep-breasted nymphs of the mountains are numbered neither among mortals nor among immortals; they live for a long time and they eat food of ambrosia and they dance with the immortals. They make love with the Sileni and with Hermes in the shelter of pleasant caves. When they are born, pine trees and oaks are also born with them, magnificent trees which look up to the sun from lofty mountainsides. Mortals do not cut these trees with axes; when it is the time for these nymphs to die, these beautiful trees first dry up, the bark wastes away, the boughs fall; and then the souls of these nymphs leave the light of the sun.

Nereus and his fifty daughters. Nereus, the son of Oceanus and Gaia, was often personified as the sea itself. He was often regarded as one of the old men of the sea and he was considered wise,

POLYPHEMUS. Hellenistic marble head. The one-eyed Cyclops, later wounded by Odysseus, fell in love with the nymph Galatea. *Courtesy, Museum of Fine Arts, Boston.*

truthful, trustworthy, and kindly. He had the gift of prophecy and, like Proteus,[1] he could change his shape. His fifty daughters, the **Nereids**, were sea nymphs; like their father, they could change their shapes. They seem to represent various forces that are intrinsic to the sea, such as favorable signs, waves, islands, beaches, shores, colors, and hues of the sea, maritime trade and commerce, and so on.

Of these fifty daughters, two are particularly important: Galatea and Thetis. The one-eyed Polyphemus once fell in love with **Galatea**; it was the first time he had fallen in love so he agonized for the nymph. When he realized that she was devoting all her interest to a young man named Acis, he was filled with jealousy and threw a part of a mountain upon Acis, killing him.

Even more important was **Thetis**. She was said to have been brought up by Hera. She also aided Hephaistus when he was cast off Olympus and into the sea by Hera. Thetis saved the infant god, took him to her sisters, and for nine years harbored and sheltered him. On another occasion, Dionysus, fleeing from the rabid and violent Lycurgus,[2] jumped into the sea for protection. Thetis rescued him and sheltered him. Thus, she certainly was well accepted by the gods.

It was said that Zeus and Poseidon both wanted to marry her. There are two different accounts regarding the outcome. The first is that Themis, the Titaness of wisdom, prophesied that Thetis would bear a son who would be mightier than his father. Upon hearing this, the gods withdrew. The other account says that Thetis would not accept Zeus' advances because of her loyalty and gratitude to Hera. Zeus, being angry, then declared that she should marry a mortal. The first version is much more common and important, for it features in the Prometheus story.

The man she ended up marrying was **Peleus**, the son of Aeacus, that very honorable and just man who eventually became a judge in the Underworld. Peleus was considered to be a very holy man and at one point in his life he had become friends with Chiron, the very just and wise Centaur. At first Thetis tried to resist the advances of Peleus. She changed herself into fire, water, a bird, a tree, a tiger, a lion, and so on, but Peleus pinned her down and they were married.

The marriage had the blessings of the gods, especially Zeus, Hera, and Themis, and the wedding was a grand affair. All the gods were invited and gave wedding presents . . . all the gods except Eris, the goddess of Strife. Hurt, jealous, and indignant because she was not invited, Eris plotted revenge. It was this resentment and revenge, as we have already seen,[3] that began the chain of events leading to the Trojan War.

114   1. See page 14. 2. See page 46. 3. See page 39.

SATYR. Attic Red-Figured Cup by Epiktetos, 6th
Century B.C. *Courtesy, Museum of Fine Arts, Boston.*

When eventually Peleus and Thetis had a child, she wanted to
make it ageless and immortal. Consequently, she would put the infant each night into a fire so as to burn from him that part of him
that was mortal, and during the day she would rub him with ambrosia. One evening, however, Peleus saw her and interrupted her. She
then abandoned her son and returned to her sister Nereids. The child
was given to Chiron, the Centaur, who brought him up and fed him
lion, bear, and boar, and named him Achilles. Another story tells
that Thetis, wanting to make her son invulnerable, dipped him into
the River Styx; the only place, however, that was untouched by the
water was his heel, where she was holding him. And it was his heel
that was struck by Paris' arrow in the ninth year of the Trojan War.

Thetis was usually favored by the gods, especially by Zeus
and Hephaistus. She prevailed upon both gods to assist her son during the Trojan War, and Hephaistus forged for Achilles his famous
shield.

115

Satyrs. Silenus. Sileni. The satyrs were described and regarded in different ways during different periods. They were at first merely described as worthless and good-for-nothing and were cited as brothers of the Curetes. Sometimes they appear as part human, part goat and show a similarity to Pan. At other times their bestial appearance is more like a horse. One eye-witness described them as "red haired with tails just a bit smaller than the tails of horses. As soon as they saw us, they darted down toward our ship and pounced upon the women. They were shocking and outrageous!" The satyrs were raucous, boisterous, extroverted, lusty, fun-loving creatures; yet they could be malicious. They usually accompanied the god Dionysus; hence, they loved wine, singing, and dancing, and they were constantly pursuing nymphs.

The oldest of the satyrs was Silenus, a coarse and vulgar and gross creature. He tutored Dionysus, brought him up, and constantly accompanied him in his wanderings. From his name came the Sileni; these were the oldest of the satyrs. In fact, the Marsyas[1] who challenged Apollo to a contest, lost, and was flayed was said to be "a Silenus."

The archetypal cynic, Momus, criticizing the influence of Dionysus, commented thus about Dionysus' retinue:

> This Dionysus comes around every morning, stinking of wine, half out of his senses. And then he brings his whole troop with him, turns Pan into a god; he brings Silenus and the satyrs, a bunch of yokels, silly, goatlike, and odd. Those satyrs have horns and, as a matter of fact, resemble goats in their bottom half; with their long beards and pointed ears and bald heads, you can hardly tell the difference and Silenus, that bald old man with his snub nose, usually seated on an ass. . .!

★　★　★

There are several other forces of the land, sea and skies that might be mentioned:

Iris. She was a granddaughter of Pontus and the Earth. In mythology she appears both as the rainbow and as the personification of the rainbow. Hence she is often depicted as a messenger of the gods, especially of Zeus and Hera. Her most common epithet is "swift-footed," and she is similarly labeled as "swift as the wind" or "swift as a storm." Like the Olympians, she could change her shape; when she delivered a message to someone on Earth, she usually did so under the guise of someone else. When she did deliver a message, even if it was not a welcome one, she herself was usually treated with respect; rarely was she disregarded, and there was never any back talk. She is also said to be a sister of the Harpies.

1. See page 22.

116

Aeolus. Aeolus inhabited the island of Aeolia, a floating island, where by the appointment of Zeus he had charge of the winds; he could calm them or send them out at his discretion. Aeolus was dear to the gods and was himself a gracious host; he set a fine table and was amenable to the requests of others on how to administer his winds; but he definitely knew his place as merely a keeper of these winds and as a steward of Zeus. He was said to have been the son of Hippotas, although some say that he was a son of Poseidon. His own name seems to derive from the Greek word *aiolos,* which means "quick-moving" or "changeable," for these qualities certainly describe the winds.

Eventually he became not just a keeper of the winds but their very king, and sometimes he is even referred to as the god of the winds. In the *Aeneid* he is described as an absolute sovereign, sitting on a lofty crag, holding a scepter, and even Hera must petition him when she has a task in mind; she does not order him.

Selene (Luna). Daughter of Hyperion and Theia, Selene was the Moon. She was very beautiful; she wore a golden crown and rode in a chariot drawn by cows or horses. She did not appear as an active mythological force except for her involvement with Endymion. Selene fell in love with this very handsome young lad as she saw him sleeping. So that she might constantly be able to kiss him, she effected upon him both a perpetual sleep and a freedom from death and age. Later, she took on the role of inspiring moon-sickness or lunacy, for it is under the full moon that aberrant or atypical behavior often takes place.

Helios (Sol). The Sun was the brother of Eos and Selene, children of Hyperion and Theia. Like his sisters, he too drove a golden chariot across the sky every day as he brought light to mortals and moved from the eastern terminus of the Ocean to the western. His chariot was led by four horses: Pyroeis (the Fiery), Eous (the Morning or the Eastern), Aithon (the Burning), and Phlegon (the Blazing). He was said to return from the West to the East each night in a golden and winged cup forged by Hephaistos.

Helios saw and heard everything. He was the one who told Hephaistos of the affair between Ares and Aphrodite;[1] he was the one who saw Hades abduct Persephone.[2] Because of his knowledge of affairs on earth, people would swear "by the sun" in much the same way that the gods would swear by the Styx.

Helios could also have restorative powers. When Orion, for instance, was blinded by Oenopion, the sun restored his vision.[3]

1. See page 38. 2. See page 17. 3. See page 90.

Sicily was a favorite island of Helios and here he kept a herd of sacred cattle. It was the plundering of these cattle that got Odysseus' men into so much trouble in the twelfth book of the *Odyssey*.

Another favorite place was Rhodes. Helios married a nymph named Rhode, a personification of that island, and rituals to the sun were widespread in Rhodes. In fact, it is believed that the famous Colossus of Rhodes was inspired by Helios.

Among the offspring of Helios were Circe, Phaeton,[1] Aeetes, Pasiphae, and King Augeas.

Hesperus and the **Hesperides**. Hesperus, the son of Eos, was the Evening Star, the brightest star in the heavens. The Hesperides were sometimes thought of as Hesperus' daughters, sometimes as the daughters of Night. They lived in the far West out of the range of the sun's light, way beyond the stream of the Ocean. They had beautiful voices and often sang. Their main function was to guard the golden apples that Gaia gave to Zeus as a wedding present when he married Hera. They assisted and tended to Ladon, a dragon with a hundred heads, born from Typhon and Echidna. The whole area was under the sway of Atlas, whose kingdom was the northwestern part of the world. There were three Hesperides: Aegle, Erythia, and Arethusa (or Hespera). When the Argonauts appeared, they changed themselves into dust and ashes but, on being importuned by Orpheus, took their conventional shape respectively as a willow, an elm, and a poplar tree.

The **Pleiades** and **Hyades**. Atlas had several daughters and one son. The son, Hyas, was killed by a boar or a lion, and several of his sisters, mourning for him, became the constellation known as the Hyades. These sisters were Phaeto, Ambrosia, Coronis, Eudora, Polyxo, Pedile, and Thyene (Dione). There are, however, several other explanations regarding their name. Some say that they are called "Hyades" because in the sky they seem to have the shape of the letter "Y." Still others say that they come from the word *hyein,* which means "to rain," for the Hyades seem to appear each autumn and hence usher in the rainy season, the season of bad weather. Still another version claims that the Hyades protected and nursed Dionysus when he was a baby and were changed into stars by Zeus.

Their sisters, the Pleiades, were surrounded with similar tales. Some say that they mourned so dearly when their sisters, the Hyades, were turned into stars that the gods rewarded their loyalty by also changing them. Others say that Orion pursued them all over the earth and that they not only refused his advances but also fled from him: Zeus finally took pity and turned both them and Orion into stars.

1. See page 91.

118

Others say that they were first turned into doves, after the Greek word for dove, *peleia,* and then into stars. Still others say that their name comes from the Greek word *plein,* which means "to sail," for the Pleiades appear in the sky during the spring months and hence usher in the fair weather and the time safe for sailing. Still others derive their name from their mother, Pleone, a daughter of the Ocean.

There were seven Pleiades: Alcyone, Merope, Celaeno, Electra, Sterope, Taygete, and Maia. They alternate in the sky with their sister Hyades. The Pleiades are summer stars and the Hyades are winter stars.

Several of them had affairs with mortals or gods. Of their offspring, the most important were Hermes, by Maia and Zeus; Lacedaemon, by Taygete and Zeus, who was the subsequent founder of Sparta (Lacedaimon); and Dardanus, by Electra and Zeus, who later founded Troy.

As even now it is very difficult to see one of the stars in the constellation, so it was thought that one of the Pleiades was either hiding or withholding her light. Some say that it was Electra, in mourning because of the loss of her son Dardanus when Troy fell; others say that it was Merope, being ashamed because she had married a mere mortal, Sisyphus, while all her sisters married gods.

Oceanus. Oceanus, the son of Ouranos and Gaia, was one of the Titans. He was the Ocean itself. The massive ocean formed a continuous stream around the flat and circular earth[1] and was the source of all rivers, many of which joined it through underground channels. On the borders of the Ocean were the Ethiopians and Pygmies to the South, the Cimmerians and the entrance to the Underworld at the West, the Hyperboreans to the North, and the Phrygians at the East.

The Ocean had an enormous number of offspring, some of which are here listed:

Doris, mother of the Nereids
Electra, mother of Iris and the Harpies
Callirrhoe, mother of Geryon, the three-headed monster
three thousand rivers
three thousand nymphs
Eurynome, mother of the Graces
Idyra, mother of Medea

Pontus. Pontus was the oldest body of water, born along with Ouranos and the Mountains from Gaia. Pontus usually refers to salt water bodies such as the Mediterranean, but later it is the specific name for the Black Sea. Its common epithet is "restless" or "barren," probably since it does not produce crops.

1. See map, page 60.

Among the offspring of Pontus were:

Nereus, the father of the fifty Nereids

Thaumas ("marvel") who with Electra ("gleaming") bore Iris (the Rainbow), and the Harpies.

Eurybia, who with Crius bore Astraeus, Pallas, and Perses. Astraeus and Eos bore the Winds and the Morning and Evening Stars. Perses fathered Hecate. Pallas and the River Styx produced Cratos and Bia (Force and Strength), Zeus' companions.

Ceto, who with Phorcys begot many dangers of the sea, such as the monster Ladon, who guards the golden apples, the Gorgons, who live in the western limit of the Ocean, the Graeae, two women with attractive faces but very gray hair (who have been thought to represent the foam of the waves as they break and then recede).

Phorcys, who with Ceto fathered the creatures just mentioned. Phorcys was another "old man of the sea." His daughter, the Nymph Thoosa, bore Polyphemus, the Cyclops. It is said that Phorcys fathered Scylla.

CHAPTER XII

THE TRANSFORMATION MYTH

The story of Pygmalion

The island is Cyprus, a place sacred to Aphrodite, and the city is Amathus. It had a sordid history of degeneracy. There were, for instance, the Cerastae, a people so savage that some think they were changed into bulls. They kept a monument to Zeus, a monument that was all blood-stained — stained not with the blood of animal sacrifices but of humans: guests and strangers were slain there. Aphrodite, totally offended by these people, had transformed them.

Then there were the women called Propoetides. They had snubbed Aphrodite and had given their bodies to whomever they wanted. So shameless were they that the goddess changed them into rocks. So hardened to any decency had they become that the change was but a slight one.

On this island lived Pygmalion. When he saw the women there leading such dissolute and wanton lives and engaging in such frequent crimes against man and god, he decided to renounce the company of women and to live alone. He, with consummate craft and skill, carved a statue out of pure white ivory; he gave it the shape of a woman and he endowed it with unprecedented beauty. It looked so much like a real woman that one would have thought that it was alive, that it was merely at rest.

So realistic was it that its creator fell in love with it. He would caress it, its hands, thighs, shoulders, neck. He would kiss it, speak to it, hold and embrace it. When he saw an imprint from his fingers, he would move back, frightened lest he might have given it a blemish. He brought her presents: shells, trifles to amuse her, flowers, pet birds, playthings. He even adorned her with jewelry and clothing; he placed rings on her, a necklace, even earrings. These new blandishments only enhanced her beauty. He even slept with her, sharing his bed with her and thinking of her as his bride.

Now, there happened to come the time for the festival to Aphrodite. All over the island people were preparing for the sacrifice. Pygmalion too prepared his sacrifice and as he was standing before the altar fragrant with incense, he prayed: "O gods, if indeed you can do everything, then let my wife be . . ." and he paused, reluctant to say "this statue" but instead said "like this statue." Aphrodite saw him and was taken by his piety and by his unusual love. She sent him an omen: three times the fire before him soared into the air. He left the temple and went home. He retired to his bed where he lay by his beloved. He kissed her; she seemed to become warm; again he kissed her; now she seemed to move; he felt a beat within her breast; the hard ivory began to soften. He was reminded of how wax, originally hard, becomes soft and pliable under the sun and how it takes whatever shape the fingers impress upon it.

Pygmalion was amazed; he was overjoyed but at the same time frightened lest this be a trick of some sort. He touched her again: it was no trick; she was real; he felt the blood pulsing within her veins. Elated, he immediately thanked Aphrodite with all the skill that he could summon, and he kissed the girl again. This time she responded. They were married; Aphrodite herself attended the service. Within a year they gave birth to a daughter named Paphos, who in turn gave her name to a city on the island. The wife was given the name Galatea.

Echo and Narcissus

Tiresias, after he had been blinded by Hera and in compensation had been given the gift of prophecy by Zeus,[1] became famous throughout the cities of Boeotia. Once the nymph Liriope, daughter of Tethys and Oceanus, asked the blind prophet about her son, the one that she had conceived when the River Cephisus swirled around her with his waters and, having her secure, raped her. The offspring of this violent union was a beautiful child called Narcissus. When asked if the child would live to a ripe old age, the prophet answered cryptically, "Yes, as long as he never recognizes himself." No one understood what the old man meant by these words, at least not until much later; they eventually found out, however.

Narcissus was now sixteen years old, both a boy and a man at the same time. Boys and girls alike sought his affections but that proud creature rejected the advances of everyone.

One day the nymph Echo saw him as he was driving deer into his nets. The more she watched him as he sauntered through the pathless forests, the more did she fall in love with him, and she would follow him everywhere.

1. See page 34.

At this time, Echo was a full bodied being, not just a voice as she is now. She was always garrulous, never could learn to hold her tongue after someone else had spoken, but never would speak first herself. Now she is quite different; Hera changed her. Oftentimes when she was out in the woods trying to find Zeus redhanded with some nymph, Echo would keep her occupied with all kinds of chit-chat until the young girls had gotten to a safe distance. Hera eventually realized that she was being duped. "So you've used your tongue to deceive me! Well, I'll make short use of that tongue, nor will you have much use for that voice of yours, my irreverent young friend." Consequently, all she can do now is to repeat the words that she hears. As she saw Narcissus, she so much wanted to call out to him, to gain his attention. But she could not. All she could do was to be ready for his voice, ready to return to him whatever she heard.

One day the youth accidentally got separated from his friends. "Is anyone here?" he shouted out, and Echo answered "Here." He was surprised; he looked everywhere but saw nothing. "Come!" he exclaimed. "Come!" replied Echo. "Why are you avoiding me?" he said, and he heard the same words in return. "Now come, let us be together here," he finally remarked, and Echo repeated the words, words which have never expressed a keener desire: "Let us be together here!" She ran up to him and was about to throw her arms around him when he repelled her: "Take your hands from me. I would rather die than let my body be turned over to you." "Body be turned over to you!" she repeated dejectedly. She left him, hid in the woods, concealed her face red from blushing and embarrassment. From then on she lived only in caves; still, her love remained; in fact, it grew. She ate no more but merely pined away, sad and lonely and dejected. Now only her bones and her voice remained. She can still be heard in the mountains but never seen; still in hiding, only her voice remains.

Meanwhile others received the same rejection from Narcissus that Echo had received. Finally someone in anger and frustration exclaimed, holding his hands up toward the sky, "If ever he does love, may he not be able to enjoy that love." The goddess of Retribution, Nemesis, heard the prayer and thought it a just one.

Nearby was a spring, clear and clean, still pristine, untouched by shepherds, birds, and beasts. There was a thick coppice of grass nourished by the water from that stream, and overhead was the hanging bough of a thick tree. One day, the youth, wearied from his hunt and running from the heat of the sun, rested here. He went to drink from this stream, but as he was satisfying one thirst, another thirst grew within him.

While he was drinking, he happened to see the reflection of his own features in the water. He was attracted to those features and fell hard in love with that form, not knowing it to be what it was. He stared at what he saw: he admired the star-like eyes, the slender fingers, the hair similar to Apollo's, the graceful ivory neck, the blushing cheeks, the sensuous mouth, the rosy complexion, and the snow white skin. All the features that he saw in this pool he admired. He fell hopelessly in love with the gorgeous creature. How often he tried in vain to kiss that youth! How often he tried in vain to embrace that object of his love! But always in vain.

He cared nothing about food or sleep. No bodily need distracted him. He lay along the bank of the coppice, gazing down upon that deceptive image.

"Was there ever anyone more hopelessly in love than I am," he mused. "O woods, you who have seen many loves and have aided them with your shelter, have you ever seen one who has loved more dearly? This object of my love, whatever his name is, seems to want me; when I reach out to him, he reaches out to me. When I try to kiss him, he tries to kiss me. When I extend my hand to him, he extends his hand to me. But a little water seems to get in our way. A little water seems to be the only thing that is preventing our union. Why, my fair-haired creature, do you resist me? Why do you disappear when I come up to you? Why do you suddenly vanish when I get very near? Certainly I am not unattractive. Nymphs have been after me as long as I can remember. And then, too, you do encourage me. You smile when I smile; you weep when I weep; when I speak, I see you answer me even though I can't understand your words; and when I give you those very telling looks of mine, you give me the same kind of looks."

He began to weep, his tears disturbed the water, and the reflection in it seemed to become deformed. And when the water began to move and the image began to disappear, he became very alarmed. "Where are you going? Stay. Even though I cannot hold you, let me at least be able to see you." For by then he had realized the nature of his loved one. Echo looked on. Although still hurt and angry, she pitied the boy. And as often as he would strike himself with his hands, so she would echo these sounds. And as often as he would cry out a sound of woe, so she would re-echo that woeful tone.

He spoke his final words, still lying on that bank: "Alas, my beloved! loved in vain." And the words were repeated. And finally, "Farewell!" Echo repeated, "Farewell!" He shut his eyes and died.

124

Even in the Underworld he would behold himself in the waters of the Styx. The Naiads all grieved for him; the Dryads too, those nymphs of the trees, as well as Echo herself, who replied to all their sounds of mourning. And when the body was searched for, it was not to be found; instead there was a golden flower with smooth petals of white.

The story of King Midas

The satyr Silenus, the tutor of Dionysus in his youth and his constant companion in his mature years, was always eager to take a nip from that wine bag that he always had with him. Once, that fat old man, having had too much to drink, got separated from the god and his company of satyrs and maenads. A group of Thracian country people came across him staggering with wine and old age, and they brought him to Midas, their king. Midas recognized the old man with wreaths and garlands on his head, and he welcomed him warmly. For ten days and nights he and Silenus partied, and both stories and wine flowed freely. Finally on the eleventh day when Midas heard that Dionysus was in the area, he sent his old companion back to him. Dionysus was so pleased to see his old tutor again and so grateful to Midas for his hospitality that he offered the king a gift of his own choosing. "Let whatever I touch," replied the king without much thought, "turn into gold." Dionysus felt that this was a rather foolish request but, since he had made his promise, he did what Midas had asked.

Midas now left joyously, excited with his new gift. He tested his new power; he saw a leaf on a tree; he touched it and Midas scarcely believed what he saw when that leaf became golden. He lifted a stone from the ground; it, too, became gold from his touch. He touched an ear of corn; it became gold. The same happened to an apple, a doorknob, a pillar supporting a house. They all turned to the precious metal. Even when he washed his hands, a stream of gold left them. He became more and more excited thinking of the possibilities of his new power.

He entertained these thoughts as he sat down to supper. The table had already been set and there were all sorts of delicacies before him. But problems beset him from the beginning. He lifted a piece of bread, but before he could bring it to his lips, it was hard and golden. When he tried to bite into a piece of meat, it too became as golden as the dish on which it was being served. Even the wine

125

changed as soon as it touched his lips. The foolish king didn't know what to do; this was not what he had planned on. He became frightened and wished he had not made such a rash request.

Becoming thirstier and hungrier, he realized his folly. Lifting his hands up to heaven, he prayed to Dionysus. "I've been foolish; please pity me, I pray, and take back this gift which once seemed to me so wonderful but which has turned out to be so disastrous." The god was understanding and pitied the foolhardy king. He took back the gift. "Go to the river," he told the king, "if you want to rid yourself of your newly acquired powers; put your head under the spring where it is the fullest and then plunge your whole body so that you may wash away your folly."

The king did as he was instructed. He bathed in the stream and the waters washed away his power. Even now the banks of that river are hard since they were touched by the waters tinged with Midas' touch.

But that was not the end of Midas' folly. Despising riches, he turned his affection to Pan and spent much of his time in the woods and in the country. His lack of judgment, however, got him into a new trouble. One day Pan was bragging to some nymphs about his prowess with those pipes that he had discovered. He even boasted that he was a better musician than Apollo himself. Apollo met his boast and the two of them had a contest. Midas happened to be present; Tmolus, a divinity of the local hills, was judge. Pan played; what came out was not music but merely odd sounds; in fact, that description is a euphemism – his playing was terrible. Then Apollo followed; he took his lyre and after just a few strains it was clear who had won. Tmolus declared Apollo the winner and no one disagreed, no one except Midas. He thought that Pan's playing was splendid and remarked that Tmolus' decision was unfair. Apollo lost patience with such stupidity. "This Midas has the ears of a jackass," thought the god to himself; "then let it be so." And before he knew it, the ears on Midas' head had lengthened; white hairs covered those ears and the king found that he could move them. Every other part of his body stayed the same, just the ears changed.

Midas was chagrinned, embarrassed, mortified; he, a king, with the ears of an ass! Trying to hide them, he wore a large turban. But one of his domestics was one day cutting his hair and happened to see those silly ears. This was too good a piece of gossip to keep secret, but the servant knew that he dare not tell anyone. Still, he itched to share his secret with someone. What he did was this: he dug a hole in the ground and whispered the secret to the earth. Then he

126

covered up the hole and, he thought, the secret. But reeds grew up out of that hole, and the reeds whispered the secret to the winds and the winds spread the rumor far and wide.

What could Midas do, now that he was an object of laughter all over the land! Some say that he committed suicide, unable to endure the embarrassment that came from his folly.

The story of Cyparissus

On one of the Cyclades Islands lived a young man named Cyparissus. He would spend most of his days in the woods where he took particular delight in caring for a large stag. This stag was a favorite of the nymphs, who had adorned its neck with a precious necklace; there were golden horns on its forehead, and it was as friendly an animal as any that had ever wandered the forests. Cyparissus would lead it to grazing fields and to streams, he would garland the stag with flowers, and sometimes he would even ride the animal, so gentle was it.

One day, as the two of them were resting under the shade of a tree, Cyparissus accidentally wounded the stag with the point of his javelin. When the stag died, the youth was filled with such grief that he too sought death. He mourned constantly for several days and nights until Apollo took pity upon him and changed him into a cypress tree, the tree of mourning. "Always will I mourn you," said Apollo, "and always will you mourn others; you will always be present among those who are in sorrow for the dead."

The story of King Tereus

King Tereus of Thrace was a son of Ares. He had married Procne, a daughter of King Pandion of Athens, and with her fathered a son named Itys. His love, however, was not stable and he soon lusted after Procne's sister, Philomela. Exactly how he managed to satisfy his passion is uncertain; what is certain, however, is that he did manage to satisfy it. He arranged for Philomela to visit her sister. Having had his way with her, he then locked her up in a hideaway of his in the forest and, so that she could never tell anyone of his bestiality, he cut out her tongue. Then he pretended to his wife that Philomela had met with a terrible accident in the woods; he wept so profusely that Procne was convinced, and time eventually soothed her sorrow.

Meanwhile, Philomela, although still imprisoned and suffering, was not daunted. She embroidered a large robe and in it wove the story of what had happened. She then gave that robe to one of her guards and instructed that guard to give it to Procne. The guard, of course, knew nothing of the situation and faithfully delivered the garment.

When Procne received the robe and interpreted the embroidery, she immediately freed her sister from imprisonment, and the two of them plotted revenge. First they killed Itys, the son from that barbarous father, boiled his limbs, and Procne served them as a meal to Tereus. Tereus ate, entirely unaware of what he was eating. Then he called for his son. Procne, unable to restrain her hatred any longer, told him that he had inside him that whom he was requesting. Then Philomela entered and showed the king the head of the boy.

The king went into a rage. He grabbed an axe and went after the two sisters. They each fled in different directions, Procne into various houses and Philomela into the woods. During the chase each was changed into a bird: Philomela into the nightingale, Procne into the swallow, and Tereus into the filthy lapwing.

One of the most common types of tale in the study of mythology is the metamorphosis, or transformation myth. Whether these tales are actually myths is a moot point depending upon one's definition of myth. But if one acknowledges that a myth is essentially a traditional story, then one will have little difficulty in admitting these tales of transformation into the ranks of mythology.

We have already seen many transformation myths — for instance, the stories of Lycaon and of Philemon and Baucis. As mentioned in the remarks following those stories, [1] the transformation often reflects a sort of poetic justice. A person often is changed into something that reflects his nature when he or she was alive. For instance, someone overcome by the death of a loved one and in inconsolable sadness is changed into a cypress tree, the tree of mourning. Not only does the tree symbolize sadness because of its drooping limbs and almost barren branches, but the tree was also planted near graves, and coffins were often made of cypress wood.

Another person who was hard-hearted in life will be changed into a statue or a stone or a rock. Someone else who shed excessive tears, usually out of grief from the death of a loved one, may be turned into a fountain or a river.

People are frequently changed into birds, and the type of bird will often reflect that person's nature. In fleeing from the evil Tereus, Procne

1. See page 71.

takes refuge in inhabited houses and hunts for the child she killed in her madness; she becomes a swallow, a bird that frequently nests in eaves or attics. Her sister Philomela flees to the woods and hides there; she is changed into a nightingale, a bird that even now nests in thickets; furthermore, having been deprived of her voice by the sadistic king, she is rewarded with a most glorious voice in her transformation. Tereus himself, that sordid king who was unable to catch the two fleeing sisters, becomes the slow lapwing, a bird that revels in filth.

Whether we are dealing with stories that come before or after the fact is another question. Again the cypress tree illustration is a good one. Is the cypress tree associated with the sadness of death because of the unfortunate Cyparissus? Or is the story of Cyparissus merely a figurative explanation for the already existing practices?

The metamorphosis often works etymologically. What a person is changed into often is the Greek or Latin word for that person's name. Cycnus is the Greek word for swan, Cyparissus for cypress, Arachne for spider, Crocus for the flower crocus, Hyacinthus for hyacinth, Myrmidon (from *murmex*) for ant, Daphne for laurel, and so on. Similarly, many people who are transformed into places give their names to that place: the Marsyas River, the rock-monster Scylla, the Acis River, the constellations Orion, Callisto, Ariadne, the Atlas Mountains.

Transformation stories often fall into certain categories:

a. Moralizing tales of reward, such as Philemon and Baucis, Daphne, Arethusa, or Ariadne. The most common reason for a reward transformation is loyalty: loyalty to the gods, to friends, parents, children, husbands, wives.

b. Moralizing tales of punishment, such as Lycaon, Niobe, Arachne. The most common reasons for such punishment are arrogance and disloyalty. A human must always remember his place, for if he pushes the gods too far, they will usually strike him down.

c. Explanations of living genera: birds or trees or flowers in particular, such as the hyacinth, the lotus tree, the swan, etc.

d. Explanations of customs.

e. Explanations of the names of places.

f. The romanticizing of actual historical events by poets and story tellers. For instance, it is possible that the original Arachne was an actual person known for her embroidery. Since Athena was also associated with sewing and weaving, and furthermore, since the Greek word *arachne* means spider web and since complex embroidery can resemble the complexity of a web, these diverse facts perhaps became amalgamated into the contest between the girl Arachne and the goddess Athena. There are, however, several other ways to explain the myth. Another example concerns the story of Marsyas.[1] One theory is that there

1. See page 22.

129

was actually a youth named Marsyas who was so skilled in flute playing that he challenged a priest of Apollo; chagrinned at his defeat, the boy jumped into a river, and the story of the encounter between Marsyas and Apollo is merely a romanticizing of the original event. One might use the story of Pygmalion as a third example. One explanation is that the story is allegorical; that there was a man on Cyprus named Pygmalion; that he was indeed offended by the looseness of most of the women on the island; that he found one whom he became attached to and trained her and moulded her to fit his own standards; that he secluded her from the other women on the island while he was reshaping her; and that he finally succeeded in remodeling her to such an extent that her behavior and personality became transformed into such delicacy and sensitivity that Pygmalion married her. Again, all explanations of this type are speculative. What is safe to say, however, is that the ancients did enjoy giving mythological or figurative analogues for historical events, natural phenomena, and various types of flora and fauna.

Whether people actually believed many of these transformation myths is doubtful. Rather, the myth appealed to their sense of imagination and helped to tie them just a bit closer to the gods. In early times, the myth most likely did help to explain the complex of phenomena that people met from day to day. Furthermore, the absence of science or of any kind of scientific principles gave way to a much more figurative view of the world.

Ovid in his *Metamorphoses* compiled fifteen books of transformation myths, ranging from the beginning of creation until the time of Julius Caesar. His ultimate aim was to show how Rome was a transformation of the city of Troy, but what he really did was to give us one of the most complete compendia of myths that exists from classical sources; in fact, he is the source of many of the stories that have been bequeathed to posterity, and even though his version of a particular story may be different from an earlier and more accurate account, and even though he may have added details from his own imagination, it is often his version that has come down to us. The tabulation in Appendix II lists some of the important metamorphoses as told by Ovid. Many of them are very rich stories, well worth reading in their entirety. The stories sometimes are precious, and a reader occasionally gets the feeling that Ovid is forcing a transformation. Although the reader must keep in mind that Ovid has often put in his own twist, Ovid does usually tell a good story.

CHAPTER XIII

PROPHETS AND ORACLES

An undercurrent in the thought of the ancient Greeks was the belief that, to one extent or another, the future was in the hands of the gods. Though they believed that individual fates were predetermined by the Moirae, they did not believe in rigid predestination, particularly for a people or a state. Human actions did have their effects, but the Greeks believed that it was foolish to pursue a course of action that was opposed by the gods. Thus they sought, through several means, to know the will of the gods, to see the consequences of a certain course of action, and when possible to see what the Moirae had determined for individuals.

There were many ways of learning the will of the gods. Dreams were said to come from Zeus and, obviously, were a vehicle available to all. Likewise, anyone could interpret certain omens, such as the sneeze, which was said to portend something good. Some omens, however, required the interpretation of one who had a special god-given gift for understanding communications from the gods. These prophets were called seers or soothsayers or augurs. The activities of birds, the entrails of animals that had been sacrificed to the gods, and, particularly with the Etruscans and Romans, the formation of the livers of certain animals were some of the means seers used to learn the will of the gods. Still other seers had ecstatic visions in which they saw the future. The Greeks in most historical periods rejected witches and wizards with their various kinds of magic, though the Romans, particularly in the second century A.D., embraced magic wholeheartedly. The Romans also formalized the interpretation of the flight of birds and called the ritual "taking auspices."

The most authoritative means of knowing the will of the gods was through an oracle. Oracles were the spokesmen of the gods and functioned in specific sacred sanctuaries. The sanctuary of Zeus at Dodona and the sanctuary of Apollo at Delphi housed the two most famous oracles in Greece, though there were others throughout the Greek world.

Prophets

Of the hundreds of prophets who were undoubtedly involved in the lives of the Greeks in ancient times, a few have come down to

131

us in ancient literature. We have already seen[1] how **Tiresias**, the blind seer of Thebes, gained his prophetic powers. In the *Odyssey* Odysseus visits him in the Underworld where he still retained his powers. He also appears as a seer in several of the Greek tragedies, including Sophocles' *Oedipus* and Euripides' *Bacchae.* He appears in the background of many different periods of history, and his seeming omnipresence is explained by the fact that he was said to have lived for a very long time. He is usually depicted as a very old man, poking his way step by step with a walking stick, severe and humorless. Tiresias was the chosen prophet of Zeus; his prophecies were reliable and he was always to be taken seriously.

Melampus, who also appears in the *Odyssey,* was skilled in both prophecy and medicine, not an unusual combination in that disease was often seen as a curse sent by the gods. We have already seen[2] how Melampus cured the madness inflicted by Dionysus on the daughters of King Proetus, and this is a good example of the blending of prophetic and medical skills. Melampus gained his skills when he was a boy. His parents' servants discovered a nest of snakes and killed them, but not before he was able to rescue the young. When the rescued snakes were mature, they once licked his ears and cleared them out. From that point on he was able to understand the speech of birds, and later on he was able to understand the speech of all animals. He became a friend of Apollo from whom he learned the art of soothsaying and the reading of auspices.

Two other seers who received their gifts from snakes were **Helenus** and **Cassandra**, twin children of King Priam of Troy. When they were children, they went to a birthday celebration held at the temple of Apollo. The children played for a while in the temple and then fell asleep. Meanwhile, the adults drank quite a bit, forgot the children, and returned home. The next day the children were found still asleep, but with snakes washing out their ears with their tongues. The spectators screamed, the snakes retreated into some laurel bushes, and from that point on the children had the gift of prophecy. During the Trojan War, Helenus supported the side of Troy. When his brother Paris was killed, however, he and his brother Deiphobus quarreled about who should get Helen. Helenus lost and retreated to Mount Ida, where Odysseus captured him and forced him to reveal how Troy might be taken.

Another tradition tells a different story of how Cassandra, Helenus' twin sister, gained her gift of prophecy. Apollo, having fall-

1. See page 34.
2. See page 47.

RAPE OF CASSANDRA. Attic Red-Figured Vase by the Altamura Painter,
5th Century B.C. As Ajax tries to abduct her, Cassandra clings to the Palladium. The Palladium was the most sacred object in Troy; the city could not be
taken as long as it remained within the walls of the city. *Courtesy, Museum of
Fine Arts, Boston.*

en in love with her, gave her the ability to see the future on the condition that she would bed with him. She accepted his gift, but then reneged on her part of the bargain. Apollo could not take his gift back, so he added to it the stipulation that she would always tell the truth but that no one would believe her. Hence, while she did make accurate predictions, her moments of articulate speech were punctuated by so much incoherent and unintelligible babble that she was not heeded. She is an example of a seer who saw the future in ecstatic visions. During the Trojan War she was raped by the Greek warrior Ajax, and after the war Agamemnon took her back to Mycenae where both of them were killed by Clytemnestra and Aegisthus. The full story will be told later.[1]

Still another Homeric seer, who appears in the *Iliad*, was **Calchas**. He accompanied the Greeks to Troy, predicted that Troy could not be taken without Achilles, recommended that Iphigenia be sacrificed so that the Greeks could get a favorable wind to take them to Troy, suggested the building of the wooden horse, revealed that Athena was angry because of Ajax's rape of Cassandra, and pointed out that Heracles' bow and arrows were essential for the Greeks to capture Troy. One of his most famous predictions occurred in Aulis, just before the Greek contingent sailed. A snake attacked a nest of sparrows, devoured the eight fledglings together with their mother, and turned to stone. Calchas interpreted this to mean that the Greeks would eventually take Troy, but only after nine years.

It was fated that Calchas would die whenever he met a prophet mightier than himself. This happened at Colophon, when he met **Mopsus**, son of Apollo, who made predictions that Calchas could not make.

Finally, a seer who appears in Vergil's *Aeneid*, but who is best known through a dramatic Hellenistic statue depicting his death and the death of his sons, was the Trojan prophet and priest of Poseidon, **Laocoon**. He said that the wooden horse left in front of Troy by the Greeks should not be admitted into the city and he struck the horse with his spear. Later, as he was sacrificing to Poseidon, two immense serpents came out of the sea to Laocoon and strangled both him and his two sons and then slithered off into the shrine of Athena. The Trojans interpreted this event to mean that Laocoon had profaned the horse, which they felt must be something sacred; hence they admitted it into their city.

In both Greek and Roman literature **Sibyls** often appear. The Sibyl was probably originally a woman who was able to predict the

1. See page 148 ff.

future, but the word eventually became a generic name for a host of women in a variety of locations who claimed the gift of prophecy. Sibyls were usually connected with Apollo and their statements were usually ambiguous and cryptic. The most famous was the Sibyl of Cumae in southern Italy. Aeneas consulted her and was told of his future in Italy, and she guided him through the Underworld.

Associated with the Sibyl of Cumae were the **Sibylline Books,** nine volumes of prophecies, rituals, and rites by which to appease the gods. A curious legend concerns these books. An old woman offered to sell the volumes to Tarquinius Superbus, the last of the legendary kings of Rome. He refused to pay her exorbitant price and she burned three of the volumes. She made the offer again, asking the same price now for only six volumes, was again refused, and burned another three volumes. Finally when she made her offer a third time, the king was so curious that he bought the remaining volumes. When he saw what the books were, he was chagrined at his foolishness in having lost the other six volumes.

Oracles

The word oracle usually refers to a pronouncement, made in answer to an inquiry, by a qualified interpreter who was in direct or indirect communication with a god. Sometimes, however, the word is used to refer to the site of the shrine where such communication took place or even to the interpreter himself. The two most important sites of oracles in ancient Greece, both mentioned in Homer, were Dodona in northwestern Greece, near the modern city of Ioanina, and Delphi, on the side of Mount Parnassus, overlooking the Gulf of Corinth.

Dodona was probably the most ancient oracle in Greece. The sanctuary was sacred to Zeus, and there, through the rustling of leaves in a sacred oak tree, he made known his will to priests who then interpreted the sounds to those who had made inquiries. Both Achilles and Odysseus had occasion to consult the oracle at Dodona. In classical times it was definitely overshadowed by the prominence of Delphi, though it was still a functioning oracle when Herodotus visited it in the fifth century. We know little of the procedures used in later times, though it would appear that after the sacred oak died, some sort of lot took the place of the wind in the leaves.

We have already seen the story of Apollo's conquest of the

snake-like Python at **Delphi**.[1] It is clear that Delphi was a spot sacred to an earth goddess at least from the second millenium B.C. on, and the story of Apollo's conquest of Python may be symbolic of an actual historical change in worship from an earth goddess to the new male god. There was a stone at Delphi called the *omphalos,* a word which means "center" or "navel." Zeus was said to have released birds simultaneously from the opposite ends of the world and, because they met at that spot, it was regarded as the center of the world.

Apollo made known his father's will through the oracle at Delphi, and we know that in both myth and history the words from Delphi carried significant weight. No one is sure exactly what the procedure for consulting the oracle at Delphi was. It was common knowledge to the ancients, so no one bothered to write it down. From what can be pieced together from ancient references, however, we get a rough idea of what went on. In early times it seems that the oracle was available for consultation only during one day out of the year. Later, however, this seems to have been expanded to one day out of each month. During the winter months, while Apollo was with the Hyperboreans, the oracle was closed and the site was sacred to Dionysus. It would seem, then, that there were at most a total of nine consultation days a year — but during those nine days, the oracle was available from dawn to dusk and hundreds stood in line waiting for their turn.

Delphi was an international site, and anyone could consult the oracle. After ritual purification and the offering of an expensive cake to the god, the petitioner would sacrifice an animal; if this sacrifice was accepted, he would then go into an inner chamber. There, a woman known as a *pythia* sat on a bronze tripod and uttered ecstatic sounds. How she reached her ecstatic state is a matter of debate, but there is no basis for the story that she inhaled fumes emitted from a fissure in the rocks. Whatever the cause, the sounds she made were said to be the utterances of Apollo. A priest who listened to these sounds would then translate them into hexameter verses for the petitioner. There is evidence that, at times, when the oracle was not in session, petitioners could get an "either/or" answer through sacred lots. The oracle at Delphi continued to make pronouncements well into the fourth century A.D., when it was closed by a Christian emperor.

1. See pages 21 and 24.

CHAPTER XIV

PERSPECTIVES

The purpose of this chapter is to present some insights and observations that may help put the reading of mythology into some perspective and to clarify a few of the confusions that the myths can sometimes present.

I. Historical Periods. There are several different ways to divide the periods of ancient history, but for the purposes of mythology, the following divisions may help. *a.* The Prehistoric period, which saw the advent of settlements in the Greek-Mediterranean area. *b.* The Minoan-Mycenean period, from about 2000 B.C. to 1100 B.C. The Minoan civilization flourished on Crete; during that time the Cretans built enormous palaces, such as the one at Cnossos, developed a system of writing, and produced significant art work. Around 1400 B.C. the culture began to wane, whether from foreign invaders or from natural cataclysms is uncertain. From that time on, Mycenae on the Peloponnesus was the leading force. The Myceneans, from their vantage point on the Aegean, engaged in extensive commerce. They built massive palaces such as the ones at Mycenae and Tiryns, and also devised a system of writing. It was during this time that the Trojan War occurred and that many of the gods in the Greek pantheon evolved. *c.* The Dark Age, from about 1100 B.C. to 800 B.C. There were almost no significant improvements in culture or life style. Rather, there was a period of regression, much like the Dark Ages in Europe fifteen centuries later. There was little art, writing, or architecture. It was a time primarily of farming and of fragmented but closely knit small social bodies. Tales from the past were romanticized and passed on orally by wandering poets and minstrels. Personal honor and physical prowess were considered very important. *d.* The Preclassical age, from about 800 B.C. until 500 B.C. This is the age of Homer, Hesiod, and the great lyric poets. Literature and art began to thrive again; the city-state became important as a social unit, and there was colonization throughout all the shores of the Mediterranean. *e.* The Golden Age or classical period, from about 500 B.C. to 300 B.C. During this time culture thrived. This is the period of the most significant Greek art, literature, and philosophy, the age of Pindar, Aeschylus, Sophocles, Euripides, Aristophanes, Plato, Herodotus, Thucydides, Aristotle. *f.* The Hellenistic age, from about 300 B.C. on. This was a period of cultural decline, of imitation rather than inspiration. Writers and artists lost the sense of discovery and innovation that they had had in the previous centuries. They were content to be cute and clever. A so-called cultural center was Alexandria, where all the would-be litterati congregated, each one trying to outdo the other in his knowledge of esoteric allusions, in saying in twenty obscure words what might have been said in ten clear words. Here is an example from the poet Lycophron: "I see the wooden bark endowed with wings speeding toward the plundered prize of the shy one, the dog of Pephnos, whom the vulture, that hovers around water, gave birth to in a curved shell." All the poet means is that he saw Paris sailing impetuously toward Helen, who was born in Laconia from the egg that Leda laid. Unfortunately, such periphrases and such verbal bombast were widely imitated by many Roman writers, who are often described as writing in the Alexandrian tradition.

II. Geography. Nowadays we refer to Greece and to the Greeks, but what we call the Greeks were originally a collection of small communities. These communities eventually became city-states, but many kept their autonomy.

In the time of the myths, each community had its king; the concept of king is nothing like what it is in modern times; rather, it is merely a term for a ruler of a city together with its environs, much like a medieval fiefdom. Menelaus was a king of Sparta, a city in Laconia; Agamemnon was a king of Mycenae in Argolis; and just a few miles away was Tiryns, where Perseus was a king.

Rather than calling themselves Greeks, they would identify themselves by their township or by their larger geographical area or by the mythical founder of the area. Hence there are Achaians, Argives, Myrmidons, Thebans, Athenians, and so on. There was a word *Hellas* of much larger scope, but this was a very broad word. It did not refer to any specific geographical area but rather embraced every area where there was some Greek culture, whether in southern Italy or in Asia Minor.

III. Religion. The study of ancient religion is vast and complex. Only a few comments need be made here. First of all, the gods were originally female oriented, and they tended to represent fertility and reproduction, such as Rhea and Gaia. Eventually, however, the masculine oriented gods tended to usurp much of the female influence, until by the Dark Ages there was an equal distribution between male and female. But even that balance is deceptive since the

138

male gods were much more active and their influence much more assertive than that of the females.[1] Secondly, the Greek gods were anthropomorphic. In other words, the Greek saw his gods as an extension of himself. The gods had the same lusts, interests, and weaknesses that a human has. But the gods were much more magnified. Furthermore, they did not seem to be subject to the same laws and moral standards that humans must acknowledge. The gods could get away with behavior that a mortal could not get away with. The gods to a Greek did not provide a model for human behavior. Thirdly, there was no such thing as a national religion with standardized beliefs. One might almost say that the Greeks lived with their gods constantly; every form of life was teeming with a divinity. The gods were there when you needed them, and they sometimes heard you. They were there when you had good fortune, and they expected your thanks. But the Greek did not go to church once a week in order to give the gods their due. Fourthly, in no way did reverence for the gods demand physical mortification, at least in the earlier periods. The Greek would have found such a concept absurd. Self-mortification, penance, and the like are more a Judeo-Christian phenomenon or a phenomenon connected with a cult, such as Orphism. The Greek religious attitudes, if they encouraged anything, encouraged a person to enjoy with moderation what was available in the world. These attitudes were not predicated on the words "Do not." Fifthly, there was no canon of belief. Each community would have a different set of religious traditions, a different set of stories about the gods. Therefore, as we have said so many times in our remarks throughout this book, one must not look for consistency in the stories of the gods and in the myths.

   IV. Sin. There were not many things that were "forbidden," but there were a few. First of all, family relations were sacred. If you abused your parent, you might be subject to the vilest of punishments from the gods. Similarly, if you abused any relative, you could well expect trouble. Perhaps one of the reasons for such strong feelings was that in the early periods there were no courts of law. Since many of the people in a particular area were likely to be related, the sacredness of the family was a way of maintaining order and harmony. Secondly, abusing a host or a guest was a terrible offense. The guest-host relationship was one very dear to Zeus, for Zeus himself might appear on one's doorstep in the form of a mortal traveler. Furthermore, in an age where there were no hotels or guest houses, one had to depend upon the hospitality of strangers. Similarly, if one

1. See page 11, note (b) and page 13, note (a).

were a host, one would have to have no reservations whatsoever about one's guest. There had to be an implicit relationship of trust, and if one violated that trust, the worst misfortunes possible could befall. Thirdly, there is the sin of hybris.[1] Hybris is arrogance, recklessness, pride; hybris is assuming the role of the gods, defying or challenging the gods; hybris above all is excessiveness. The sixth century poet Bacchylides expresses the sentiment aptly.

> When great misery comes to a man, it is not from Zeus; man brings it upon himself. The man who honors Justice and Orderliness and Righteousness is happy; but fearless Hybris flourishes on profit that is alluring and wily and on lawless recklessness and foolishness; very swiftly does Hybris allow a man to have wealth and power, only so that when she removes it just as swiftly, he will feel his fall more dearly. For it was she who destroyed those two very reckless ones, the Giants.

Pindar, a fifth century poet, reiterates:

> It is necessary that we ask from the gods only such blessings as are fitting for mortals, always keeping in mind just who we are. We must not strive for the life of the gods but rather we should enjoy totally that which is given us.

V. Mention should be made about one phenomenon that appears quite a bit in mythology — that is, the **blood guilt**. If you murdered someone, you had that person's blood on your hands, and before you could find peace in your life, you had to be purified. Purification usually meant that you indentured yourself to someone as a vassal for one blood year or nine standard years. Hence, Heracles had to undergo purification twice in his life: once for the murder of his children and the second time for the murder of Iphitus. Even the gods were not necessarily exempt. Apollo, for instance, had to serve Admetus for the murder of the Cyclops.

VI. Correlative to what is sinful is what is not sinful. An important difference between the Greek times and our own times concerns that which we would define as "dirty." Greek art is full of what we would call obscenity but which would have been regarded as totally natural and acceptable in Greek times. For instance, on the most expensive cups and even on funeral urns, explicit sexual activity is sometimes depicted. Greek comedy abounds with both visual and verbal ribaldry. None of this was considered obscene, and in order for us to understand and appreciate the Greek mind, we must make a conscious effort to suspend our notions of obscenity. Secondly, our culture tends to look askance on those who would *seek* fame and reputation and glory. This jaundiced view does not apply to the

---

[1] See pages 22 and 96.

140

Greek mind. It was noble to seek fame. It was much better to lead a short but glorious life than a long but inglorious life. Similarly, there was nothing inherently wrong with bragging or boasting about what one had done or what one would do as long as one remembered one's place in relationship to the gods. Compare the same attitude in Anglo-Saxon poetry . . . for instance, the boasts in *Beowulf.*

VII. There were, however, limits to the Greek sense of aesthetics and propriety, and these limits changed with the passing of time. The Furies, for instance, originally horrible and terrifying forces, became the Eumenides, a name with distinctly positive connotations. In the early story of Ganymede, Zeus personally took the youth to Olympus; later writers found this behavior undignified and had the boy carried up by an eagle. In the earlier stories Zeus was actually deceived by Prometheus' trick; later stories claimed that Zeus knew of the deception all along.

VIII. The first reading of mythology is inevitably confusing. Here are some of the reasons. First, the ancients themselves would have known the stories; they would not have written them down in the way that a mythology book does. A Greek writer would use a myth as a springboard for his own work. If you were writing about a person who had just done something exceptional, you might compare him to a hero such as Theseus or Heracles. If you wanted to write about the effects of destructive love, you might refer to Jason and Medea. The point is that what we know of mythology is often the result of references to a myth rather than a retelling of a complete myth. Secondly, the myths were constantly changing, taking on new details throughout the historical ages and, thirdly, various communities would embellish a myth to suit their own purposes. Hence, there are all sorts of different versions to almost any myth. Fourthly, the names can often be confusing. There are five different people named Cycnus, for instance, two named Diomedes (one a son of Ares, one a foe of Ares), three named Helenus. Eventually one does get a feel for these various similarities, but one should not feel frustrated if at first the names appear as a jumble.

IX. By now you have probably noticed that there is a great deal of violence in mythology. Indeed there is. Mythology often reflects the very violent instincts in man himself and the violence in the world of nature.

X. It may be distressing to us, living in an age of increasing interest in equal rights, to reckon with the Greek attitude toward women. The Greek world was not a woman's world. Pandora, the first woman, was considered the source of evil; Hesiod is explicit: Zeus created woman as a punishment. A century later the poet Semonides supports Hesiod in a lengthy and explicit diatribe against women: "Women — the greatest evil that Zeus made." Later the philosopher Democritus comments: "There is no greater outrage for a man than to be ruled by a woman." It is women like Helen, Phaedra, Medea, and Pasiphae who have come down to us with an unfair stigma.

Chapter XV

MYTHS OF THE GREAT FAMILIES

In order to appreciate the subtleties of the Greek tragedies and of the Homeric epics, a reader must certainly know something about the Olympian gods and about the lesser deities. But more than this, he also needs to know the history of several great families of mortals that appear again and again. In the tragedies, the two most important families were the **House of Atreus** and the **House of Labdacus.** The former is focal in Aeschylus' *Agamemnon, Libation Bearers, Eumenides,* in Sophocles' *Electra,* and in Euripides' *Iphigenia in Tauris, Orestes, Iphigenia in Aulis, Electra,* and *Helen.* It also provides the cause for the war in Homer's *Iliad* and figures large in the *Odyssey.* The latter family is focal in Aeschylus' *Seven Against Thebes,* in Sophocles' *Oedipus the King, Oedipus at Colonus, Antigone,* and in Euripides' *Bacchae.* It too is frequently mentioned in both the *Iliad* and the *Odyssey.* One further family, the **House of Laomedon,** provides the background for the Trojans in the *Iliad* and the *Odyssey* and occurs with some frequency in many of the tragedies.

A Greek citizen watching a tragedy performed at the theater of Dionysus in Athens or at Epidaurus or at Delphi would have known the genealogies of these families and the stories associated with them. It is hard for us to realize this, but it is surely true that the Greek audience knew the plot of a play before it started. Rather than waiting for surprises, the audience waited to see what the dramatist would say through a well known story — i.e., what interpretation he would provide in his play. Thus, even to approach an equal footing with the Greek audience, we too need to know this background.

The House of Atreus

The House of Atreus started with Tantalus, the son of Zeus, and ended with Orestes, the son of Agamemnon, lasting five generations. From beginning to end, the house was embroiled in violent disputes and blood feuds. No other family in myth or recorded history comes close to bringing the horror that this family brought upon its own members.

143

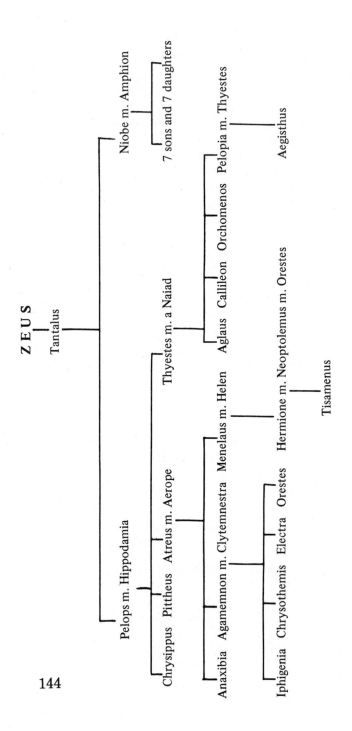

The genealogy of selected names in the House of Atreus

Tantalus, whose deeds have already been mentioned,[1] was king of Lydia in Asia Minor. A favorite of the gods, he abused his friendship with them. Among other things, he invited them to a banquet at which he served them his son, **Pelops,** to test whether they could distinguish between human and animal meat. The gods saw through his deception and refused to eat — all except for Demeter, who was so distracted over the loss of her daughter Persephone that she didn't notice. Outraged at Tantalus' behavior, the gods punished him and restored Pelops to life. All the parts were there except for the shoulder that Demeter had eaten, and they replaced that with a piece of polished ivory. Tantalus' other child was Niobe, whose disastrous boast we have already seen. [2]

Pelops, a youth of rare beauty and a favorite of Poseidon, left Lydia and traveled to Greece, where he sought the hand of **Hippodamia,** the daughter of King Oenomaus of Pisa, which is near Olympia on the Peloponnesus. Oenomaus did not want to give up his daughter, some said because he had an incestuous passion for her, some said because he had heard an oracle that his son-in-law would destroy him. Therefore, the king had set a test that a suitor had to pass before he could have Hippodamia. Essentially it was a race; the suitor had to take Hippodamia in his chariot and race to a finish line near the Isthmus of Corinth. Oenomaus would give him a head start, but if he caught him, he would kill him. Oenomaus, moreover, had rigged the race in his favor. His secret advantage was the fact that Ares had given him his horses, and he had never been beaten. If the suitor lost the race, he also lost his head. Though Pelops decided to accept the challenge, he felt a bit uncomfortable as he faced the dozen heads of previous suitors nailed to Oenomaus' house.

Poseidon provided Pelops with horses and a chariot, but remembering the dozen heads, the young Lydian wanted to be doubly sure; thus, he devised a strategy. Having learned that Myrtilus, Oenomaus' charioteer, was secretly in love with Hippodamia, he went to him and made a bargain. If Myrtilus would guarantee that Pelops would win the race, Pelops would guarantee that Myrtilus would be the first to sleep with Hippodamia. Myrtilus agreed and either took the linch pins out of Oenomaus' chariot or replaced them with wax ones. Whatever he did, however, he was successful, and midway through the race, the wheels flew off and Oenomaus, tangled in the reins, was dragged to his death.

1. See page 79.
2. See page 93.

Since blood guilt was on his hands, Pelops had to leave Pisa to seek purification, and Hippodamia accompanied him — but so did Myrtilus, who wanted his end of the bargain satisfied. Pelops stalled. Then one day, when Pelops had gone to get water, Myrtilus could wait no longer and tried to rape Hippodamia. Though he was unsuccessful, Hippodamia told Pelops what had happened, and he tossed the charioteer into the sea, drowning him. Before he died, however, Myrtilus put a curse on the house of Pelops.

Later, after he had been purified of his blood guilt by Hephaistus, Pelops returned to Pisa to rule. He was a voraciously successful king, ultimately controlling much of the Peloponnesus, which he named after himself. The story of his success in Arcadia gives an indication of his political strategy. While he was taking the Peloponnesus, Stymphalus, one of the local kings, provided strong resistance. Pelops realized he could not win militarily; so, under the guise of friendship, he invited the rival king to dine with him as his guest. When Stymphalus arrived, Pelops attacked him, cut him up into pieces, and scattered the pieces over the countryside.

By Hippodamia, Pelops had three children, Pittheus, **Atreus**, and **Thyestes**. In addition, he also had a bastard son, Chrysippus, who was his favorite and about whom we will hear in the story of the house of Labdacus.[1]

Atreus and Thyestes were always brutal rivals. Atreus married Aerope; Thyestes then had an affair with her. This deception was to have important repercussions. The rivalry between the two brothers was even intensified when the Myceneans, having learned through an oracle that they should choose a Pelopid as their new king, invited Atreus and Thyestes to be considered for the role. A means was needed for deciding which brother would be king.

Some time before the brothers had received their call from the Myceneans, Atreus had made a vow that he would sacrifice to Artemis the finest of his flocks. When he found a lamb with a golden fleece, however, he reneged on this vow by killing and stuffing the creature and keeping it locked in a trunk. From his bragging about the prize, Thyestes knew about the lamb and persuaded Aerope to get it for him. Soon afterwards, when the Myceneans were trying to decide between the two brothers, Thyestes suggested that they resolve their decision from a divine sign; for instance, he suggested, if either he or his brother could produce a lamb with a golden fleece, surely that would be a sign. Atreus, not suspecting treachery, agreed heartily and was aghast when Thyestes produced the prize and was made king.

1. See page 155.

146

Zeus was angered by Thyestes' trickery and told Atreus to suggest to the Myceneans that they needed a more convincing sign and he said that he could make the sun reverse its journey across the sky. When he did perform this feat, aided by Zeus, the Myceneans were convinced, and they made him king in place of Thyestes. Once he had assumed his throne. Atreus banned Thyestes from the kingdom.

After he had ousted his brother, Atreus learned of Thyestes' earlier adulterous affair with his wife Aerope and plotted revenge. Under the pretense of friendship he invited Thyestes to return; he then prepared a banquet to celebrate their reconciliation. Having slaughtered Thyestes' three sons beforehand, Atreus cooked their torsos and served them to the father. After dinner, he revealed what he had done and showed Thyestes the hands and feet and heads of the boys, which he had carefully saved so that there could be no doubt about the identity of what had been eaten. Satisfied with his revenge, Atreus again expelled Thyestes from Mycenae. Again blood guilt was on a member of the family.

Thyestes went to Delphi to learn how he might avenge himself. He was told that revenge would be accomplished only by a son of a union of Thyestes with his own daughter. Determined that Atreus would be paid back for his crime, Thyestes disguised himself and went about meeting the terms of the oracle. He raped his daughter Pelopia; in the scuffle, however, he lost his sword. **Aegisthus** was the child born as a result of this rape. Several years later it was through the lost sword that Thyestes recognized his son, and Pelopia, realizing that she had committed incest, killed herself in shame. Some say that Pelopia had married Atreus, who did not know that she was the daughter of Thyestes and who had adopted Aegisthus. Whatever the details, revenge was accomplished when Aegisthus killed Atreus and restored Thyestes to the Mycenean throne.

Agamemnon and **Menelaus**, Atreus' sons, were still children when their father was killed. With the help of an old nurse they had escaped from Mycenae and had fled for their lives. After several years of exile, they returned to Mycenae seeking to avenge the murder of their father; with the help of King Tyndareus of Sparta, they expelled Thyestes. In addition, they each married one of Tyndareus' daughters.

The paternity and even the maternity of Tyndareus' children is one of the more complicated genealogical questions in Greek mythic history. All writers are agreed that Tyndareus and his wife **Leda** brought up the following four children: **Castor, Polydeuces**

(Pollux), **Clytemnestra**, and **Helen**. All agree that Zeus had something to do with the birth of the children; but agreement stops there. The most famous story is that Zeus, attracted by her beauty, fell in love with Leda and, turning himself into a swan, had his will with her in that form. As a result of that union, Leda laid an egg – or perhaps two eggs – out of which her children were hatched. One version says that Tyndareus slept with her the night after Zeus had her and that Helen and Polydeuces were Zeus' children, Castor and Clytemnestra were Tyndareus'. Still another version says that Zeus in the form of a swan caught Nemesis, that she laid an egg and somehow got Leda to hatch it for her. In all versions, at least Helen was the daughter of Zeus.

Agamemnon wanted to marry Clytemnestra; therefore, he first killed her husband and their newly born child; then he forced her to be his bride. Of their children, Orestes, Electra, and Iphigenia are important in ancient literature. Menelaus married Helen and peacefully succeeded Tyndareus to the Spartan throne. Agamemnon remained in Mycenae as king.

It was Helen's beauty that led to the Trojan War. As we have seen,[1] Aphrodite had promised Helen, the most beautiful woman in the world, to Paris, prince of Troy, for judging in her favor in the beauty contest with Hera and Athena. Menelaus, after Paris had absconded with his wife Helen, got the support of the various kings in Greece to help him retrieve her. Since Homer's *Iliad* gives a full account of the war, just those few details that directly affect the House of Atreus need be mentioned here.

Agamemnon, King of Mycenae, was the head of the Greek forces against Troy. When the assembled ships were ready to sail from Aulis to Troy, the winds died. Through oracles the Greeks learned that Artemis was angry, possibly because Agamemnon had once boasted that he was as good a hunter as she was, possibly because she was still indignant that the golden fleeced lamb promised to her by Atreus had never been properly sacrificed. Whatever the cause, the winds would not blow until Agamemnon sacrificed his daughter **Iphigenia** to the goddess. Agamemnon managed to trick the girl away from her mother to Aulis by saying that he had promised her to Achilles, the greatest of the heroes, as his wife. There are two versions of what happened once she arrived. In one, he simply killed her on the altar; in the other, as he was about to kill her, she was carried away by Artemis to be a priestess in the land of the Taurians. In both versions, Clytemnestra thought the girl was dead and was furious

1. See page 39.

148

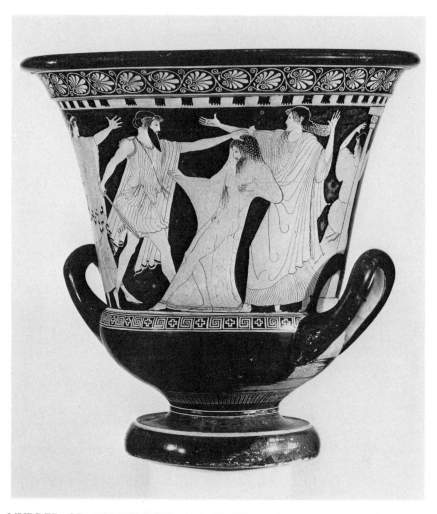

MURDER OF AGAMEMNON. Attic Red-Figured Vase by the Dokimasia Painter, 5th Century B.C. Agamemnon has just been stabbed by Aegisthus. As he stepped out of the bath, his wife, Clytemnestra, dressed him in a robe that had no openings for his head or arms. Clytemnestra stands behind Agamemnon, cheering on her lover, Aegisthus. *Courtesy, Museum of Fine Arts, Boston.*

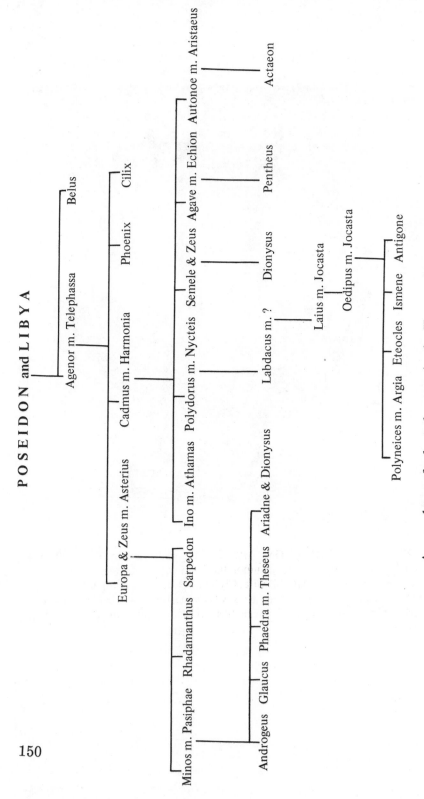

A genealogy of selected names in the House of Labdacus

with her husband; and in both versions the winds then blew and took the Greek forces to Troy.

While Agamemnon was away fighting, Clytemnestra took Aegisthus as her lover. Each had reasons to hate the king. He had killed Clytemnestra's first husband and her first child and then he had killed Iphigenia. As the son of Atreus he was obviously hateful to Aegisthus since Atreus had butchered Aegisthus' older brothers. Therefore, the two plotted to destroy Agamemnon on his return.

The final insult came when Clytemnestra learned that Agamemnon was bringing home a mistress, **Cassandra**. One of the daughters of Priam, King of Troy, Cassandra was a woman of remarkable beauty. Apollo had fallen in love with her and had given her many gifts trying to get her to give in to him. His final gift was the gift of prophecy, but when she still refused him, he gave up in anger. Unable to take back the gifts, he added a clause to the final gift: she would always know the truth but no one would believe her.

On the day of his return, Clytemnestra greeted Agamemnon with open arms, pretending to be a faithful wife overjoyed at the return of her master. Lovingly she prepared a bath for him so that he could luxuriously wash off the grit and grime of travel. As he stepped from his bath, she helped him into a new robe; but the robe had no arm or neck holes, and as Agamemnon struggled to free himself, Aegisthus slipped into the room and stabbed him. Triumphantly, Clytemnestra cut off his head with an axe and carried it through the palace. She also killed Cassandra.

Electra, a daughter of Agamemnon and Clytemnestra, realizing that Aegisthus might out of jealousy want to kill her young brother **Orestes**, took charge and smuggled him out of Mycenae to Crisa, at the foot of Mount Parnassus, where she found him a home with an old man, Strophius. Pylades, Strophius' son, was about the same age as Orestes, and the two of them became closest of friends. Several years later, when he had reached maturity, Orestes went to Delphi to consult the oracle to find out what he should do. Advised to avenge his father's death, he went, with Pylades, to Mycenae. There he was secretly reunited with his sister, Electra, and he murdered both Aegisthus and his mother, Clytemnestra.

The House of Labdacus

The House of Labdacus began with Agenor, son of Poseidon and Libya, and ended several generations later with the children of

Oedipus: Polyneices, Eteocles, Ismene, and Antigone. While savage and bloody acts appear in generation after generation of the House of Atreus, the House of Labdacus is characterized by unintentional crimes followed by divine punishment in generation after generation. Among the members of the House of Labdacus, there is no one to equal the viciousness of an Atreus, who served up his brother's children at a feast of "friendship."[1] Rather, the crimes of most of the members of the House of Labdacus result from ignorance, from blindness, or from misguided enthusiasm.

Agenor, the first mortal in the line of males that leads to Oedipus and his children, had a twin brother, **Belus.** Their father was Poseidon, and their mother was Libya, after whom the region of Libya was named. She, in turn, was the daughter of Memphis, the daughter of Nile, after whom the city of Memphis was named. Here we are clearly dealing with geographical myths; however, with the mortal twins, we begin a clear geneaology. Belus' line ultimately led to the heroes Perseus and Heracles, about whom much more will be said later;[2] we have already seen[3] Belus' children Aegyptus and Danaus and the catastrophic marriage of their children.

While Belus remained in North Africa, his birthplace, Agenor went to Phoenicia when he was still a young man, and he ultimately ruled there as king. By his wife, Telephassa, he had four children: Europa, Cadmus, Phoenix, and Cilix. Of the four, Europa and Cadmus and their descendants are particularly important in classical literature. Phoenix and Cilix seem to have been invented as ancestors of the Phoenicians and the Cilicians, and they have little additional mythology.

Cadmus was the father of the line that led to Oedipus and his children, but we should first take a brief detour and follow the offspring of Europa, for they too are important in ancient literature.

When **Europa** was a tender, young girl, living with her father in Phoenicia, Zeus fell in love with her. Visiting her daily in the form of a tame, white bull, he gradually gained her confidence and romped with her in flower-full fields. Europa became so fond of the bull and so comfortable with it that one day, when it knelt in front of her, she climbed on its back. This was what the bull had been waiting for; with the girl on his back, he ran to the sea and with his feet barely touching the water carried her across to Crete where he had his pleasure with her. The offspring of this union between Zeus and Europa were **Minos, Rhadamanthus,** and **Sarpedon.** On Crete, Europa married the prince Asterius, who helped bring up her children but with whom she had no more children.

1. See page 147. 2. See Chapter XVI. 3. See pages 80-81.

When the three sons of Europa reached maturity, they quarreled. Their quarrel was provoked by their love for the beautiful boy, Miletus, son of Apollo. When Minos saw that Miletus was more attracted to Sarpedon than he was to him, he managed to expel both of his brothers. Sarpedon became king of Lycia, where he lived for three generations. Rhadamanthus fled to Boeotia and on his death became one of the judges of the Underworld, as did Minos.

When Asterius died, Minos vied for the Cretan throne. When he met opposition, he claimed that the gods wanted him to be king. Needing a sign, he prayed to Poseidon; he promised the god that, if a perfect bull were to come from the sea for all the Cretans to see, he would sacrifice that bull to him. Poseidon did send the bull and Minos became king; but instead of the bull from the sea, he sacrificed another and kept the sacred bull as his own. As we will see later,[1] Poseidon was angry at Minos' double-cross, and as a result Minos' wife Pasiphae fell in love with the creature and gave birth to the Minotaur. Minos had eight offspring by Pasiphae, three of whom are important in ancient literature: **Phaedra**, wife of Theseus, **Ariadne**, Theseus' savior and wife of Dionysus, and **Androgeus**, whose death at the hands of the Athenians led to Minos' declaration of war on them. There were no significant offspring from any of these children, and the line of Europa ends here.

We return to the line that leads to Oedipus and his children. When Agenor learned that Europa had disappeared, he sent his sons to find her, telling them that they should not return until they had. His wife, Telephassa, went with Cadmus, and after much wandering and no success, the two of them settled in Thrace. Many years later, after his mother had died, Cadmus went to Delphi to find out what he should do — should he continue to seek Europa or should he seek a life of his own? The oracle told him not to worry about his sister but to follow a cow and found a city wherever the animal dropped from exhaustion. Following the oracle, he wandered on and ultimately came upon a cow, which he recognized to be the cow chosen for him. After gathering a band of men, he followed the animal across Boeotia, and when she fell down, he decided to sacrifice her to Athena. But when his followers went to a nearby spring to get the water necessary for the sacrifice, they found a vicious dragon protecting the spring. Remembering the words of the oracle, Cadmus was not deterred; he fought with the dragon and killed it. Athena came to his aid and advised him to throw the dragon's teeth over his shoulder, which he did. When the teeth hit the ground, armed men called the Spartoi sprung from the soil. These newly born creatures fought with

1. See page 199.

each other and in the fight all were killed, except for five, who were said to be the founders of the noble families of Thebes. But Cadmus was guilty of blood guilt for slaying the dragon, and he had to serve Ares to be purified.

After the period of purification, Athena gave him Thebes as his land and Zeus gave him Harmonia, the daughter of Aphrodite and Ares, as his wife. The marriage feast was one of the most famous in mythology. All the gods were present. As a wedding gift, Cadmus gave his wife a golden necklace, crafted by Hephaistus, which we will see again in the history of this family. The children of Cadmus and Harmonia were Autonoe, Ino, Semele, Agave, and Polydorus.

Each of Cadmus' daughters met an unfortunate end. **Autonoe** married Aristaeus, whose son, Actaeon, perished savagely, as we have already seen.[1] **Semele** was loved by Zeus but, though she was instrumental in the birth of Dionysus, she too met a miserable end.[2] **Agave** married one of the Spartoi, Echion, and their child was Pentheus, whose destruction by his mother and aunts has already been described.[3] Though the myths associated with **Ino** are vague, they all suggest that she went mad and probably was responsible for killing her own children and her husband, Athamas.[4]

Of Cadmus' children, only Polydorus remained. He is a vague character in ancient literature, and all that is known is that he was king of Thebes and married Nycteis, who bore him Labdacus. He is really just a connecting link in the ancient genealogy.

Cadmus, having given up the throne of Thebes, left, and according to one tradition he became king of the Illyrians; according to another he returned to Thebes, only to see the destruction of his grandson and heir, Pentheus. According to both traditions, both he and Harmonia were transformed into serpents. Euripides' *Bacchae* treats this final story.

Polydorus had a son **Labdacus**, who had a son **Laius**. Labdacus died when Laius was only one year old, and Lycus, a son of one of the Spartoi, ruled Thebes in the child's place for twenty years. Lycus' destruction came about because of a promise he had made to his brother, Nycteus. Zeus had fallen in love with Nycteus' daughter, **Antiope**, and had slept with her. When the pregnant girl came to her father and tried to explain that the child belonged to Zeus, the father threw her out of the house. She fled to Sicyon and married Epopeus, the ruler of Sicyon. In deep depression at the disgrace which his daughter had brought upon his house, Nycteus made Lycus promise that he would punish Antiope and Epopeus, and then he killed himself. Lycus honored his brother's final wish, marched on Sicyon,

154   1. See page 27. 2. See page 45. 3. See page 47. 4. See page 45.

killed Epopeus, and took Antiope as captive. Before the party returned home to Thebes, Antiope gave birth to twins, Zethus and Amphion, whom Lycus exposed on a Boeotian hillside. Once he had her home, Lycus imprisoned Antiope and treated her miserably; but his wife, Dirce, treated her even worse.

Found by a shepherd, Zethus and Amphion survived. While Zethus devoted himself to cattle breeding and athletics, Amphion, much to his brother's disgust, spent his time practicing on a lyre that Hermes had given him. After many years, Antiope magically escaped from Thebes and found the cottage where her sons were living. When they learned of the outrages their mother had suffered, they went to Thebes and killed Lycus outright. Because of the brutal treatment Dirce had given Antiope, however, Dirce met a much more horrible fate. Amphion and Zethus tied her to the horns of a wild bull and thus she was battered to death. The two brothers then assumed control of Thebes, expelling the now mature Laius because they felt that he had been an accomplice in their mother's pain, and they built the walls of Thebes.

Laius fled south and was received by King Pelops, with whom he lived for some time. As a nobleman, Laius was skilled in the use of the chariot, and he gave Chrysippus, Pelops' favorite son, many lessons in its use. While teaching the boy, however, he fell in love with him and carried him off, thus violating the sacred laws of hospitality and bringing a curse upon his house.

Meanwhile Amphion, who was now ruling Thebes, married Niobe, daughter of Tantalus, whose fate we have already seen.[1] On the death of Amphion, Laius returned to Thebes as Cadmus' rightful heir, where he married **Jocasta**. Laius had been warned by an oracle that he would be killed by his own son; therefore, when his wife bore a son, he had the infant exposed on a hillside after he had pierced his ankles with brooches.

The child was discovered exposed on Mount Cithaeron by shepherds of King Polybus of Corinth, who gave him to his wife, Merope. The child was adopted and brought up as their child and was called **Oedipus**, which the ancients interpreted to mean "swollen feet." The child matured to be an exceedingly strong and clever young man. Somehow he heard a persistent rumor that he was not the son of Polybus and Merope, and though he was heir to the Corinthian throne, he wanted to know the truth; therefore, he went to Delphi to consult the oracle. There he was advised to keep away from his native land because he was destined to kill his father and sleep with his mother. Horrified at the thought, he was determined

1. See page 93

not to return to Corinth, and he headed east on foot on the road toward Thebes. At a mountain crossroad he met a carriage coming the other way. There the coachman commanded that the pedestrian get out of the way, and the passenger insolently demanded that he move. Oedipus hit the coachman, and the passenger leaned out, striking Oedipus with his staff. Enraged, Oedipus killed the driver, the passenger, and those accompanying him. Needless to say, the passenger he had killed was his father, Laius.

When news of Laius' death reached Thebes, **Creon**, Jocasta's brother, became regent, but great calamities fell upon the city. The **Sphinx**, daughter of Typhon, a monster with the body of a lion, wings of a bird, and face of a woman, was sent by Hera to plague the city. She proposed a riddle to all who wanted to pass by her; if they failed, she ate them. Many Thebans had been eaten by this creature, and Creon had promised that whoever solved the riddle would have both Thebes and Laius' wife.

When Oedipus heard of Creon's promise, he decided to face the Sphinx. Her riddle was, "What goes on four feet in the morning, two feet at midday, and three in the evening?" Oedipus solved it: "Man," he said; "man crawls as a baby, walks upright as an adult, and needs the aid of a cane in old age." The furious Sphinx killed herself when the riddle was solved, and Oedipus went to Thebes to claim his prizes. By his wife and queen he had four children: **Polyneices, Eteocles, Ismene,** and **Antigone.**

Ultimately Oedipus discovered how fate had tricked him into marrying his mother and killing his father, and the events surrounding this discovery form the subject of Sophocles' play, *Oedipus Rex.* Jocasta killed herself on learning the truth, and Oedipus blinded himself and left Thebes. Sophocles' *Oedipus at Colonus* deals with his final years, when he was accepted by Theseus in Athens. There are several versions of what happened to Oedipus during the final years, and each of the major dramatists wrote plays about him, though only those of Sophocles survive.

After his abdication, Oedipus' sons, Polyneices and Eteocles, made an agreement to rule Thebes on alternate years. However, once Eteocles had assumed the throne, he would not give it up. The angry Polyneices went to Argos to convince King Adrastus to give him support in regaining his rightful inheritance. Though he managed to convince Adrastus, the seer Amphiaraus predicted that only Adrastus would return alive from the expedition, and the seer tried to discourage the venture. Polyneices, using the necklace that Cadmus had given Harmonia as a wedding gift, managed to bribe Amphiaraus' wife

156

SPHINX. Sculpture from the top of an archaic Greek gravestone, 6th Century B.C. Rarely do Greek artists emphasize the unseemly or the horrifying attributes of creatures or monsters. *Courtesy of the Metropolitan Museum of Art, New York, Hewitt Fund, 1911 and anonymous gift, 1951.*

Erphyle so that she might persuade her husband to support the cause; thus it was undertaken. Adrastus, with seven leaders under him, waged war on Thebes, the subject of Aeschylus' *Seven Against Thebes.* Ultimately Eteocles and Polyneices met in individual combat and killed each other, and Creon again became king of Thebes. The aftermath of the war of Argos on Thebes is the subject of Sophocles' play *Antigone.* Ten years later, the sons of the original seven who had been killed at Thebes waged war against Thebes. Known as the Epigoni, they were successful and destroyed the city.

Alcmaeon, son of Amphiaraus, learning how his mother had manipulated his father and hence had unwittingly brought about his

157

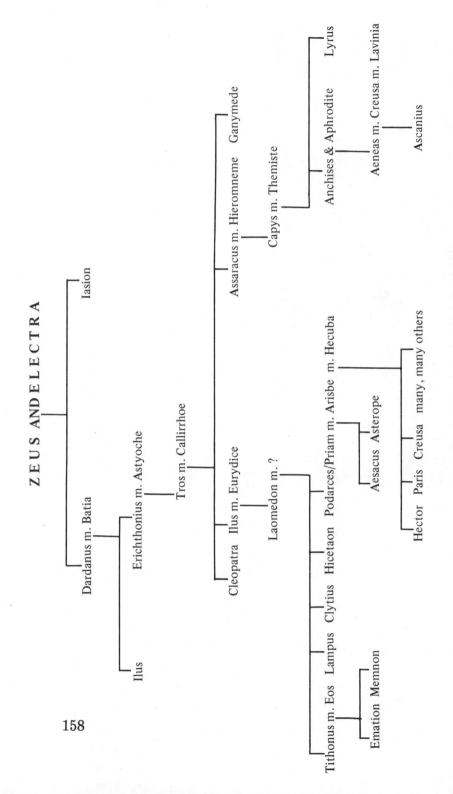

158

A genealogy of selected names in the important families of Troy

father's death in the battle, killed her and as a result went mad, pursued by the Furies.

With the death of Oedipus' children, the line that began with Agenor ended. Though crimes abound in this family, they are of a very different sort from those of the House of Atreus.

The Trojan House

The history of the Trojan ruling family is rather mild compared with that of either the House of Labdacus or the House of Atreus. Blood guilt is never on the hands of any member or any of the generations, and few crimes against the gods were committed. Beginning with Dardanus, son of Zeus and the Pleiad Electra, the line ended with the death of Priam and his sons and the destruction of Troy by the Greeks. If anything can be singled out as a problem-causing trait in the several generations, it would be the extreme beauty found in many individuals. The gods were often enamored of individuals in the line, and divine jealousy naturally followed.

Zeus violated the Pleiad Electra who, as a result, delivered two sons, **Dardanus** and **Iasion,** on the island of Samothrace in the northern Aegean. Demeter, in the one moment of feminine weakness she ever experienced, lay with Iasion after much drinking at a marriage feast. We have already seen how Zeus punished Iasion by destroying him with a thunderbolt.[1] Dardanus, in grief at the loss of his brother, left Samothrace and sailed to the mainland to the east of the island. There he was received by King Teucer, who gave him both land and the hand of his daughter, Batia. Dardanus built a city on his land, naming it after himself, and when Teucer died, he took over his lands as well, naming the area Dardania. By Batia he had two sons, Ilus and Erichthonius.

Ilus died childless, and when Dardanus died, **Erichthonius** inherited his kingdom. Tremendously wealthy and particularly successful at breeding horses, Erichthonius lived a long and full life. On his death, his son **Tros** succeeded to the kingdom and renamed it Troy, after himself. Tros had one daughter and three sons, Ilus, Assaracus, and Ganymede by his wife Callirrhoe.

Ganymede was the most beautiful youth who had ever lived. When Zeus saw the boy, he fell hopelessly in love with him and, either in his own shape or in the shape of an eagle, he took him up to Olympus to be his cup bearer, displacing Hebe who had, up to that point, filled that role. When Tros learned that his son had disap-

1. See page 18

peared, he grieved, not knowing what had actually happened. Zeus, feeling sorry for the father, sent Hermes with a gift of several glorious horses and a message that Ganymede would live forever on Olympus, deathless and always young. When Tros learned this, he was overjoyed, totally eager to welcome his son's success.

Tros' second son, Assaracus, lived a rather normal life. He married Hieromneme and had one son, Capys. Capys in turn married Themiste and had two sons, Anchises and Lyrus. Lyrus died childless, and Aphrodite's love for Anchises and the offspring of their union, Aeneas, have already been mentioned.[1]

Tros' oldest son, **Ilus**, left home and went to Phrygia, where he participated in the games set up by the Phrygian king. Winning the wrestling competition, Ilus was given a prize of fifty youths and fifty maidens. In addition, in accordance with an oracle, the king gave Ilus a dappled cow, told him to follow it and to found a city wherever the cow lay down. Ilus followed the instructions and founded the city of Ilium. There is obviously some confusion in the original myths, because Ilium and Troy are usually interchangeable names for the same place. After praying for an additional divine sign that he was doing the right thing, he found the Palladium, the story of which we have already seen.[2] By Eurydice — not the Eurydice loved by Orpheus — Ilus had one son, **Laomedon.**

After his father's death, Laomedon inherited the city of Ilium/Troy. He had five sons: Tithonus, Lampus, Clytius, Hicetaon, and Podarces. With the help of Apollo and Poseidon, he walled the city, a story mentioned earlier;[3] however, he reneged on his promise and refused to pay them. As a result the hero Heracles sacked Ilium, killed Laomedon and his sons Lampus, Clytius, and Hicetaon. He spared the life of Podarces, the youngest, but made him a slave until he was ransomed by his sister Hesione. Once ransomed, Podarces' name changed to **Priam**, which the Greeks saw as etymologically related to the word meaning "to buy or ransom." Heracles magnanimously made Priam ruler of Ilium.

Tithonus, Laomedon's oldest son, escaped destruction by Heracles because earlier he had been taken to Ethiopia by Eos, the goddess of dawn. Eos had fallen in love with Tithonus' beauty, had taken him away, and had asked Zeus to grant him immortality, a request which was granted. Better that Tithonus had fallen under Heracles' club! Eos forgot to ask that her lover also have eternal youth. In the early years of their love while his beauty remained, there was no problem and Eos bore Tithonus two sons, Emathion and Memnon. But when the first grey hairs showed on his head, Eos

160   1. See page 38. 2. See page 32. 3. See page 15.

EOS AND TITHONUS. Attic Red-Figured Vase by the Tithonus Painter, 5th Century B.C. Eos, the Dawn, is advancing upon Tithonus. He should have escaped! *Courtesy, Museum of Fine Arts, Boston.*

didn't want to sleep with him any more, though she did continue to be a dutiful wife, providing him with nectar and ambrosia. Then, when old age set in and his limbs became stiff and his mind feeble, Eos, forever young and beautiful, decided that she would have to lock him away someplace. Thus she put him in a room where he lived forever and babbled endlessly, forgotten by all. In fact, some writers say that he shriveled up into a grasshopper or cricket.

Priam married Arisbe, by whom he fathered Aesacus. Then, tiring of her, he gave her to a friend and married Hecuba. In total, he had fifty sons, nineteen of whom he fathered by Hecuba. **Hector** was his firstborn by her. When she was pregnant a second time, she had a dream that she had given birth to a flaming torch, the fire from

161

which spread across the whole city. When Priam consulted his son Aesacus, who was a seer, he learned that this meant that the child in Hecuba's womb would bring about the destruction of Ilium. Following the seer's advice, he had the child exposed as soon as it was born. The infant, however, survived and, after five days of exposure, was found by one of Priam's servants, Agelaus, who took the child and brought him up. As he grew, the child, called **Paris** or Alexander, astounded all with his strength and his beauty. Ultimately he discovered who his parents actually were and was received by them. We have already seen how Paris was chosen by Zeus to judge the beauty contest among Aphrodite, Hera, and Athena,[1] a judgment which led to the abduction of Helen and consequently to the Trojan War, thus fulfilling his mother's dream. Priam also had four daughters, Creusa, later to become the wife of **Aeneas**, Laodice, Polyxena, and Cassandra. The fate of Priam and his family is the subject of Homer's *Iliad* and Vergil's *Aeneid* and continues in the early parts of the *Odyssey*.

1. See page 39.

CHAPTER XVI

MYTHS OF THE HEROES

Perseus

In the discussion of the House of Labdacus, we traced the ancestors of Oedipus and his children back to Agenor, the son of Poseidon and Libya, and we mentioned that Agenor had a twin brother, Belus. When Agenor went to Phoenicia, Belus remained in North Africa and had two sons, Danaus and Aegyptus, who produced a total of one hundred offspring — Danaus had fifty daughters and Aegyptus had fifty sons. The brothers quarreled about who was to rule their father's kingdom and Danaus, the weaker of the two, retreated to Argos. Some time later, the sons of Aegyptus followed Danaus and his daughters and asked to marry the fifty girls so that the two houses might be joined. The frightened Danaus yielded to their request but gave each of his daughters a dagger, ordering them to kill their respective husbands on their wedding night. We have already seen the success of this plan and its consequences.[1] However, one of the fifty girls, Hypermnestra, had fallen in love with her husband, Lynceus, and spared his life.

Lynceus ruled Argos on Danaus' death and had a son Abas, who inherited the throne from him. Abas, in turn, had two sons, the twins Acrisius and Proetus. Just as their great grandfather had quarreled with his brother, these twins were also destined to be rivals. In fact, before they were born, they quarreled in their mother's womb. When Abas died, they waged war against each other for the throne of Argos. When Acrisius won, Proetus went to Lycia, where he was taken in by King Iobates. After having married the king's daughter, Stheneboea, who later became famous for her inappropriate passion for Bellerophon,[2] Proetus returned to Argos with Lycian forces to challenge his brother again for the throne of Argos.

This time the war was a draw and the brothers negotiated an agreement: they would divide the territory. Acrisius would continue to rule Argos while Proetus would rule the neighboring Tiryns. Using the skill and the labor of seven Cyclops he had brought with him from Lycia, Proetus then built the fortifications of Tiryns, which can still be seen today.

1. See pages 80-81. 2. See page 95.

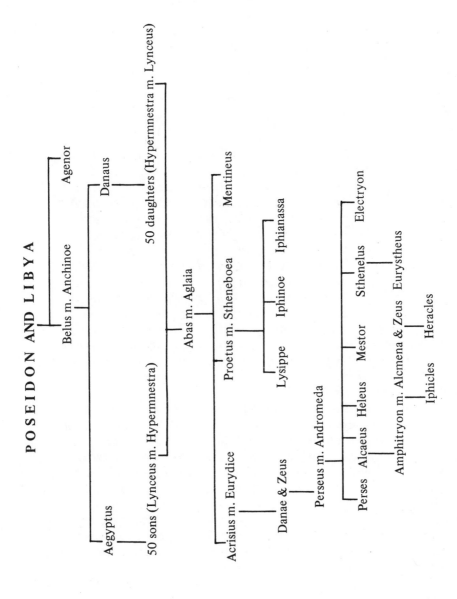

A genealogy of selected names among the relatives of Perseus and Heracles

POSEIDON AND LIBYA

Belus m. Anchinoe — Agenor

Aegyptus — Danaus

50 sons (Lynceus m. Hypermnestra) — 50 daughters (Hypermnestra m. Lynceus)

Abas m. Aglaia

Acrisius m. Eurydice — Proetus m. Stheneboea — Mentineus

Danae & Zeus — Lysippe — Iphinoe — Iphianassa

Perseus m. Andromeda

Perses — Alcaeus — Heleus — Mestor — Sthenelus — Electryon

Amphitryon m. Alcmena & Zeus — Eurystheus

Iphicles — Heracles

Acrisius, King of Argos, had several children, but they were all girls. With no male heir, Acrisius had no one to inherit his kingdom, and all his battles with his brother seemed to be in vain. In despair, he consulted an oracle to find out whether or not he would have a male heir — or perhaps to find out how he might have one — but the oracle gave him information he wasn't expecting. He was told that he would not have a son but that his daughter would give birth to a son who would kill him. Having only one daughter still alive, **Danae**, he decided on a scheme by which he could trick his fate. Thus, he had a bronze chamber constructed underground, and he imprisoned Danae there so that there would be no chance of her conceiving a son. Little did he know, however, that Zeus had fallen in love with the girl and was determined to have her. While Danae sat in her prison, Zeus penetrated the chamber through its ceiling as a stream of gold, which she caught in her lap. In such a way was Perseus conceived.

After some time, when Acrisius discovered that Danae had had a child in spite of his precautions — and a male child at that — he was furious. When Danae tried to explain how it had happened, he wouldn't believe her. However, not wanting to kill the child with his own hands and thereby incur blood guilt, he put the infant with Danae into a chest and cast it into the sea. The chest was carried by the waves to the island of Seriphos, where it was discovered by the fisherman Dictys. There Perseus was reared as the son of the fisherman, but when King **Polydectes**, Dictys' brother, saw Danae, he wanted her.

By this time Perseus had reached manhood and was an impressive young man. Polydectes was intimidated by him and had to find some ploy to get him out of the way. Therefore, he conceived a ruse: he pretended that he was going to seek the hand of Hippodamia, daughter of Oenomaus, whom we have already met in the story of Pelops.[1] He held a feast at which each of his countrymen was to bring him a gift that he might use in winning Hippodamia's hand. Everyone who came to the banquet brought a horse as a gift, except Perseus, who, being the stepson of a fisherman, could not afford one. Not to be outdone, however, he boasted that he would get anything the king demanded of him; taking his cue from this boast, Polydectes suggested that he would like to have the Medusa's head, and Perseus agreed.

Medusa was one of the Gorgons, three dreadful daughters of Phorcys and Ceto. Of the three, Medusa was the only mortal one.

1. See page 145.

DANAE WITH PERSEUS IN THE CHEST. Attic Red-Figured vase by the Danae Painter, 5th Century B.C. Acrisius, Eurydice and a friend look on as the lid is about to close on Danae and Perseus. *Courtesy, Museum of Fine Arts, Boston.*

Once beautiful, her hair had been turned into serpents and she was so ugly that a mortal, looking on her, was instantly turned to stone. She lived with her sisters, Stheno and Euryale, on the other side of Oceanus on the edge of the realm of Night.

When Perseus accepted the task, Athena and Hermes came to his aid and explained how he could accomplish it. First he went to the Graeae, also daughters of Phorcys, to find directions to the

166

nymphs who could provide tools necessary for his task. The Graeae were three women, old from birth, who shared one eye and one tooth. Perseus crept up on them, grabbed their one eye, and demanded the information he needed before he would give it back to them. They obliged him, and from the nymphs he got winged sandals that allowed him to fly, the cap of Hades that made him invisible, and a wallet in which to put the Medusa's head. From Hermes he received a sickle-like sword made of adamantine. Then with these aids Perseus swooped down on the Gorgons and decapitated Medusa. Looking at the Medusa's reflection in his shield, he avoided being turned to stone, and some say that Athena guided his hand. From the trunk of Medusa emerged the winged horse Pegasus and the giant Chrysaor, whom she had conceived by Poseidon. Her sisters tried to pursue Perseus but failed because of the cap that made him invisible.

On his way back from the nether regions of the world, Perseus passed over Ethiopia. Drops of blood from Medusa's severed head fell on the sands of the desert, and vipers sprung from them. As he flew over the coast, he looked down at one point and saw a beautiful girl chained to a rock. Dropping closer, he saw an ugly sea monster churning up the sea near her. Instantly in love with the girl, he decided he had to have her, and realizing from her beauty that she must be the daughter of the king, he devised a scheme. Perseus went to King Cepheus, father of the girl **Andromeda** chained to the rock, and offered to save her if the king would promise that he would give her to him as his wife. The king agreed at once, and Perseus went to save the girl.

Andromeda was the daughter of Cepheus and Cassiopia. Some time earlier, Cassiopia had indiscreetly bragged that she was more beautiful than the Nereids. The nymphs had complained to Poseidon, who had little tolerance for such hybris, and he had sent a great flood and a sea monster to plague the Ethiopians as punishment. When Cepheus had consulted the oracle of Ammon to find out how he might rid his land of these plagues, he had learned that he would have to sacrifice his daughter to the monster. Compelled by his people, he had chained Andromeda to the rock as Perseus found her.

After a brief battle Perseus destroyed the monster. Some say he killed it with his curved sword, others say he turned it to stone by showing it the Medusa's head. Whatever his method, he had Andromeda as his own. But he faced one further problem. Cepheus had pledged Andromeda to his brother Phineus, and when Phineus learned that she had been saved, he demanded that she be given to him. When confronted by Phineus and his many friends, Perseus used

167

the Medusa's head to turn them to stone. Then, with his new wife, he returned to Seriphos.

While Perseus was away, Polydectes had actively resumed his suit of Danae. He had never been seriously interested in Hippodamia but had merely pretended interest in her in order to rid himself of Perseus. Though Danae continued to resist him, his demands had become so intense that she fled for refuge in a temple. He decided to starve her out. Though he could not take her from the altar, he could see to it that she got no food. Ultimately, he reckoned, she would have to give in. When Perseus returned and discovered the situation, he was furious and he went to Polydectes' palace. He burst into a celebration, exposed the Medusa's head, and turned the king and his friends to stone. Later Athena took this head and made it an emblem on her own shield.

After making Dictys king of Seriphos, Perseus left the island with Andromeda and Danae. He had learned who his grandfather was and wanted to make peace with him. Since he had learned of the prophecy that he would kill Acrisius, he wanted to assure the old man that he had nothing to worry about. But when the trio arrived in Argos, they learned that the king had left for Larissa in Thessaly. Acrisius had heard that his grandson was returning and did not want to take any chances. Perseus, however, followed Acrisius to Larissa, determined to be reconciled with him. They ultimately met and in celebration of their meeting, the Larissans held a series of games. Perseus, an athlete at heart, couldn't resist and joined in the competition. When he threw the discus, however, it went off course and struck Acrisius on the foot, killing him. Perseus was humiliated at what he had done. He gave his grandfather a proper burial but felt that he could not rule Argos. Thus he arranged with Megapenthes, the ruler of Tiryns, to trade kingdoms. Megapenthes would rule Argos and Perseus would rule Tiryns.

As ruler of Tiryns, Perseus expanded his domain and founded Mycenae. By Andromeda he had five sons, one of whom, Alcaeus, was to be a forefather of Heracles. Another son, Perses, whom Andromeda had borne before they left Seriphos, was to be the founder of the Persian race.

a. While Perseus is certainly a local hero, associated with the Argive people, his popularity spread far beyond the confines of the Peloponnesus. In the above account of Perseus' activity, specifically local traditions, such as the murder of Dionysus,[1] have not been included. Students of mythology should realize that since there was no canon, myths varied radically from region to region, and the stories were often created to bolster a particular hero's repute.

168   1. See page 49, note (f).

b. A minor variant on the conception of Perseus says that Proetus slept with Danae before she was put in her bronze chamber.

c. Some versions of the Andromeda story say that she was chained to a rock off Palestine and that she was from Joppa. The Ammon that Cepheus consulted was an Egyptian god, equated by the Greeks with Zeus.

d. According to some versions, when Perseus was returning to Seriphos he argued with Atlas and ultimately showed him the head of Medusa, turning him into stone — thus the origin of the Atlas mountains.

e. Ovid tells in Book V of the *Metamorphoses* of a gruesome battle that Perseus was involved in against Phineus in order to assure himself of Andromeda's hand. One wonders why he would have gone through that agony and loss of friends if all he had to do to win was to show the Medusa's head.

Heracles (Hercules)

From the marriage of Perseus and Andromeda came six sons; one of them, Perses, went to Persia; the other five — Alcaeus, Sthenelus, Heleus, Mestor, and Electryon — remained in Mycenae. Alcaeus had a son named **Amphitryon,** who married a woman named **Alcmena.** Now, Zeus developed a passion for Alcmena and one evening, pretending that he was her husband, slept with her. Amphitryon and Alcmena eventually learned of the deception from the prophet Tiresias; consequently, when Alcmena found herself pregnant, neither she nor her husband knew who the actual father was.

Meanwhile, Hera had learned of Zeus' deception and she vowed vengeance against both Alcmena and her child. When she heard that the next descendant of Perseus was going to be the ruler of Mycenae, she ordered Eileithyia, the goddess of childbirth, to delay the birth of Alcmena's child, and she brought it about that Sthenelus' wife would deliver hers immediately. Thus, Sthenelus' child, **Eurystheus,** was born prematurely; nonetheless, he was the prophesied descendant of Perseus and hence he would be the inheritor of Mycenae, thereby depriving Alcmena's child of that honor. Meanwhile, Alcmena was shrieking in agony during the seven days and seven nights of her labor pains; Eileithyia, however, was unmoved, constantly imprecating charms to hold back the child. Finally, Galanthis, one of Alcmena's servants, being unable to stand the cries of pain, tricked Eileithyia. She went to the goddess and told her that Alcmena had already given birth; the goddess, caught off guard, relaxed her spell for just a moment, and Alcmena's child was born.

169

Whether that child was fathered by Zeus or by Amphitryon is unknown, although it is said that she actually bore two sons, **Heracles** by Zeus, and the next night **Iphicles** by Amphitryon.

Hera had been thwarted, but her hatred and resentment for both Alcmena and her children only grew. When Heracles was eight months old, for instance, she sent two snakes to destroy the baby as it lay asleep. Just as the snakes were about to engulf the baby in their monstrous jaws, he awoke, seized them and strangled them; Iphicles, on the other hand, bawled and fled. Alcmena summoned the prophet Tiresias for advice, for she was totally upset and perplexed by this very bizarre affair. He assured her that all would be well, that she would be highly honored because of her son, and that he was destined to be a hero among men and eventually to live with Zeus upon Olympus. From that point on, there was little doubt that the boy had not been fathered by a mortal.

Heracles received a thorough training. He learned archery and marksmanship, music, the moves of wrestling, the art of boxing, horsemanship, accuracy with the spear, and fencing. His teachers were professionals, world renowned in their respective skills. One of the most prominent was Linus, brother of the famous Orpheus, who taught him music. Heracles was less interested in music than he was in some of his other studies, and once, when he had had an especially poor lesson, Linus scolded and struck the boy. At this, Heracles flew into a rage and smashed his lyre over Linus' head, killing him.

Heracles' family had changed residence from Mycenae to Thebes in Boeotia. When he was eighteen years old, he visited his neighbor, King Thespius, and the two of them went on an expedition to kill a lion from Mount Cithaeron that was menacing the area. The king, being impressed by the valor and stamina of the young man, wanted his descendants to have some of the hero's blood. Therefore, each night, he sent one of his daughters to Heracles' bed chamber. Heracles thought that he was sleeping with the same daughter each night; but, in fact, he had fathered offspring by fifty different women.

On the way from Thespius, he came upon some ambassadors of King Erginus of Orchomenos, the capitol of the Minyans, who were on their way to Thebes. The Thebans, according to an unfair treaty, were required to pay an annual tribute to Erginus. Therefore, when the ambassadors learned that Heracles was a Theban, they demanded their tribute. Heracles cut off their ears and noses and hands; he tied these severed parts together and fastened them to the ambassadors' necks, saying that they could take that as their tribute for the year.

170

HERACLES. Graeco-Roman marble statue. The mature Heracles stands with the two symbols of his strength: his club and his lion skin. *Courtesy, Museum of Fine Arts, Boston.*

Erginus declared war. Heracles, having been armed by Athena, killed Erginus, routed the Minyans, and demanded double the tribute from them. In the fight Amphitryon was killed. Creon, King of Thebes, rewarded Heracles with his daughter **Megara** and he gave his younger daughter to Iphicles. Alcmena later remarried a son of Zeus named Rhadamanthus, who had left Crete.

171

Not much later Heracles again suffered one of his spasms of violence. In his madness he threw his own two sons, whom he had had by Megara, and Iphicles' two sons into a fire. The madness had been sent by Hera, who had not by any means put aside her hatred for the descendants of Alcmena. When Heracles came to his senses, he realized that he had blood guilt on his hands and therefore would need purification. He went, therefore, to the Oracle at Delphi to seek advice. He was told that he should enthrall himself to Eurystheus, his relative, serve him for twelve years, and complete ten tasks that Eurystheus would require; when these tasks were completed, he would be purged.

The first labor was that he kill the lion of Nemea and bring its skin back to Eurystheus. Eurystheus, now king of Mycenae, was weak and cowardly and, fearing Heracles' might, hoped that the lion would kill him. Nemea was an area in Argolis that was being ravaged by a monstrous lion. The lion was just like a roaring river in the way that it would consume anything it came upon. Nonetheless, the undaunted Heracles took his bow and quiverful of arrows and his club and set out. The club was one that he had found on Mount Helicon, and, bark, roots and all, had designed for himself. Heracles was all alone in the area: no one of the local inhabitants dared to leave the security of the home. The bones and carrion of the lion's victims were strewn everywhere. When Heracles saw the lion, it was on its way to its den, licking its mouth to wash off the gore from the day's ravages. Heracles shot his arrow, but it just bounced off. Another arrow hit the lion just where the lung is located; but again the arrow had no effect. He then clubbed the beast, but the weapon broke. No weapons could hurt this creature. Heracles finally trapped it in a cave, got a stranglehold on it and managed to kill it. But then he was faced with the problem of how to flay the lion. Inspired by the gods, he took the lion's own claws and used them to tear the skin from the carcass.

When Eurystheus saw him coming clothed in the lion's skin and jaws, he flew into a panic. Terrified, he ordered his servants to build for him a large jug, and from that point on, he would hide in the jug whenever Heracles approached. He even went so far as to have the jug put in the ground. Meanwhile, Heracles made himself completely at home in Eurystheus' palace. Finally, terrified of Heracles, but still indignant, Eurystheus, through his servants, sent Heracles off on another mission.

A serpent was menacing the land of Lerna, a water snake called the Hydra with nine heads. Heracles and his nephew Iolaos —

HERACLES, IPHICLES, AND THE SNAKE. Attic Red-Figured vase attributed to the Nausikaa Painter, 5th Century B.C. Horrified mortals see the
snakes in the babies' bed. Iphicles, to the right, screams for the protection of
his mother, while Heracles takes charge of the situation and strangles the
snakes. Athena stands in the background, calmly watching the scene. *Courtesy, Metropolitan Museum of Art, Fletcher Fund, 1925.*

for the two of them had become close friends — approached the
swamp where the snake had its lair, but approach was difficult. Heracles had to drive the beast out of the swamp in order to tackle it; this
he did by shooting flaming arrows at it. When the raging beast attacked Heracles, it wound itself around the hero; as often as he
would smash one of its heads with his club, two more grew; and, to
compound the difficulty, a huge crab assisted the snake and kept on
biting Heracles' foot. Heracles killed the crab and ordered Iolaos to
take a burning stake and to singe the roots of the Hydra's neck in order to prevent new ones from growing. Now, the middle head of the
nine was immortal and Heracles realized that this was the most important of the heads. He then chopped off that head, putting it under a rock so that it could do no more damage. Then he dipped his
arrows in the poisonous blood of the creature; from that point on,
nothing could survive those arrows.

   When Eurystheus heard that Iolaos had helped Heracles, he
refused to accept this labor as part of the ten, and he sent Heracles
off on another exploit.

There was a savage boar in the land of Erymanthia in Arcadia. Capturing this beast could have been very risky, for one wrong move could have seen Heracles impaled on the boar's mammoth tusks; but the task actually proved quite easy for Heracles. He pursued it until it was exhausted, cornered it in a snow bank, and overcame it. When he brought it back to Eurystheus, the king again fled to his jar and hid.

While Heracles was on this mission, he had been entertained by the Centaur Pholus. Once, while they were supping, the scent of their wine allured other Centaurs, who immediately started a fight with Heracles. He routed them and they took refuge with Chiron, the best and wisest of the Centaurs. But in the process, Heracles accidentally wounded Chiron with one of his arrows. Now, Chiron was immortal; at the same time, a wound from Heracles' arrows was incurable. Therefore, rather than spend his days in perpetual agony, Chiron exchanged his immortality with Prometheus and thus died.

Heracles' fourth labor was of a different nature, requiring more finesse than ferocity. Eurystheus ordered him to fetch a marvelous stag with golden horns. Since it was sacred to Artemis, Heracles dared not kill it. Therefore, he pursued it all over the world for a whole year, going as far north as the Hyperboreans. Artemis challenged him when he finally caught it, but, explaining that he was merely following the injunction of Eurystheus, he mollified the goddess.

The next task was to rid the city of Stymphalus in Arcadia of a brood of man-eating birds that had feathers and claws and beaks of metal, and were the size of cranes. When Heracles saw how many of them there were, he realized that his arrows would be useless; fortunately, however, he was inspired by Athena; she gave him a pair of cymbals which created such cacophony when Heracles smashed them together that the birds flew off in terror.

King Augeas of Elis had an enormous flock of cattle that lived in a stable which had not been cleaned for years. The smell was overwhelming and the manure seemed to be piled to the roof itself. Heracles' sixth venture was to clean this stable but he had to do it unassisted and in one day. When Heracles interviewed Augeas, he promised to clean the stables if the king would give him a portion of the cattle. Augeas agreed. Heracles then rechanneled the course of two rivers to flow through the stable; the waters rapidly washed the stables clean of the filth. The mission was accomplished, but Eurystheus, hearing that Heracles had done this for profit even though Augeas had reneged on his promise, refused to admit this task as one of the ten.

HERACLES BRINGS THE ERYMANTHIAN BOAR TO EURYSTHEUS.
Attic Black-Figured vase, 6th Century B.C. Athena looks on as Heracles holds
the boar above Eurystheus, who is cowering in the great jar he has had prepared to protect him from Heracles. The scene is a very popular one in Greek
art. *Courtesy, the Metropolitan Museum of Art, Rogers Fund, 1941.*

The seventh labor took Heracles away from the area of the Peloponnesus into Crete, where he had to capture a wild and mad bull. The task was easy: he grabbed it by the horns and subdued it; in fact, he tamed it so well that he rode it to the beach where his ship had been anchored. The next two labors, however, proved more demanding. He had to enter the uncivilized area of Thrace and capture the man-eating mares of King Diomedes, son of Ares, and then to go even further north to the no-man's-land where the Amazons lived and steal a girdle from Hippolyte, the queen of that savage tribe of women. First, he and his companion Abderos entered Diomedes' stables; while Heracles wrestled with some of the mares, several of the Thracians, hearing the commotion, attacked. Heracles left Abderos to hold the horses while he himself resisted and routed the assailants. When he returned to the stables, the horses had trampled Abderos. Heracles shot some of them with his venomous arrows and then established the city of Abderos in memory of his friend. It is even said that he fed Diomedes to the horses in order to tame them. Eurystheus gave the horses to Hera, and they ran wild in the North Country. It is said that their offspring continued to the time of Alexander the Great of Macedon.

The Amazons were a wild brood of women who had no use for men except as breeders, who trained themselves as warriors, who cut off the left breast of their female young so that they would be able to use their bows more easily, and who destroyed all their male young except those who were needed to continue the species. They lived in Colchis on the eastern shores of the Black Sea, not far from the borders of the Ocean itself. Hippolyte, the Queen of the Amazons, had a belt that Eurystheus' daughter wanted; therefore, Heracles was ordered to fetch it. When he entered the land with his group of companions, he saw Amazons everywhere; they were all prepared to fire their arrows at him; therefore, he knew that an assault would be useless. Apparently Hippolyte was not eager for a pitched battle either, for she requested a private interview with the hero. A deal was made and she forfeited the belt. But Hera, still bearing her hatred for the sons of Alcmena, had entered the scene and told the Amazons that Heracles was abducting their queen. They attacked; he counterattacked; the leader of the Amazon band was killed in the skirmish; and Heracles left with the belt and gave the Amazon Antiope as a gift to his companion Theseus.

On the way back from Colchis, he happened upon Troy. This city was fortified by a network of fabulous walls built by Poseidon and Apollo. They had taken the shape of men and had offered to

Laomedon, King of Troy, to fortify the city for suitable remuneration. When they finished their labors and Laomedon refused to pay their wages, Apollo sent a plague and Poseidon sent a sea-monster to ravage the land. Laomedon consulted oracles to see what he should do, and they informed him that he could clear himself and remove these pestilences if he would give his daughter Hesione to the sea monster. He tied her to a rock near the sea just about the time when Heracles came by. He saw the poor girl and offered to rescue her if Laomedon would give him the horses that Zeus had given Tros when he took Tros' son Ganymede to Olympus,[1] for these horses were still at Troy. Laomedon promised, Heracles killed the sea monster, rescued the girl, and claimed his reward. Needless to say, Laomedon devised another deception and cheated Heracles. But that was not the end of it. Years later Heracles returned. He vanquished Laomedon and most of his family and turned the city over to the young Priam.[2]

Since Eurystheus had refused to admit two of Heracles' previous labors, there were still three more left before the instructions of the oracle could be fulfilled, and these final three took Heracles all over the world, to the island Erytheia in Oceanus itself, where Geryon, a three-bodied monster lived with his two-headed dog, Orthos. Geryon was the mightiest of all mortals; he, his dog, and a herdsman named Eurytion guarded a flock of cattle belonging to Hades, and it was Heracles' job to bring that flock back to Greece. At first the dog attacked; it was clubbed; Eurytion then attacked; he also was clubbed; finally Geryon himself came forth; he was shot with one of the poisoned arrows and perished.

On the way to Geryon's island, Heracles had gone through the deserts of Libya. On one occasion, being overwhelmed by the heat of the Sun, he aimed his arrow at Helios himself and threatened the god. The Sun, so impressed with Heracles' audacity, lent him the use of the golden goblet that he used each night to cross from the West to the East. This goblet now came in very handy when Heracles had to find a way to get Geryon's cattle off Erytheia. So, Heracles now left the Ocean; as he sailed in Helios' goblet, he looked down at the massive Pillars at Gibraltar that he had designed on his way to Erytheia, and he was pleased.

The mission accomplished and the goblet returned to Helios, having now spent just a little over eight years accomplishing these ten tasks, he now had to return to the western extremities of the world, for he had to steal the golden apples, the wedding present of Gaia to Hera and Zeus. These were situated in Hesperia, and were guarded by a savage dragon, Ladon, who had a hundred heads and was immortal

1. See page 160. 2. See page 160.   **177**

and whom the daughters of Hesperus guarded. Not knowing where the gardens of Hesperus were located, he consulted Nereus, an old man of the sea, who, like Proteus, could change himself into whatever shape he wanted and would do so to avoid giving information to mortals. Advised by Themis, Heracles pounced on Nereus as he slept, remaining unintimidated as Nereus tried all the tricks at his disposal, and secured his information. The journey was a long one. On the way he passed through Libya, where he encountered the giant Antaeus and subdued him.[1] In Egypt he slew Busiris, who had been butchering strangers. Then he traveled north to the Caucasus and killed the vulture that was torturing Prometheus[2] and unbound the Titan. Prometheus repaid this kindness by advising him not to go personally after the golden apples but rather to send Atlas, who was holding the world on his shoulders in the land of the Hyperboreans. Atlas agreed provided that Heracles would hold up the globe in his absence. Heracles complied, but when Atlas returned, he was unwilling to reassume such a burdensome weight and intimated that Heracles would now be stuck with this chore. Heracles, knowing that Atlas was not very bright, agreed, but he asked that Atlas take the world for just one second while he put a cushion on his shoulders. Atlas fell for the ruse, took the earth, and Heracles scampered away with the apples. Eurystheus, when the apples were handed to him, gave them back to Heracles; he gave them to Athena, and she, in turn, returned them to the daughters of Hesperus, for it would have been improper for these wedding presents to have fallen into unworthy hands.

Finally the twelfth task, the most demanding of the series: to bring the dog Cerberus up from the Underworld. First he went to Taenarum at the southern tip of Laconia, where there was a deep cavern which led to Tartarus. He saw the shades of many dead, most of whom instantly fled; he saw Medusa, the Gorgon, tried to slash her with his sword, but she merely evaporated through his blade; he saw Theseus stuck on a slab of stone together with his friend Pirithous; they had tried to steal Persephone as a bride for Pirithous; Hades had caught them and attached them permanently to the seat. Heracles managed to detach and rescue Theseus but was unable to free Pirithous. Then he saw Ascalaphus, the one who had divulged the fact that Persephone had eaten pomegranate seeds while she was in Hades' charge: Ascalaphus was punished by being crushed under a heavy rock; Heracles rolled away the stone and freed him, and Demeter turned the wretch into an owl. He killed one of Hades' cattle desiring to give the food of blood to some of the ghosts; when accosted

178   1. See page 103. 2. See page 57.

by Menoetes, who had charge of the cattle, he wrestled and broke the herdsman's ribs; he would have crushed him to death had not Persephone interceded. He then interviewed Hades himself, who gave his consent for Cerberus to be borrowed provided that Heracles use no weapons. Consequently, Heracles girded himself for the encounter; he dressed himself in his lion's skin, embraced the beast's heads with his mighty hands, and, even though the dragon-part of his tail bit him, did not loosen his hold one bit.

Eurystheus meanwhile was sitting smugly in his palace thinking that he had finally managed to get rid of Heracles, for surely no one could ever survive the Underworld, to say nothing about subduing Cerberus. But when he heard the thundering roar of the watchdog of Hades and when he saw its three snake-filled heads, its dragon-like tail, its back crawling with serpents and the venom drooling from its mouths, he was terrified. He ran for his jar, taking cover as usual, and from that point on Heracles was absolved of his guilt and from his vassalage to the cowering king. Eurystheus lived quite a while longer; his death, however, was as inglorious and unattractive as his life: after Heracles' death, Eurystheus went after some of his sons; there was a fight; Eurystheus sped off in his chariot and, in his attempt to flee, was killed; his head was cut off and given to Alcmena, who gouged out its eyes with a pin.

Heracles, having returned Cerberus, was indeed now a free man in his mid-thirties. But his adventures had by no means ended, and for the rest of his life he would be involved in one exploit after another.

In his wanderings throughout the world, he is said to have rid many areas of Europe of their cruel men and wild beasts; he cleaned up some parts of the desert in Africa and made some areas arable and productive; he founded the Olympic Games in honor of Zeus; he brought trees from the land of the Hyperboreans so that there might be the comfort of shade at Olympia, where the games were held. Appreciative of the hospitality shown him by King Admetus, he wrestled with Hades himself in order to bring Admetus' wife Alcestis back to the land of the living.[1] He fought with the Olympians in their battle against the Giants and was of invaluable assistance.[2]

In Italy, as he was driving Geryon's cattle back to Greece, he came across Cacus, a son of Hephaistus. Cacus lived in a cave; all around this cave were the bones of people that Cacus had slain; along the entrance to the cave hung human heads and arms, other trophies

1. See pages 87-88. 2. See page 50.

to Cacus' savagery. Cacus himself was enormous and hideous; from each mouth on his three heads came flames. Heracles with his club bashed him to death. He then took a group of men into Gaul and purged many areas of their habit of wantonly killing strangers; he forged a pass through the Alps from Gaul into Italy. In fact, throughout his wanderings, he constantly warred against barbarity, lawlessness, and incivility; furthermore, he frequently founded cities, created lakes, established festivals to the gods, and always rid lands of savagery, whether in man or beast, wherever he found it.

A bizarre incident occurred as he was dispatching Diomedes' horses back to Eurystheus. At one point the horses disappeared; while Heracles was looking for them, a strange creature came up to him, half woman and half snake; she said that she would effect the return of the horses if Heracles would sleep with her. He did so, and she bore him a son named Scythes, who began the race of the great kings of Scythia.

At one point in his travels he came upon Cycnus, a son of Ares. They got into a fight and even Ares entered the fray; hence, Heracles fought with the god himself. Zeus had to intervene by throwing a thunderbolt in their midst in order to break them apart. Then there was a villain named Termerus, a giant who would run against all strangers and crush them with his rock-like head. He tried this on Heracles, ran against him like a cannonball, but when the two heads met in collision, Termerus' smashed apart. A far less dramatic incident occurred when Heracles was trying to get rid of the two Cercopes who were pestering him. He tied their tails to a pole, but as he was carrying them off, they saw his black and hairy posterior and started laughing so hard that Heracles himself began to laugh and released them.

He participated in the expedition against the Calydonian boar; he joined Jason in his expedition for the Golden Fleece. He even helped to repair the walls of Troy that Apollo and Poseidon had previously constructed.

The gods looked kindly upon him and bestowed him with gifts. Athena gave him a robe, Hephaistus a club and a coat of arms, Poseidon gave him horses, Hermes a sword, and Apollo a bow and arrow.

The details that eventually led to Heracles' death are as involved as those concerning his labors. But, in brief, here is what happened. We saw earlier that he had been given Megara as a wife before he began his twelve labors. Well, after the labors he gave her to his friend Iolaos and sought a new wife. During his wanderings he came upon a young man named **Iphitus** who triggered his temper to such an extent that Heracles killed him. Having blood guilt on his hands and overcome by physical illness, he sought purification. An oracle told him that he must serve as a vassal for three years in order to secure expiation. Hence, he put himself up for sale and was bought by an old woman named **Omphale**. She treated him well, was terribly amused by his abilities, dressed herself in his lion skin, made him do all sorts of chores around the house but also gave him sufficient freedom to roam and to be adventurous.

When at the end of his stay with her he was freed, he fell in love with a woman named **Deianira**. She was being wooed by the River Achelous, who changed himself into a bull and challenged Heracles to wrestle him for Deianira's hand. Heracles wrestled, beat the river, breaking off one of his horns, and married Deianira. One day as they were about to cross a river, the Centaur **Nessus** offered to carry her across. Heracles himself reached the other side but Nessus, while he was in the midst of the river, tried to rape Deianira. Heracles barraged the Centaur with his poisoned arrows and fatally wounded him. But before he died, the Centaur told Deianira that his blood was magical and contained a substance that served as a love potion. Deianira, knowing that Centaurs were often very learned in the occult, put some of Nessus' blood in a small bottle, hoping that she would never have to use it but feeling that it would be prudent to have it on hand just in case. Such a situation occurred a few years later. Heracles came upon a flame of his from the past, a woman named Iole. Fearing that that flame might be rekindled, she smeared her love potion over one of her husband's cloaks. When he put on the cloak, he was consumed by the poison which, like an acid, began to eat away his skin. The cloak, furthermore, stuck to his body and when he tried to remove it, he tore off his flesh. Deianira hanged herself and Heracles climbed to Mount Oeta, set up a large pyre, and requested that it be lit. No one would accommodate him; finally the Greek warrior Philoctetes came along and, lighting the fire, took Heracles out of his misery. To him Heracles bequeathed his bow and arrows. Then, as the fire blazed, there was a blast of thunder, and a cloud took Heracles up to his father on Olympus. There he married Hebe and lived forever as one of the gods. Zeus even effected a conciliation between Heracles and Hera, and she eventually adopted him with all the love of a mother.

Heracles is probably the most famous, most popular, and most ubiquitous figure in all of mythology. Only a portion of his exploits have been cited in this chapter; another chapter of double or triple the length would scarcely cover all the various phenomena that have been attributed to him.

From a logical point of view, there is much that makes no sense. Take, for instance, the chronology. Heracles is supposed to have assisted the gods in their battle with the giants; he is supposed to have freed Prometheus in the Caucasus; he is said to have freed Theseus from the Underworld; and he is said to have killed Cacus in Italy. Each of these events is separated by myriads of years. Then there is the question of geography. Take, for instance, Heracles' alleged wanderings after the theft of Geryon's cattle: from Mycenae (Eurystheus' palace) to Illyria (to consult Nereus) to western Africa (Antaeus) to Egypt (Busiris) to Rhodes to Arabia to North Africa to the Caucasus (Prometheus) and eventually to the Hyperboreans where he finally interviewed Atlas. Ancient sources pass off these thousands of miles as if they were trips to the local supermarket.

Then there are the tasks themselves. In some versions of the Heracles-story, the Cerberus task is the eleventh, not the twelfth. Sometimes he kills Ladon and personally fetches the golden apples. Sometimes Geryon's island is in the Ocean, sometimes it is in the Mediterranean or the Iberian Sea, sometimes it is not an island at all but a place in southern Spain. Sometimes Atlas is in Africa, sometimes in the land of the Hyperboreans. One could make a list of variations as long as the story itself.

It has been stated regularly in the remarks throughout this book that one must not expect consistency among classical myths and that one must not look for a canon of accepted beliefs. This is especially true of the Heracles stories. The name Heracles was known throughout much of the ancient world; localities would then associate various phenomena with the feats of this hero. If there had been a lake which was now dried, Heracles would probably be credited with its draining. All sorts of local customs and rituals were attributed to Heracles. Almost any region might have claimed a visit by Heracles as he was purging the world from giants, villainous humans, or wild beasts. Hence, there are literally hundreds of Heracles stories. Cicero in his *De Natura Deorum* cites at least six different Heracles: the most ancient one being the one that toured the area of Greece; the Egyptian Heracles; the Gallic or Celtic Heracles; the Heracles of Spain; of Phoenicia, and so on. Now, if each geographical unit could have kept its stories intact, there would be less of a problem; if each small locality had done the same, the problems would be still less. But the stories of one area began merging with the stories of another area, and throughout periods of history the story of one area was borrowed by another area, and that second area added a few details here and there, perhaps changing a name. Then, when hundreds of years later someone tried to codify, compile, and organize these diverse stories, we have what must appear as utter chaos.

The various adventures usually fall into three categories: the *erga*, or the actual twelve labors done under the auspices of King Eurystheus;

the *parerga,* or the side-labors he performed while performing the twelve tasks; and the *praxeis,* or the tasks he performed after he had been freed from Eurystheus. The *erga* — or at least some of them — are probably the original stories; the *parerga* and the *praxeis* are a combination of local folk legend, an embellishment of actual natural phenomena, and the romanticizing of specific historical events and processes as various localities wanted to buy into the Heracles mystique.

Heracles is certainly a mixture of qualities, and it is difficult to get much of a feeling for his personality. At times he seems to be the incarnation of violence and rabidity: smashing Linus' head with his lyre; cruelly mauling Erginus' envoys; flinging his own children into a fire; throwing Iphitus off a cliff. One can say, however, that his madness is Hera-sent. Nonetheless, one does see a savage temper, one which he could control when he had to, for how many times would he have liked to smash the pusillanimous Eurystheus!

In complete contrast to that temper is a certain gentleness. His relationship with Omphale is remarkable for his kindness and cooperation and patience. Nonetheless, he is certainly an act-now-think-later person. He rushes into encounters precipitously. Rarely does he think first; he is definitely a man of action. Sometimes, however, one wonders whether he is going too far: fighting Ares should be hybris by anyone's standards; challenging the sun is absurd; and it is said that when he first consulted the oracle after killing Iphitus, the oracle refused to answer. He got so indignant that he grabbed the sacred tripod, intending to start his own oracle somewhere else. Apollo came to retrieve it and the two of them wrestled until Zeus himself intervened.

Sometimes he appears to be little more than a spoiled child who, if he doesn't get his own way, will rant and rave. The incident with the sun, just mentioned, illustrates this facet of his personality. It gets too hot: the precious little baby can't take the heat, and he tries to intimidate the Sun itself. He has a need for vengeance; no one who injures him or who cheats him ever does so with impunity. He certainly lacks no confidence. When he hears that Alcestis has been taken by Hades, he immediately decides to take matters in his own hands and to tackle Hades himself.

Then there is the comic side to this hero. His sleeping with the fifty daughters of Thespius and not knowing what was happening is amusing enough; but when one realizes that another version of the scene claims that he slept with all fifty in one evening, the feat becomes absurdly hyper-herculean. Eurystheus' jumping into his jar, a popular scene in Greek art, is ludicrous. Certainly the picture of Heracles and the two Cercopes laughing at his black and hairy rear-end is an absurd moment. And the picture of him at Admetus' house[1] is comically painful; this bumbling oaf, laughing, backslapping, this hail-fellow-well-met who doesn't realize that the entire household is in mourning over the death of Alcestis.

1. See page 87.

There is no doubt, however, that Heracles does represent a civilizing force throughout the world, righting wrong wherever he finds it, eliminating brutality and savagery, and above all ridding the world of those who would use their strength to prey upon the weaker. Heracles, therefore, becomes a model for action, a model for the heroic tradition. We can't do what he did, but at least he is someone who shows us something of the human potential.

There is some pathos among the outrageousness and extrovertedness of the Heracles stories. Certainly the death of Chiron, the noblest of the Centaurs and a figure as close to a saint as the Greek mind would allow, is moving. The story of Deianera illustrates a sad end to an illustrious career. And the ironies in Heracles' last moments are touching ones: he who had been a superman is now helpless and in terrible agony; he seeks death and no one will assist him; he who has always fended for himself is now totally dependent upon someone else . . . anyone else.

Finally, mention should be made of a story attributed to the young Heracles. As he was moving from boyhood into manhood, two women approached him. One was gorgeously seductive and alluring, the other plain but with a certain intangible dignity. Each asked him to follow her. The first promised him a life of comfort, luxury, self-indulgence, and the realization of every desire that he might have. Her name was Happiness, but her enemies called her Pleasure. The other woman said that her path would require much effort on his part; she offered him no luxuries and no creature comforts; but she did offer him respect from both god and man. Her name was Virtue. The two women continued their presentations, each challenging the other, each building up her own gifts, and each inviting Heracles to select her own particular path. When all was said and done, they left, each on a separate path, and Heracles had to make the choice of which road to take. According to tradition, Heracles chose the path of Virtue. Whether he wandered from that path is up to the reader to decide.

Jason
and
The story of the Argonauts

Athamas, son of Aeolus, was king of Boeotia. With his wife Nephele he had a son named Phrixus and a daughter named Helle. Later he took a second wife, Ino, a daughter of Cadmus and Hermione. Wanting to get rid of her two stepchildren, Ino devised a complex plan. She first scorched the seeds for the year's wheat crop. When the earth bore no wheat that year, she then persuaded Athamas to consult the Oracle at Delphi so that he might be advised what

to do in order to remove the blight from the land. Ino then per-
suaded the ambassadors that Athamas had sent to the Oracle to say
that the Oracle had proclaimed that Athamas must sacrifice Phrixus
to Zeus. Just as he was about to slay his son, Nephele snatched up
both Phrixus and Helle on a golden-fleeced ram that she had received
as a present from Hermes. As they were in the air, Helle fell off the
ram and plunged into the sea at the place named after her, the Helles-
pont or Sea of Helle. Phrixus managed to arrive safely in Colchis at
the palace of King Aeetes. The King then sacrificed the ram to Zeus,
hung its fleece in a grove sacred to Ares, and put a dragon to guard it.
The story of the fleece spread and it was generally regarded as a high-
ly valued treasure.

Pelias was King of Iolcus in Thessaly. He had usurped the
throne from his brother **Aeson**. He had then effected a reign of terror
against his brother's family, although he would not touch Aeson himself, for they were of the same blood. When Aeson had a son, however, Pelias would have had the infant killed if the boy's mother had
not pretended that the child was still-born. With Pelias thinking the
boy was dead, Aeson's friends smuggled the infant out of Iolcus and
left him with the wise Centaur Chiron.

Pelias ruled for several years. As he was getting older, he consulted an oracle which told him that he must beware of a person
wearing only one shoe. At first he paid little attention and went
about his business. A few years later, however, he was going to offer
a sacrifice to Poseidon, and he had invited company from far and
near to celebrate with him. Jason, now a strapping young man, heard
about the sacrifice and decided to participate; he furthermore saw
this as an opportunity to regain the rightful inheritance that his uncle
had deprived him of. In his journey to Iolcus, Jason met an old woman at the bank of a river; she asked him to carry her across. Jason
agreed, but in the process of crossing, he lost one of his sandals. The
woman was Hera in disguise, and being angry at Pelias for not sacrificing to her, she had determined that Jason should be the agent of
her vengeance. Hence, Jason arrived at Pelias' court with one foot
bare. The king recognized him as the person described by the Oracle,
and he instantly resolved to get rid of the young man. When Jason
claimed his birthright, Pelias feigned compliance; but first, he said,
Jason would have to undertake an expedition to secure the Golden
Fleece, that very desirable treasure. After the Fleece was secured, Pelias would hand over the throne.

Such a venture appealed to young Jason. Here was a chance

185

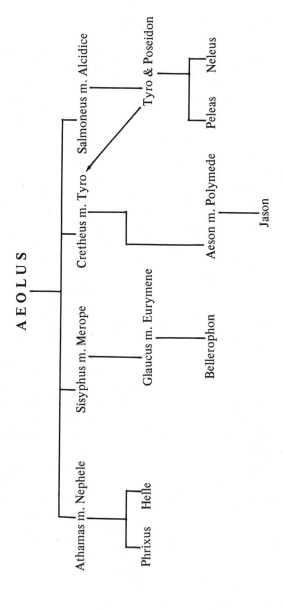

The ancestors of Jason. Tyro was the wife of Cretheus, but since she had once slept with Poseidon, Aeson and Pelias were at least half brothers. The four sons of Aeolus each were rulers: Athamas of Boeotia, Sisyphus of Corinth, Cretheus of Iolcus in Thessaly, and Salmoneus of Salmone in Elis. Eventually Peleas settled in Thessaly and took the throne from Aeson.

to prove himself, to gain a reputation, and to leave his mark on the world. Consequently, he recruited a crew and asked Argus, the leading shipbuilder of the day, to design him a vessel. It was the largest ship ever built, could seat fifty oarsmen, and even had one beam from the sacred wood of Dodona, the seat of Zeus' oracle; it was from a tree that Athena herself had planted and because of this one sacred beam, the ship itself could talk. The builder called the ship the *Argo* after himself.

The crew was a veritable catalogue of heroes. Everyone who was anyone was there: Orpheus, Zetes and Calais, Castor and Polydeuces, Theseus, Heracles, Admetus, Atalanta, Iphitus, Meleager, Peleus, and Telamon among others. It was the most prestigious adventure of the time, and the crew was the finest that had ever sailed the seas. As they embarked, Chiron and Thetis with the baby Achilles in her arms wished them Godspeed, and even the fish followed their path wherever they went.

They first touched on Lemnos, an island in the northern Aegean, inhabited only by women. Much earlier, these women had slighted Aphrodite and she, in retribution, had inflicted them with such a horrible smell that their husbands sought bedmates elsewhere. The women then killed all the men – all the women, that is, except Queen Hypsipyle, who hid and saved her father. When the Argonauts visited these women, they bedded with them, the smell apparently having disappeared with the departure of the husbands. Through these several unions, the Argonauts fathered a race of men who were later to be known as the Minyans.

They then passed the harbor at Cyzicus and landed near Mysia in Phrygia. There Hylas, one of their crew, while he was fetching water, was carried off by nymphs who fell in love with his beauty. While Heracles was looking for him, the crew sailed, thinking that both he and Hylas had been lost, and this terminated Heracles' involvement with the good ship *Argo*. The sea god Glaucus then assured the crew that Zeus had other plans for Heracles and that they should continue without him.

By now the *Argo* had already passed through the Hellespont and was deep into the Propontis, a total no-man's-land, whose shores were inhabited by barbarous and fierce people, unaccustomed to foreigners and hostile to them. Entering the land of Bithynia, they came upon King Bebryces, a son of Poseidon and the haughtiest of all people. He would challenge every newcomer to his shores to a boxing match. He did so to the Argonauts, and Polydeuces, the son of Zeus and Leda, accepted the challenge. The fight was a good one, but

187

Polydeuces eventually killed the insolent king with one stiff cuff.

They continued their voyage into Thrace, where they came across the wretched Phineus. Phineus had once been a prophet, but when he had divulged certain secrets of the gods, Apollo punished him by blinding him and by inflicting him with the terrible Harpies. These were enormous creatures, part woman and part bird, with long claws and sharp beaks, who could fly as fast as lightning. Whenever Phineus would try to eat, these creatures would pounce upon his food, steal whatever they wanted for themselves and so foully pollute the remainder of the food that the stench was unbearable. They left only enough food for Phineus to survive. When the Argonauts came upon this miserable creature, they were eager to kill the Harpies, and Zetes and Calais, the sons of Boreas, the North Wind, would have done so had not Iris interceded. The Harpies were her sisters and they had been sent by a god; it would be wrong, therefore, to kill them. She, however, went to Zeus and effected Phineus' release from his punishment.

Phineus was so grateful that he told the Argonauts how to avoid the Clashing Rocks. These two rocks, sometimes called the Symplegades, were located at the mouth of the Black Sea. These two rocks would smash together whenever anything passed between them. Phineus advised the crew to let fly a dove; the rocks would then smash together and the ship could speedily pass as the rocks were pulling apart. They took his advice; the only damage that occurred was to the dove; it lost a few of its tail feathers.

They were now at the far east of the Black Sea; they sailed past the island of Philyra where Cronos was said to have fathered Chiron; they saw the Caucasus Mountains and heard Prometheus' groans of agony; finally they reached the land called Colchis, where the Fleece was being guarded by King **Aeetes**. He had dedicated the Fleece to Ares, and had put a dragon in charge of it, for he had heard from an oracle that his life depended upon his keeping the Fleece. Therefore, when Jason told him of his mission, the king had no intention of handing over the Fleece; but he thought it best to hide his real intentions. Thus, he told Jason that the Fleece would be his if he would perform two tasks: yoke unaided a pair of wild bulls, and sow the teeth of a dragon using that pair of bulls.

Jason accepted. As he was puzzling how he might single-handedly yoke these two huge, savage, bulky creatures who had feet of bronze and breathed fire, gifts of Hephaistus to Aeetes, a woman entered the scene. She was **Medea**, daughter of Aeetes, and a witch of considerable power, and she was to be very much of a mixed blessing for Jason.

188

Her father was a brother of Perses, father of Hecate, that very notorious sorceress. Hecate was extraordinarily clever at mixing potions and testing them on humans. She even poisoned her father and then married Aeetes, bearing by him two daughters, Medea and Circe. Circe, like her mother, had mastered the arcane art of brews and potions, poisons and herbs, spells and transformations; but she eventually became less of a menace when she took over an island in the western Mediterranean.

Medea, meanwhile, stayed with Aeetes. She had learned to use all the powers that her mother and sister had, but unlike them she used them for good purposes. Whenever possible she would rescue strangers about to be killed by her cruel father. As she grew more and more hostile to her father's behavior, Aeetes, beginning to fear her, put her in custody. She escaped and came across the Argonauts just as they were entering the land. She warned them of the dangers, told them of her father's custom of slaying strangers, and asked their assistance in escaping, promising to cooperate with them, using her powers whenever necessary to help them accomplish their mission. Jason even promised that he would marry her when the deed was accomplished.

Now, as Jason had been pondering how to yoke the bulls, Hera, who had been watching everything from up above, had begun to worry. Jason was part of her master plan to destroy Pelias and here he was all but stymied. Then she got an idea. She asked her sister Aphrodite to send Eros on a visit to Medea. Eros went down to Colchis and struck Medea with one of his arrows, and she was hit as hard as any person has ever been hit. Wanting Jason, she realized the plight she was in and, therefore, she resolved to use all her powers to aid him. She gave him a potion and told him to bathe his body and his weapons in that potion; the potion gave invulnerability to both fire and iron for one day. He did what she recommended and managed to yoke the two creatures. Then she advised him about the dragon's teeth. She told him that as soon as he had put these teeth in the ground, armed men would spring up, for Aeetes had secured half of the teeth which Cadmus had planted in Thebes.[1] When the armed men arose from the ground, he threw stones in their midst; this caused them to fight with each other, and as they were so occupied, Jason killed those who had not already been killed.

Two labors were now completed, but Aeetes refused to hand over the Fleece, planning to burn the ship and slay the Argonauts. But Medea drugged the dragon guarding the Fleece, stole the Fleece,

1. See page 153.

˳nd herself handed it over to Jason. They entered the *Argo* and sailed away. Following Phineus' advice, they did not retrace their course but took the northern route along the Black Sea. Aeetes followed in hot pursuit. To slow him down, Medea killed her brother Absyrtus and cut up each of his limbs and threw them overboard. Aeetes would have to go after each piece in order to give Absyrtus a proper burial and the *Argo* would escape.

Zeus now entered the scene. He was angry at the murder of Absyrtus and sent a terrible storm that drove them off course; then the ship itself spoke, saying that they would have to travel to Circe's island in the western Mediterranean in order to be purified. They followed these directions and encountered many of the same phenomena that other ships had met in that area: the seductive Sirens, the monster Scylla, the whirlpool Charybdis, the Wandering Rocks or Planctae; but Thetis led a band of Nereids and guided their ship safely through these dangers. They visited Alcinoos' island, where Jason and Medea were married by Queen Arete. Then they sailed east toward home.

When they were about to enter Crete, they were prevented by Talos, a gift of Hephaistus to King Minos. Talos was a robot-like man, made all of metal. He had just one vein in his body, and it ran from his neck to his ankles; his limbs were unbreakable. He was vulnerable in only one spot: his ankle; here was a vein of ichor with only a tender covering of skin. Talos was a watchman for the island. Whenever a ship would come near, he would pelt it with stones and prevent its landing. Jason despaired of landing, but Medea took matters into her own hands. Talos accidentally scraped his ankle against a jagged rock, the ichor rapidly flowed from his body, and then the giant fell with a mighty crash.

On the way back to Colchis, when Jason told Medea the outrages of his uncle, Medea vowed to assist him in his revenge. She then dressed herself as a terribly aged crone, put on make up that shriveled her skin, bent herself over and walked with a distinct limp. She then entered Iolcus in this guise of an old woman. She announced that she had magical powers and offered a demonstration to Pelias' daughters. She entered a closet-size room with her magic charms; actually her charms in this case were nothing but fluids to wash out the gray dye from her hair and the artificial wrinkles from her skin. Then she presented herself: a young and attractive woman. She could transform anyone, she claimed. Pelias' daughters were totally taken in. They were even more convinced when she took an old ram, cut it up into pieces, put it in a cauldron of boiling water, and turned it

190

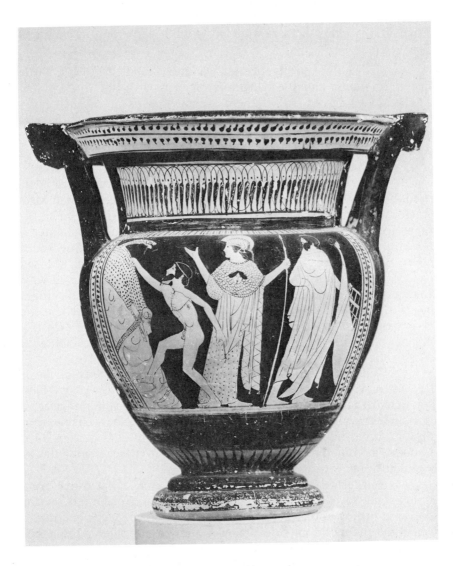

JASON GETS THE FLEECE. Attic Red-Figured case attributed to the Orchard Painter, 5th Century B.C. Jason reaches for the fleece, which is guarded by a serpent-like dragon. Athena, wearing her helmet and her aegis with the Medusa's head mounted on it, oversees the operation. A man to the right tends to the *Argo,* on the bow of which is a small head, indicating the ship's power of speech. Note that this artist has represented a variation on the traditional story told in the text: Medea is missing. Note too the Greek tendency not to depict the horrible: neither the dragon nor the head of Medusa is very lurid. *Courtesy, Metropolitan Museum of Art, Harris Brisbane Dick Fund, 1934.*

191

into a young lamb. If there were any doubts, those doubts were now dispelled.

Medea now subtly planted an idea that Pelias might be restored to youth and the daughters pleaded with her to do so. Of course Medea agreed. All of them except Alcestis cut up their father into bits and pieces, following the procedure used with the ram, threw the pieces into the cauldron, and waited for his rejuvenation. As might be expected, the magic didn't work this time. Pelias was dead. Hera had her revenge.

When Acastus, son of Pelias and cousin of Jason, heard of the deed, he expelled Jason and Medea from Iolcus, a stigma which Jason graciously accepted. The two of them went to Corinth and settled there for ten years. But Jason fell in love with Glauce, daughter of the king. He planned to marry her and divorced Medea. But Medea, never one to take any sort of affront, plotted revenge. She sent Glauce a robe as a wedding gift. The robe was poisoned, and when Glauce put it on, she was consumed by fire; her father, rushing to her aid, also perished. Fire spread throughout the household and everyone perished save Jason. Medea and her son Medus flew off to Athens on a chariot drawn by winged dragons, a gift from Helios. At Athens she settled in with King Aegeus.

Medea, Medus, and Aegeus lived happily for several years. But when Aegeus' long-lost son Theseus showed up one day, Medea was afraid that Theseus would displace Medus. She almost succeeded in killing the young man, but when Aegeus caught her scheme in the nick of time, he banished her from Athens. She did quite a bit of wandering from that point on. Of her death, if in fact she did die, we know nothing.

Neither is there any story left to Jason. He had lost everything; some say that in despair he committed suicide. Others say that the gods turned upon him for violating his oath to Medea and that he wandered the world ingloriously, eventually dying when a beam from the *Argo* fell upon him.

Alcestis, the only one of Pelias' daughters who did not dissect him, married Admetus.[1] Medus, Medea's son, extended the southern territory of his grandfather's kingdom and gave his name to the Medes, the group of people who live southeast of Colchis.

Compared to the other three major heroes — Perseus, Heracles, and Theseus — Jason is indeed very pale. He has almost no personality. Scarcely, in fact, do we ever see him actually acting; most of the time he is acted upon. Almost the only decision he ever makes on his own

1. See page 86.

MEDEA AND THE RAM. Attic Red-Figured Vase, 5th Century B.C. As a youthful ram springs out of Medea's cauldron, one of Pelias' daughters is convinced of Medea's powers and encourages her father to undergo rejuvenation. *Courtesy, Museum of Fine Arts, Boston.*

initiative is the one to divorce Medea, and ironically it is that decision that leads to his destruction and the destruction of everything he loves.

Compared to the missions of the other heroes, Jason's is quite easy. All he has to do is to yoke two bulls and trick a group of warriors. He has it quite easy compared to Perseus, Theseus, or Heracles. There are some inconveniences, but nothing that really tests him. The Harpies don't bother him; the Symplegades he maneuvers not through his own devices but through Phineus' advice; Polydeuces, not Jason, defeats King Bebryces. He sheds no tears when Hylas is lost. In fact, we don't see him doing anything; until Medea enters the scene, members of his crew do what needs to be done; from that point on Medea takes care of everything.

Jason goes on a mission, as do all the other heroes, but the purpose of that mission doesn't seem very prominent in his mind. He doesn't seem to be that committed to getting back his rightful kingdom. He seems, in fact, much more interested in the immediate moment than in the long range goal.

Unlike the other heroes, Jason doesn't accomplish much. He doesn't clean up beasts, he doesn't right wrong, he doesn't rid the world of injustice, he doesn't even put down a bully. Furthermore, he is the only hero who ends ingloriously. He is the only hero who doesn't accomplish his goal. He gets the Golden Fleece, but he does not get Iolcus. And no locality would point to Jason as one of its historical figures in the way that localities turned to Theseus, Perseus, or Heracles.

The real hero of the story is Medea. She is as intense as Jason is passive. She has her quest — to realize and fulfill her love for Jason — and she does everything she can to get and keep what she wants. She is totally committed to Jason; she lies, cheats, and steals for him; she commits incredible horrors — the murder of her brother and the butchery of Pelias for instance — and yet she is not a villain. Her strength and dedication contrast markedly with the absence of those qualities in Jason. It is even claimed that Medea ended up in the Elysian Fields — i.e., the Land of the Blessed — where she and the spirit of Achilles consort together.

There are several variations to the Jason story, just as there have been variations to every other story in classical mythology. Medus is sometimes Aegeus' son, for instance, not Jason's; sometimes Medea personally kills her sons, sometimes they die from the fire that spreads from the burning Glauce; sometimes Medea flees with a son named Thessalus, who later founds Thessaly; sometimes Jason and Medea are said to have had seven sons and seven daughters. Furthermore, there are several more scenes in the corpus of Jason stories, most of which are colorful and spicy but few of which add any significant details.

Ovid in his retelling of the Jason-Medea story builds up Medea's power as a witch. He describes how Jason became so upset when, upon returning home, he saw how old and decrepit his father had become that he asked Medea to use her powers to take some years from his own life and add them to Aeson's life. Medea, being moved by such filial affection, went a step further. Using all her knowledge and allying herself with Hecate, she went out in the middle of the night under a full moon and invoked all the occult spirits. A dragon-harnessed chariot swooped down from the sky and took her to the hills of Thessaly where for nine days and nights she gathered herbs, then returned to Iolcus, made a powerful potion, added all sorts of witch-like substances — such as sand from the ocean, frost gathered by moonlight, the wings of an owl, the scales of a snake, the entrails of a wolf, the liver of a stag, and the head of a crow — and then, cutting Aeson's throat, draining him of his blood, she infused him with her potion, and totally restored to him the vigor of a young man.

194

Theseus

I. – Birth and First Adventures

Aegeus was one of the four sons of Pandion, a king of Athens living in exile in Megara. After Pandion's death the brothers waged war against those who had usurped their father's throne, and ultimately Aegeus became king of all Attica. His position, however, was not secure. His brothers were jealous of him, and after two wives and many years he had still not produced a son. In despair, Aegeus went to Delphi to find out from the oracle how he might father a male heir. As usual, the oracle gave a cryptic response, telling him not to loosen the mouth of the wineskin until he returned to Athens. Confused by this advice, Aegeus decided to return to Athens by the way of Troezen, where he might consult with King **Pittheus**, who had a reputation for being able to interpret oracles.

Pittheus did indeed understand the oracle and decided to use this understanding to his own advantage. He saw the advantage of having a link between his country and Attica, the latter being much stronger and far wealthier than his. That night, Pittheus invited Aegeus to dine with him and in the course of the evening managed to get him very drunk. Then he took his drunken guest to a bedroom and provided a girl to sleep with him – the girl being his daughter **Aethra**. When Aegeas woke in the morning and saw the girl next to him and realized what he had done, he was deeply upset. He had indeed opened the wineskin both literally and figuratively. What he did not know, however, was that on that same night, before she had come to him, Aethra had been deflowered by Poseidon. Nonetheless, Aegeus, just in case there might be a son resulting from their night together, made Aethra promise that she would not reveal to the son who his father was. Then he placed his sword and sandals under a huge rock and instructed Aethra that, if and when the child could move the rock, he should bring them to him in Athens. The frustrated Aegeus then returned home, where he was soon joined by the exiled witch Medea, who became his consort.

A child was indeed born to Aethra: his name was Theseus, and he was brought up by Pittheus. He was a bright and lively youngster. When he was seven, Heracles visited his family, and from that time on Theseus was determined that he too would be as daring and courageous as Heracles was. Heracles became his hero: he was, however, to differ from that hero; whereas Heracles relied primarily on massive strength, Theseus would rely more on ingenuity and intelligence.

195

By the time he was sixteen, Theseus had grown to manhood. Aethra took him aside and told him of his father and of the sword and sandals beneath the rock. With no difficulty, Theseus moved the rock and retrieved the objects. Then he immediately announced that he would go by land to Athens to present himself to his father. Both his mother and his grandfather tried to dissuade him from taking the overland route: Athens was at most a two-day sail from Troezen, while the overland route would take him twice that time; but, more important, the country between Troezen and Athens was overrun with outlaws and rogues who would slit his throat for a drachma. But Theseus was adamant. His model, Heracles, wouldn't be afraid of robbers and the like, and after all, perhaps he could do a service for mankind by dispatching the worst of the brigands. That's it, he'd clear the way so that it would be safe for others.

So off he went by himself, overland, to Athens. But he had gotten only as far as Epidaurus when he ran into his first problem. There, in front of him in the path, was a hairy rogue coming at him with a huge bronze club. His name was Periphates, and he was said to be a son of Hephaistus. He was well known in those parts and was called "Club-man," because he waylaid passersby and smashed their skulls with his club. But Theseus was too quick for him, and before long the young hero was on his way again, now with Periphates' club, which he kept with him from that time on just as Heracles had a club.

Theseus trudged on and, when he reached the Isthmus of Corinth, he met his second challenge. Another hairy rogue, called Sinis, came after him. Like Periphates, Sinis had his own technique for dispatching travelers, and, in fact, was known as "Pine-Bender" because of his technique. Sometimes, when he saw a traveler coming, he would start tugging on a rope tied to the top of a tall pine tree. When the traveler reached him, still tugging he would ask for help in bending the tree down so that he could use it as a spring. Sinis was tremendously strong and did most of the pulling himself, and when the top of the tree had almost reached the ground, he would let go. The unsuspecting traveler would thus be catapulted to his death. On other occasions, when he didn't feel like playing games, he would simply catch a traveler and tie him to two trees that were already bent over — the feet to one tree, the arms to the other. Then, simultaneously he would cut the ropes that held both trees and as they sprung up the traveler would be torn in two. Theseus fought with Sinis and, when he had subdued him, he tied him to the bent trees that were meant for his own destruction. Gleefully he cut the ropes and watched the death of another enemy of justice and law and order.

196

One night when he was staying outside of Megara, Theseus learned of a vicious sow called Phaea, who was rampaging nearby at Crommyon. This miserable creature had destroyed many crops and had killed many men. Though Crommyon wasn't really on his route to Athens, Theseus decided that he would hunt the sow. If he didn't go out of his way at least once, people could say that his victories over various brigands had been a result of necessity rather than choice. More than that, he had committed himself to making the world a safe place for good people to live, and this sow was clearly an enemy to good living. And after all, Heracles wouldn't have avoided such a challenge. Thus, he made a brief detour, dispatched the sow, and was on his way again.

Near Megara, on the route from Corinth to Athens, there is a place where steep cliffs reach down to the sea. There the path was narrow and treacherous, and the traveler had to take great care as he moved along it, lest he tumble into the sea. To make matters worse, a rogue by the name of Sciron often waylaid travelers as they worked their way along the path. A pompous fellow, he would insist that the traveler stop and wash his feet before he would let him pass. Then, as he would bend over to wipe Sciron's feet, he would kick him off the cliff into the sea where a great turtle waited to devour him. But Theseus was not about to fall for this ploy. Sciron, as usual, demanded that the young hero wash his feet. Theseus pretended that he was going to oblige him, but instead, he picked up the foot-bath, smashed Sciron on the head with it, and threw him off the cliff as food for the turtle. And on he went.

At Eleusis, a huge, hairy man by the name of Cercyon lived. Cercyon had never met a man to equal his own strenth. The classic bully, he used this strength by insisting that travelers wrestle him. If they won, they could pass by: if not, he would kill them in the fight. So far, no one had won. Theseus was clearly neither as big as nor as strong as was Cercyon, but he was willing to take him on. Using skill and technique rather than strength and size, Theseus defeated Cercyon and killed him. He had discovered the art of wrestling and later was to teach it to others.

In a house on the road outside of Eleusis lived a man named Damastes. When weary travelers passed by his house, he invited them in to rest, but his intentions were less than honorable. He too had gained a nickname because of his technique for destroying the unwary traveler — he was called Procrustes, or the "Stretcher." In his house he had two beds, a long one and a short one. When a short traveler accepted his hospitality, he took him into the room with the

197

long bed. Having subdued the guest, he took a great hammer and pounded at the fellow, flattening him until he fit the bed. If a tall traveler came, he put him in the short bed and cut off whatever extremities stuck over the ends so that he too would fit. Again Theseus was victorious. He chose the short bed for Procrustes and hammered him into shape.

When the exhausted Theseus reached the outskirts of Athens, the witch Medea, who was living with Aegeus, learned of his arrival. He was a distinct threat to her position as favorite of Aegeus,[1] and she devised a plan to get rid of him. Athens was in a state of political unrest. Aegeus had still not produced a male heir, and his brother Pallas with his sons was pressing for the throne. Medea went to the old man and warned him that she had learned of a stranger who would soon visit the palace but who was actually a traitor, intent on overthrowing the king. With Aegeus' consent, she prepared a cup of poison. Therefore, when Theseus arrived, he was invited to a feast where he would be given the poisoned cup.

Theseus accepted the invitation, but he wasn't sure how he should let his father know that he was his son. He didn't think it was appropriate simply to go up to him and tell him. After all, Aegeus had kept him in the dark all these years. Somehow he had to let his father discover who he was. So, he went to the feast. Once he was seated, he drew his sword and cut the meat with it and then reached for his cup. At that instant, Aegeus recognized the sword and knocked the cup from his son's hand before he could drink the poison. The happy father embraced his son, thankful that he had discovered in time who he was. Then, remembering Medea's advice, he turned on her and expelled her from his lands.

Anxious to help his father in matters of state, Theseus went to Marathon and killed a bull that was ravishing the countryside. The Athenians accepted him as their hero and as the heir to his father's throne. Obviously Pallas, Aegeus' brother, was not overjoyed at the news of Theseus' arrival, and realizing that it was a now-or-never situation, he waged war on Athens. With Theseus' help, Aegeus destroyed these rivals. '

II. — Theseus' Cretan Adventures

When Aegeus had returned to Athens after siring Theseus with Aethra, he had received Androgeus, son of King Minos of Crete, as his guest.[2] Androgeus was a valiant young man and a fine athlete.

1. See page 192. 2. See page 153.

He won all the contests he entered, but he aroused the jealousy of the Athenians by his success. Confident of his own strength, he had offered to kill the Bull of Marathon, and Aegeus was only too happy to have him try. He went to Marathon and, in the course of his battle with the bull, was killed — some said through the treachery of his companions, others said that the bull had done it. Whatever the cause, Minos was furious at the death of his son. He held the Athenians responsible and waged war on them. The war was a standoff, but in addition to their mortal foes, the Athenians were visited with plagues from the gods as well. No crops would grow, the rivers dried up, and a pestilence spread across the land. In despair, the Athenians sent an emissary to Delphi to consult the oracle. They learned that, to quell the anger of the gods, they would have to propitiate Minos by agreeing to whatever terms he arrived upon. Thus, they sent an embassy to Crete. Minos demanded that every nine years a tribute of seven youths and seven maidens be sent to him as fodder for his ghastly stepson, the Minotaur. The Athenians had no choice but to agree.

The Minotaur was a monster with the body of a human and the head of a bull. As we saw in the story of the ancestors of Oedipus, when Minos had met opposition to his taking the Cretan throne, he had prayed to Poseidon for a sign. Poseidon had sent a magnificent white bull, with the understanding that Minos would sacrifice it, but Minos had cheated and had sacrificed another one in its place.[1] As punishment, Poseidon had inflamed Minos' wife, Pasiphae, with a mad passion for the bull. She couldn't sleep, she couldn't eat, so profound was her passion. Finally she went to Daedalus, the master craftsman, who was then associated with Minos' court, explained her problem, and asked for his help.

Daedalus was the Leonardo Da Vinci of the ancient world. Born in Athens, Daedalus was said to be related to the royal house and was thus a relative of Theseus. He was an exceedingly clever man; there seemed to be no problem that he couldn't solve. In Athens, Daedalus had taken in his sister's son as an apprentice; but, when the boy had shown signs of surpassing the master, he threw him off the Acropolis to his death. Tried by the Areopagus, Daedalus was condemned to death, but he fled to Crete, where Minos took him in. When Pasiphae came to him with her problem, he found a solution for her. He constructed a hollow, wooden cow on wheels, which he covered with the skin of a recently slaughtered cow; then, with Pasiphae inside, he rolled the device out into the pasture where the bull was grazing. As a result, Pasiphae became pregnant by the bull, and her offspring was the Minotaur. Minos, horrified at this creature, or-

1. See page 153.

199

dered Daedalus to conceal it from the sight of everyone. Daedalus, therefore, constructed the **labyrinth,** a maze of passageways and chambers in which the Minotaur was housed. When the Athenian offering arrived every nine years, they were thrown into the labyrinth, where they either died of starvation, not being able to find their way out,or they were eaten by the Minotaur.

When Theseus returned to Athens after killing the Bull of Marathon and defeating Pallas and his sons, it was again time for the tribute to Minos. Eighteen years had passed since the tribute had first been offered, so this was to be the third. Though Theseus had already proved himself as a supporter of the Athenians, there was much grumbling when it came time to draw lots for the youths and maidens who would be sacrificed. Why, people asked, should this foreigner, and a bastard at that, be allowed to go free when we citizens of Athens have to give of our own to Minos! Aegeus was in a difficult position, but Theseus came to his father's aid by volunteering to go with the party as one of the seven youths. Though Aegeus tried to dissuade him, there was no sense arguing with Theseus once he had made up his mind. He was going but, he bragged, he would return having killed the Minotaur just as he had killed the Bull of Marathon and the sow of Crommyon.

Just before he sailed for Crete, Theseus agreed to give his father an early sign of success or failure. If he was still alive, the ship on which he returned would have a white sail; if he was dead, the sail would remain black as it was when they left, indicating the sorrowful nature of their journey.

When Theseus arrived in Crete with his companions and before the group was thrown into the labyrinth, **Ariadne**, the daughter of King Minos, saw him and instantly fell in love with him, attracted by his marvelous beauty. She found a way to talk with him and offered to help him escape from the labyrinth if he would take her to Athens as his bride. Theseus swore an oath that he would. Ariadne immediately went to Daedalus for advice and he promptly gave her a suggestion that Theseus successfully adopted. He attached the end of a ball of thread to the lintel of the door leading into the labyrinth; then as he wandered through the passages and chambers he let the ball unwind. Deep in the labyrinth, he found the Minotaur and killed him with his fists; then he followed the thread back to the entrance, leading the thirteen young Athenians with him. Finally, with Ariadne he sailed for Athens.

After the first day of sailing, they stopped at the island of Naxos to spend the night – Greek sailors sailed at night only when

THESEUS VISITS POSEIDON. Theseus has come to Poseidon's palace under the sea to get proof of his own divine parent. In one tradition, when Theseus was sailing to Crete with the youths to be sacrificed to the Minotaur, King Minos, a son of Zeus, challenged him to prove that his father was Poseidon. Minos threw a ring overboard, and Theseus dove in to retrieve it. Poseidon came to his aid. In this picture, Theseus has the ring and is about to be returned to Minos by Triton. Poseidon, holding his trident, bids him farewell, as do Amphitrite and several nymphs. *Courtesy, Metropolitan Museum of Art, Purchase, 1953, Joseph Pulitzer Bequest.*

they had to. There are many versions of what happened at Naxos. Some say that Theseus abandoned Ariadne there; others say that Dionysus absconded with her; but whatever the case, Theseus left without her and she became Dionysus' wife.

When the ship approached Athens, either out of joy at returning or out of grief at having lost Ariadne, Theseus forgot to change the sail on his ship. Aegeus, standing on the western end of the Acropolis, where the temple of Athena Nike is today, saw the black sail, assumed that Theseus was dead, and in despair jumped to his death. Some versions say that he jumped into the sea — a bit hard to do off the Acropolis — and that the sea was named the Aegean after him. Theseus on his return was welcomed as the new ruler, but he rejected the title of king and demanded equality for all. He established the Panathenaic festival, which would be open to all Athenians. Then he drew the people together from the many small towns into one large one and was the founder of the city that was to be famous throughout the world and the city known for its creation of democracy.

Meanwhile, on Crete, Minos was furious. Tired of Daedalus' subterfuges, he threw him in the labyrinth along with **Icarus**, his son by one of his slaves. But it was impossible to repress Daedalus' imagination, and the master-craftsman built wings for himself and for his son out of wax and feathers. Before they took off, he warned Icarus not to fly too high, or the sun would melt the wax, and not to fly too low, or the dampness would loosen the feathers. Together they took off but Icarus, being young, ignored his father's warnings, flew too high, and fell into the sea that was later named after him. The sad Daedalus flew on to Sicily, where he was taken in by King Cocalus.

Minos was determined to punish Daedalus, and he began a search for him which he would not give up until he found him. He set a trap. He offered an enormous reward for anyone who could work a thread through a spiral shell he carried with him. He figured that Daedalus was the only one who could possibly do it, and he knew that, by appealing to Daedalus' vanity, he could catch him that way. Ultimately he came to Sicily. When he presented the puzzle to King Cocalus, the king brought it to the hidden Daedalus. Daedalus met the challenge. He drilled a small hole in the shell, tied the thread to an ant, and thus threaded the shell. But when Cocalus brought the threaded shell to Minos, the Cretan king demanded that he turn over the outlaw, Daedalus. Cocalus agreed, but asked him to wait until the following morning. That night, when Minos was in his bath, the daughters of Cocalus came to him with cauldrons of boiling water and scalded him to death. Thus, Daedalus lived out his years in Sicily.

III — Antiope, Phaedra, and Hippolytus

When Theseus learned of Heracles' plan[1] to get the golden girdle of Ares from the Amazon queen, Hippolyte, he volunteered to go along and help. Confronting the women in their own land at the mouth of the river Thermodon on the Black Sea, they were successful in their venture, and as a reward for his valor Theseus was given one of the Amazon queens, **Antiope**, as his paramour. She came back to Athens with him, willingly in some accounts, unwillingly in others, and bore him a son, **Hippolytus**. Whatever her feelings might have been, the rest of the Amazons were determined to rescue her and thus, working their way to Athens, laid siege to the city. The siege lasted for four months, with the women holding strategic locations around the Acropolis. However, their losses were heavy, and ultimately they signed a treaty with the Athenians. Antiope remained behind.

Soon after the departure of the Amazons, Athens began negotiations with Crete. Minos was dead, and his son had inherited his throne. With the loss of their strong leader, the Cretans had also lost their maritime power and were anxious to establish ties with the up-and-coming Athenians. As a sign of good intentions and as a means of establishing a link between the powers, the new king gave his sister, **Phaedra** — also the sister of Ariadne — to Theseus to be his wife. Clearly this was a politically expedient marriage, and Theseus accepted the gift. He had never married Antiope; therefore, he was free to accept Phaedra as a wife.

On his marriage day, Theseus gathered the notables of Athens in his home for a celebration feast. After the guests were seated and just as they were about to start the meal, the doors of the room burst open and Antiope, fully armed, with several of her sister Amazons who had remained with her, entered. Theseus was her man and had no right to marry another. She threatened to kill him and his guests. But her paltry platoon was no match for the many guests, who quickly subdued her. She continued to struggle and threaten, and finally in the fray she was killed.

Theseus lived happily with Phaedra for several years, and she gave him two sons, Acamas and Demophon. As all rulers must, he faced the question of who would succeed him as ruler of Athens. While he loved Hippolytus, he did not want a bastard son to succeed him, feeling that it was only right that his rule should descend to one of his legal sons. Ultimately he resolved this problem by sending Hippolytus to live with Pittheus in Troezen. Thus, when Pittheus

1. See page 176.

died, Hippolytus would become king of Troezen and Acamas and Demophon would inherit Athens. Furthermore, he was worried about how Phaedra would feel about having an illegitimate son growing up with their two legitimate sons.

Hippolytus was a handsome, athletic lad who had devoted himself to Artemis. He loved to ride through the countryside and to hunt, and he despised women. Female charms were repulsive to him, and he scorned Aphrodite. To punish his brash neglect of her, Aphrodite made Phaedra fall hopelessly in love with him. She first saw him when he came to Eleusis to be initiated into the rites, not an uncommon practice for noble youths. Phaedra's love for him was so strong that she couldn't eat or sleep. He was constantly on her mind. She had to see him again. When Theseus suggested that they visit his grandfather in Troezen, Phaedra was elated. While they were there, she discovered that from a temple of Aphrodite she could see into the gymnasium, and daily she would go to watch the young man exercise nude. At the same time, she was disgusted by this love that she could do nothing about. She didn't want to love Hippolytus: it had simply happened. Furious with herself and frustrated at the hopelessness of her love, she would stab at the leaves on a myrtle inside the sanctuary. Ever after, the temple was called the Temple of Aphrodite Spy, and the myrtle's pierced leaves became famous.

Later, Hippolytus came to Athens to participate in games there. Some say that Phaedra found another vantage point from which to watch the object of her love. Finally, when she could stand it no longer, she invited him to her room and confessed her love for him, pleading with him to take her. Outraged and disgusted by her confession, Hippolytus fled. In retrospect, as Phaedra saw it, she had given in to a forbidden passion, and honor demanded that she kill herself. But before she did, she left a note accusing Hippolytus of trying to rape her, and she arranged her room so that it would appear as if there had been a struggle.

When Theseus heard of Hippolytus' attempt to rape Phaedra, he was quite naturally furious. At some point in the past, his father, Poseidon, had given him three wishes which he promised to grant. Theseus used one of them now, asking that Hippolytus be destroyed for his crime. While the youth was fleeing Athens in his chariot back to Troezen, a bull rose out of the surf near the Isthmus of Corinth and pursued him. His horses raced on in terror and, though he controlled them at first, his chariot overturned when one wheel hit a stump. Hippolytus was caught in the reins and dragged to his death.

Some ancient authors say that Artemis explained to Theseus

the truth of what had happened between Hippolytus and Phaedra. Others say that at Artemis' request Asclepius brought the youth back to life and was destroyed as a result of his hybris. Whatever the details, Theseus was saddened at the loss of the son he had loved.

IV — Pirithous

The stories of Theseus' successful ventures against various foes of man spread throughout the Greek world. In Thessaly in northern Greece, **Pirithous**, King of the Lapiths, heard of this new hero and was skeptical. Determined to find out if all that was said about this Theseus was true, he decided to test him. With a group of warriors, he went to the plain of Marathon, where Theseus' cattle grazed, and he began to drive the animals north. When Theseus heard of this cattle rustling, he sped to Marathon and pursued the outlaws. Instead of running, though, Pirithous turned and faced Theseus, ready for a fight. But when the two men saw each other, they were both awed at the other's beauty and courage, and instead of fighting each made a pledge of friendship to the other and each sealed his pledge with a sacred oath. From that time on they were inseparable comrades, sharing many adventures.

Their first joint adventure took place when Pirithous invited Theseus to be present at his marriage to Hippodamia — or, according to some authors, Deidameia. Pirithous' country was in a wild, mountainous region. His people, the Lapiths, shared the region with the Centaurs, creatures with torsos, arms, and heads of humans and backs and legs of horses. Ixion, whom we have already met among the criminals in the Underworld,[1] was the father of Pirithous by Dia, though some said that Zeus had slept with Dia, and he was also the father of Centaurus, who was the father of the race of Centaurs. When Ixion had tried to seduce Hera, the furious Zeus had created a likeness of Hera out of clouds to see how far Ixion would go with his hybristic passion. When he went all the way, he was thrown into the Land of the Damned where he suffered eternal punishment strapped to a turning wheel, and the cloud bore Centaurus from that union. Thus Pirithous and the Centaurs were blood relations.

When Pirithous decided to marry Hippodamia, he felt obligated to invite his kin, the Centaurs, to the marriage feast. The rowdy creatures came but were on their best behavior, pleased at having been invited. Though their intentions were good, they were unaccustomed to wine and they drank too much — unmixed wine at that.

1. See page 81.

One of the Centaurs, Eurytion or Eurytus, fired by the wine, suddenly jumped from the table, grabbed the bride Hippodamia by the hair, and tried to rape her then and there. A violent battle between the drunken Centaurs and the Lapiths followed, and with Theseus' help the Centaurs were defeated. As punishment, Pirithous and Theseus cut off the ears and nose of Eurytion and threw him out of the palace. The uneasy truce that had been in effect between the two peoples had been broken. A war between them followed and ultimately the Centaurs were expelled from their homes on Mount Pelion.

Some time later, when Pirithous was with Theseus in Athens, the two heroes decided that, since each one of them was said to be the son of a god — Pirithous by Zeus and Theseus by Poseidon — it was only right and proper that each of them should marry a daughter of Zeus. After considering the options, they decided first to get Helen, the daughter of Zeus by Leda. Thus they traveled to Sparta. When they found her, she was dancing in a temple of Artemis. Quickly they grabbed her and fled. The Spartans pursued them only as far as Tegea; therefore, they wandered leisurely back to Athens. To decide which of them would get the girl, they cast lots. Theseus won. But Helen was only ten years old — or, some writers say, twelve — so Theseus brought her to his mother, Aethra, at Aphidnae outside of Athens and asked her to take care of her until he could properly marry her.

Pirithous still needed a daughter of Zeus. He decided upon Persephone, wife of Hades, and Theseus, as his sworn friend, had no choice but to aid him in getting her. Consequently, the two heroes entered the Underworld, managed to cross the Styx, and finally were greeted by Hades himself, who knew their intentions. Hades pretended to be delighted to see them and invited them to sit on two stone thrones while he would provide them with entertainment. But the thrones were the Chairs of Forgetfulness and, once seated, neither Theseus nor Pirithous could move. Some say that they grew into the rock and it became one with their flesh; others say that they were held fast by the coils of snakes. Whatever the case, they were caught and seemed doomed to eternity with Hades. Later, however, when Heracles was in the Underworld, he saw the two, and though he was able to save Theseus and bring him back to the world of the living, he was unable to free Pirithous, who remained forever, stuck to his throne.

While Theseus was in the Underworld, **Menestheus**, a direct descendant of Erechtheus, one of the ancestral founders of Athens,

BATTLE BETWEEN THE CENTAURS AND THE LAPITHS. Red-Figured vase attributed to the Painter of Wooly Satyrs, 5th Century B.C. Having violated the laws of hospitality at Pirithous' wedding, Centaurs are in battle with Lapiths. Theseus, one of the guests
at the wedding, wields an ax in the center of the picture and a centaur holds up a pillow
from one of the couches behind him to protect himself. Behind Theseus another centaur
is clearly defeating a punch-drunk Lapith. *Courtesy, Metropolitan Museum of Art, Rogers
Fund, 1907.*

spent much time stirring up the Athenians. He was particularly successful in arousing the ancient noble families. Since Theseus' democratic policies had been particularly offensive to them, they were ripe
for an advocate. He gained unexpected success, furthermore, when
the twin sons of Zeus, Castor and Polydeuces, waged war on Athens
to retrieve their sister Helen. Though Helen was hidden in Aphidnae,
they found her with the help of an informer and took her and Aethra

207

back to Sparta. But before they left, they put Menestheus on the Athenian throne.

When Theseus returned from the Underworld, he was not well received. Menestheus' campaign to discredit him had been successful. The people had quickly forgotten the many good things Theseus had done for them. Depressed and in disgrace, Theseus retired to his family estate on the island of Skyros in order to try to regroup and plan his future moves. But Lycomedes, the King of Skyros, was not eager to have the retired hero in his land. He well remembered Theseus' successes and was worried about his own position. In addition, Menestheus probably urged him to do something about Theseus.

One day, Lycomedes invited Theseus to go with him to the top of the island's highest mountain so that he might survey the country and give the king advice on what improvements could be made. Then, while Theseus was studying the lay of the land from the top of the mountain, Lycomedes gave him a shove and he fell to his death.

Theseus' sons had gone into hiding when Menestheus had come to power, but on his death they returned and retrieved the throne, establishing a line of rulers that went down into historical times. In 473 B.C., Cimon, the commander of the Athenian fleet, sought the grave of Theseus on Skyros. Finding it, he brought the remains back to Athens where they were reburied in the Thesion, a temple near the Acropolis.

Theseus was, without any question, the most important hero for the ancient Athenians. In addition to the deeds mentioned above, he was alleged to have been a member of the party that sought the Calydonian boar and a member of Jason's crew on the *Argo*. When Oedipus left Thebes in disgrace, Theseus accepted him, and when Creon refused to allow the burial of those who challenged Thebes with Polyneices, he completed the burials.

a. While Theseus and some of the stories associated with him are quite ancient, the bulk of his deeds seem to have been attributed to him during the seventh and sixth centuries B.C. Some scholars speculate that the Athenian tyrant Pisistratus (560-527 B.C.) wanted a distinctly local hero associated with his reign. But whatever the cause, Theseus suddenly rose from relative obscurity and became another Heracles, and he remained popular long after the tyranny passed. In fact, he came to symbolize all that was good in Athenian democracy. Unlike Heracles or Jason or Perseus, he did not have a panhellenic appeal, but was specifically the hero of the Athenians. Many of his deeds, however, are clearly patterned on those of Heracles while others embrace traditional folktale motifs.

b. The details of the Hippolytus/Phaedra story vary from source to source. Perhaps the most famous account is in Euripides' play, *Hippolytus,* where Phaedra's love for Hippolytus is divulged to him through a nurse without Phaedra's consent. In an earlier version of the play, Euripides had told the tale as it appears in this chapter; however, the audience was apparently offended at the idea of Phaedra's actively seeking Hippolytus' love, and this first version was unsuccessful.

c. The oracle given to Aegeus is a good example of the ambiguity often associated with prophecies. Not only are the words themselves imprecise, but one wonders where to put the stress. Does one assume, in a positive sense, that Aegeus is now assured of one male heir and that it would be to his advantage to father that son in Athens? Or does one assume, in a negative sense, that Aegeus will forfeit the chance of having a son unless he fathers it in Athens? Though we know the outcome, it is intriguing to try to look at it through his perspective.

d. The following table lists the great rulers of Attica and some of their offspring.

Parents	Ruler	Offspring
	Cecrops m. Aglauros	Aglauros, Herse, Pandrosus, Erysicthon
	Cranaus	
Deucalion m. Pyrrha	Amphictyon	
Hephaistus & Athena	Erichthonius	
	Pandion m. Zeuxippe	Procne, Philomela, Erechtheus, Butes
Pandion m. Zeuxippe	Erechtheus m. Praxithea	Cecrops, Pandorus, Procus
Erechtheus m. Praxithea	Cecrops m. Metiadusa	Pandion
Cecrops m. Metiadusa	Pandion	Aegeus, Pallas, Nisus, Lycus
Pandion	Aegeus & Aethra	Theseus
Aegeus & Aethra	Theseus & Antiope m. Phaedra	Hippolytus Acamas, Demophon

CHAPTER XVII

MYTHS OF LOVE AND PASSION

Daphne and Apollo

The first time that the young Apollo fell in love was with Daphne, the daughter of the river god Peneus. But it was not chance that led him to that love but the spiteful arrows of Eros himself.

Once Apollo happened to meet Eros, who was practicing with his bow and arrow. "What in the world are you doing with weapons like that?" Apollo asked. "Such things aren't toys and should not be in the hands of children like you. They'd be much better off in hands like mine, for I have recently killed the wild Python at Delphi and I have killed innumerable wild beasts. If you want to play at love-making, use a torch or something else. But don't try to move in on my area of archery."

Eros was not about to tolerate such an affront. He waited a few moments as Apollo strutted off, then secured a vantage point on Mount Parnassus, and took out two arrows, a gold one and a lead one. The gold one, the one that arouses desire, he shot at Apollo, and the lead one, the one that repels desire, he shot at Daphne. Immediately Apollo fell hard; his passion and desire for the nymph were overwhelming. Daphne, on the other hand, found even the thought of love repulsive; she was content to wander the fields and woods, engaging in the hunt and devoting herself to Artemis. A number of handsome men courted her, but she had no use for them or for their courtship. Her father would try to reason with her. "Daughter, when am I to be a grandfather? You must not deprive me of that pleasure." But when she begged him to allow her to keep her vows to Artemis, he agreed.

Apollo's passion grew; he was consumed by the fires of his own heart. He looked at her hair, casually thrown to the winds, and he wondered what it would be like if the hair were artfully arranged. He saw her eyes and thought of stars. He saw her lips and wanted them on his. His eyes wandered all over and wanted everything that they beheld; and what he did not see he imagined. But she would have none of him; into the woods she fled. He begged her to stop.

210

He assured her that he meant no harm, that he was no enemy. He encouraged her not to risk injury by running so carelessly through the woods. He even announced who he was: the son of Zeus, the epitome of refinement and sophistication and culture and all that is beautiful. But she did not slow down at all. Like a greyhound, he picked up his pace. Now he was within reach, both of them sprinting just like seasoned runners. But she was getting tired; as eager as she was to avoid her pursuer, she did not have the strength of a god. Looking upon the waters of the Peneus River, her father, she prayed to him for assistance. "Father, if you have any divine power, then use it now. Let the earth divide and devour me. Make me ugly so that I will not draw anyone toward me."

She had scarcely spoken when she felt her body getting heavier, sluggish, droopy. Her torso became hardened with bark, her hair grew into leaves, her arms became branches. The only quality that remained was her beauty and elegance. Apollo recognized what had happened; he embraced the trunk of the tree and began kissing the wood. "You may not be my wife," he said, "but you will be my tree. Wherever I go a part of you will go with me. You shall crown my hair and my lyre and my quiver. You will crown the heads of heroes when they celebrate their triumphs and victories. And since the hair on my head will always remain young and alive, so your leaves will remain green throughout the year and never suffer the pangs of age." The laurel tree seemed to nod assent and shake its top just as if it were a head.

Pyramus and Thisbe

Pyramus and Thisbe were two of the most attractive young people to be found anywhere in the world. They lived next to each other in the city of Babylon and this nearness encouraged both their acquaintance and their friendship and their love. They would have married, but their parents forbade it. But the parents could not forbid with words or edicts the attraction that each had for the other. The two lovers met secretly; no one knew that there was anything between them; a cryptic glance, the slightest of nods, the raising of an eyebrow — these little signs communicated a great deal to both of them. The more they were kept apart, the more their loves grew.

There was a wall between their two houses, and there was a slight hole in one part of that wall. Both the wall and the hole were so old that no one paid any attention to them . . . in fact, no one even noticed that the hole was there. But that hole became a most important thing to the two lovers. They would meet on their respective sides of it, speak to each other, get a slight glimpse of the other, feel each other's breath, but they could go no further.

This type of meeting went on for longer than either could bear, and finally one night they decided that they would flee their homes. Each would sneak out, they would meet by a mulberry tree on the outskirts of town, and then they would leave Babylon and the restrictions of their fathers.

The next day Thisbe made her escape and got to the tree. As she was waiting she saw a lionness in the distance and ran to take protection in a nearby cave. As she fled, however, she dropped her veil. Meanwhile, the lionness, merely looking for a place to drink, had her drink, and went about her business. But as she walked, she saw the veil and tore it apart.

At about the same time, Pyramus made his way to the tree. He saw the tracks of a wild animal; he was late, and when he realized that Thisbe was not there and then saw Thisbe's veil torn to shreds, he knew the worst had happened. He cursed himself for being late, and he invoked the lion to destroy him as it had destroyed his lover. Then he took Thisbe's veil, gave it one last kiss, and plunged a sword into his body, hoping that his blood would mingle with the blood shed by Thisbe when she was attacked by the lion. The blood dripped upon the mulberry tree, and the berries darkened their color.

But now Thisbe, having given the lion enough time to leave, returned. Then she saw Pyramus' body still quivering on the ground. Recognizing him, she shuddered and then went into a panic. She tore her hair, gouged her skin, and embraced that body that could never be hers. Pyramus had just enough life left in him to recognize her. He opened his eyes, gave her one last glance, and then closed them forever.

She realized what had happened and decided to follow him in death. "Oh my parents," she soliloquized, "you have kept us apart in life, but you will not be able to do so in death." And with those words she took his blade and brought it to her own body.

Their parents recognized the error of their bans, and they buried the two lovers in the same tomb. The midsummer night's dream of the two lovers had turned into a nightmare.

Hero and Leander

Hero and Leander were two youths who lived on opposite shores of the Hellespont. Once when Leander was visiting the city of Sestus, he visited the shrine of Aphrodite, where Hero was a priestess. Immediately the two fell wildly in love. Leander returned home to Abydus on the other side of the Hellespont, but his interest in Hero only grew.

Now, for one reason or another, their parents kept them apart, but the lovers remained undaunted. Each night Leander would go to the shore and swim the mile-length of the Hellespont. Hero meanwhile would assist his swim by lighting a bright beacon to guide him. They would spend the night together and he would swim back each morning. This continued for quite a while until one night a violent storm arose. For seven nights the waters raged and for seven nights their desire for each other raged even more fiercely. Leander even thought of taking a boat across the sea, but he feared that word would get back to his family if he were seen. Three times did he try to tackle the sea himself, but the waters proved too hostile.

In one of the few moments of sleep that offered Hero some respite, she had a dream. She saw a dolphin swimming over the rough waves, but its skill was insufficient. It was dashed upon the sands, never again to brave the waters. She feared the dream was an omen. And indeed it was. One evening Leander could bear the separation no longer. He plunged into the waters and began his swim; the winds, however, had blown out Hero's beacon light. The next morning Hero found his body on shore. Unable to bear life without him, she threw herself into the sea.

Zeus and Io

In Thessaly is a beautiful and serene valley known as the Vale of Tempe. Through this valley flows a gentle river, the Peneus. Peneus was still in mourning over the loss of his daughter Daphne, and all the nymphs and rivers of the area were commiserating with Peneus, all except the River Inachus, who himself was bewailing the loss of his own daughter, not knowing whether she were alive or dead but fearing the worst.

It happened that Zeus had seen his daughter, Io, once as she was wandering near her father's stream, and the god immediately took a liking to her. She tried to flee from him, but he overtook her, embraced her in the shape of a huge cloud, and made love to her.

Meanwhile, Hera was looking down from her vantage point on Olympus and wondered why such thick clouds had suddenly deprived the earth of its light from the sun. She commanded the clouds to disperse, wondering whether her husband was again up to some infidelity, for she knew his nature all too well. Zeus, sensing that she was on her way, immediately turned Io into a white cow. But Hera was not fooled. She questioned her husband: What was he doing? Where did this cow come from? Why was he so interested in a mere cow? Zeus lied. He said that the earth had just produced this cow as a gift . . . "Why not a gift for me?" Hera interrupted, and Zeus knew he was trapped. If he did not give away this love of his, he would immediately attract Hera's suspicion.

Therefore, Zeus gave Hera the cow. But Hera, being still suspicious, summoned Argus to guard the gift. Now, Argus had a hundred eyes; while two of these eyes rested, the others would keep a close watch on the cow. No matter which way he faced, some of his eyes would be on Io. Meanwhile the poor girl had to eat the leaves and shrubbery of the area, she had to sleep upon the hard ground, to drink from the muddy streams; when she wanted to stretch her arms in order to beg for mercy from Argus, there were no arms; and when she wanted to call to him in her misery, the only sound she could make was a cow-like low, and this sound frightened her.

Zeus was full of pity for the poor girl. He saw her walk along her father's stream; he saw Inachus offer her a handful of grass and he saw Io lick her father's hand; he heard the tears from the poor creature and he could bear it no longer. He summoned Hermes and ordered that Argus be slain. The messenger of the gods disguised himself as a simple shepherd, walking the land and playing his pipe. When Argus heard the beautiful music, he invited the shepherd to sit and talk, for he had been getting lonely tending the cow all day. They talked for a while, and all the time Hermes kept playing the most soothing music that has ever been heard upon earth. When gradually all his hundred eyes shut and he fell asleep, Hermes slew the watchman, and Argus fell.

Hera was livid. First she took the hundred eyes and put them on her favorite bird, the peacock. Then she sent a gadfly which so irritated the cow that it fled over the whole earth, trying to escape those maddening stings. It even wandered to the Caucasus where it saw Prometheus and asked his assistance. But all Prometheus could say was that it would have many more miles of suffering before it

ARGUS AND HERMES. Attic Red-Figured Vase by the Agrigento Painter, 5th Century B.C. Hermes is about to kill the many-eyed Argus, who is guarding Io, the cow. The anxious Hera watches, holding her scepter. Compare this artist's version of the story with the one told in the text. *Courtesy, Museum of Fine Arts, Boston.*

felt relief. Finally it reached the Nile where it fell to its knees and prayed to Zeus to bring an end to its suffering.

Zeus could bear its misery no longer. He sidled up to Hera and swore by the River Styx that Hera would never have to concern herself with Io if only Hera would spare the maiden. Hera had mercy. She brought the girl back to her former shape, and the only remnant of her former self was the whiteness of her skin.

Eros and Psyche

There was once a king who had three daughters, all of them beautiful, but of whom the third and youngest was by far the most beautiful creature imaginable. Her beauty was compared with that of Aphrodite's and it was not long before she was reverenced as a new Aphrodite. People came from far and wide just to see her and she,

215

without realizing how powerful was her beauty, unwittingly infused both young and old with distracting passion.

The goddess Aphrodite, seeing that no one was paying her much attention and that her temples and shrines were becoming filled with dust, was pricked with contempt. "I am supposed to share my name with some flossie! No, this cannot be. I'll get her!" And she plotted revenge.

She went up to her winged son, Eros, that rash and head-strong young man who with all his bad habits was upsetting all law and order; equipped with fire and arrows he would run around from house to house during the night and spoil marriages, causing all kinds of trouble . . . in fact, doing nothing good. But was he ever caught? Well, once in a while caught, but never punished. Now, bad enough what he was able to do on his own! But Aphrodite went up to him and egged him on toward greater mischief. She pointed out her rival, whose name was Psyche, and she cajoled her son into making that young thing squirm. She persuaded him to make her fall in love with the most ugly, vile, filthy, mean, poor, loathsome creature alive. Having gained his cooperation, she left.

Meanwhile poor Psyche enjoyed none of the attention she was getting. Furthermore, though all sorts of people admired her, she wasn't getting anywhere. Her two sisters were already married to kings and here she was spending her evenings alone in boring virginity. Her father, suspecting that something was amiss, consulted an oracle of Apollo. Apollo, prompted by Eros as might be expected, said that Psyche should be dressed in funeral clothes, left on the summit of a certain high hill, and would be claimed by a husband, savage, viper-ous, and winged.

Mother, father, and Psyche, townspeople — everyone mourned the fate of this dear girl. But an oracle was an oracle: it was tanta-mount to a direct order from the gods themselves. She was left on the hill, trembling, weeping, when suddenly a gentle puff from the West Wind came upon her and led her into a deep valley laden with flowers and rich green grass. Not far from this dell was a spectacular palace with ivory carvings, pillars of gold, and walls of silver. The paths were not of cobblestone but of gems, and the place looked like one fitting for Zeus himself.

When she entered the house, the splendor there fully match-ing the magnificence of the outside, she heard a voice. The voice re-assured her that all was well, guided her through the house, con-ducted her to her rooms and to her meals; and that evening under the cloak of darkness, that voice, this time with full bodily complement,

216

joined her in bed and they consummated their marriage.

Eventually her sisters came looking for her. Her husband-voice only with greatest reluctance allowed them a visit, and a short one it was, for as soon as he could, he made sure that they were on their way. Naturally they were entertained lavishly during their stay, and Psyche gave them as much gold and jewelry as they could carry. Naturally, they were not only suspicious but incensed with jealousy as they left Psyche, especially since they hadn't even seen her husband, whom Psyche had described as being young, stately, and just beginning to put aside the bloom of his youth. "Drat," said one of them; "what right does she have to such treasure . . . and to such a husband. My husband is as bald as a pumpkin, more doddering than a baby, and whatever he has he keeps hoarded to himself." "What are you complaining about," rejoined the other sister; "my husband is lame, shriveled, and smells of salves, balms, and ointments; and he is about as potent as warm wax. I don't know about you, sister dear, but I can't bear to see our young sister flaunting such luck." And so the two of them plotted.

Meanwhile her husband, still unseen by her although she frequently felt his presence, kept on warning her about those perfidious sisters. He told her that she was going to have a child who would be a god if the identity of the father was kept a secret but who would be mortal otherwise. She was delighted, but she did wonder what was happening to herself when she saw her mid-parts begin to swell.

At the same time the envy and rancor of those two vipers was also swelling but, in spite of warnings from her husband, Psyche was overjoyed when she heard that those sisters were again eager for a visit. Of course they put on a grand show when the three of them were reunited. When they asked her about her husband, the poor little thing forgot what she had told them the previous year and replied that he was just a merchant, middle aged, who was now on a business trip. They picked up the fabrication immediately, although they remained silent. A few days later they invited her to have a heart to heart talk. They told her that her husband was a huge poisonous snake; they reminded her that the oracle had prophesied that she would marry a monster; and they told her that on their way they had seen such a creature swimming in a nearby river. Finally, they assured her that the creature's intention was to eat her up just as she was about to give birth, for monsters like that had a fondness for heavy women. Then they convinced her to take a knife with her to bed and to slay the beast when he was off his guard. Having convinced her, they left.

She did what they had advised; yet she kept that knife next to her with some ambivalence. After all, she did love her husband. Nonetheless, when the time came, she prepared herself to stab. But curiosity got the better of her; she took a lamp and lighted it when she was sure her husband was asleep. And what did she see but Eros himself in all his splendor lying next to her, the handsomest of all males: golden hair, ambrosial locks, ivory white neck, rose red cheeks, winged shoulders, and totally smooth skin; and at his feet lay his bow and arrows. In her excitement she accidentally pricked herself on one of those arrows and accidentally dripped a few drops of oil on her husband, who promptly awoke, realized what had happened, realized that his identity was no longer a secret, chastized her for lack of trust and breach of faith, and promptly fled.

She was about to kill herself out of grief and remorse when she fortunately came upon Pan sitting at the side of a river. Pan solaced her; he told her that Eros was not an adamant person, that he was very susceptible to flattery, and that she should stop crying and try to win back her husband. And so she set off on a hunt for him. In the process she came upon one of her sisters and told her what had happened. But she understood a bit more this time, and she added an important detail. She said that when her husband had rejected her, he had commented that he was going to go after the sister.

The sister, overjoyed at the thought of such a splendid union, climbed to the top of a hill and gave herself to Eros, who, she remembered, had appeared to Psyche as the West Wind when he had claimed her. She summoned the god, threw herself into the wind, but no god caught her: she left parts of her body scattered over the rocks on which she smashed. Psyche then repeated her tale to the other sister who also promptly splattered herself over the countryside.

Meanwhile, Psyche looked everywhere for her husband. She came upon a temple to Demeter, asked Demeter's aid, but the goddess had heard of Aphrodite's hatred for Psyche and thought it best not to get involved. Hera felt the same way; it was not wise to interfere with Aphrodite. And their instincts were not wrong, for Aphrodite was as livid as ever. And when she heard that the mortal was going to bear a child, her wrath grew even more severe. "I am to be the grandmother of some whim of my irresponsible son who couldn't sit still long enough to do what I had asked him to do!" Then, through her friend Hermes, she put out a summons that whoever was able to find the wretched Psyche and deliver her would be rewarded.

The summons had its effect. Within a short time the girl was before her mother-in-law. The goddess had her flogged and tortured

218

and barraged her with abusive language. Finally she took six bushel bags, each containing a different grain, emptied those bags, and mixed up all the grain. She then ordered the girl to separate the types before nightfall. The girl despaired; this was an impossible task. But an ant saw her weeping, recognized her as the wife of the mighty Eros, and enlisted the aid of all the other ants in the area, who promptly separated all the grains.

When Aphrodite returned, she was furious. Not daunted in her revenge, however, she assigned the maiden another task: to clip some fleece from a flock of especially obstreperous sheep. This time a reed in the fields gave her an idea. She waited until late afternoon when the flock napped, gently entered their midst, and easily cut off a piece of wool. Again Aphrodite was foiled. The next day she ordered Psyche to fetch her a cup of water from a particularly treacherous stream. Again Psyche was assisted: this time by an eagle, who took her jar and filled it himself. Finally, Aphrodite sent her to visit Persephone in the Underworld and to fetch some of Persephone's beauty powder.

Psyche was sure that this mission would have to be her last; after all, how could she get to the Underworld except through death. But this time, as she was about to throw herself off a tower, the tower gave her explicit instructions on how to beat death. First, she should go to Sparta and find Taenarum; in that place was a cave that led directly into Tartarus. Secondly, she should carry two pieces of bread soaked with honey and barley; this food she should give to Cerberus when she entered and when she left. Thirdly, she should have two coins to give to Charon, one to take her across the Styx, the other for her return journey. Fourth, she should pay no attention to a corpse that would beg for assistance. Fifth, she should not give any assistance to certain old women who would be weaving and asking for help. These would just be ruses from Aphrodite to get her to drop her bread and money. Finally, she was under no condition to open the box containing Persephone's cosmetics.

She did as she had been bidden; she entered the Underworld, she crossed the Styx, she resisted the wails of the corpse in the water, she ignored the plaintive pleas of the old women, she distracted Cerberus with her bread, and she paid Charon. But she could not resist the box. "Why should Aphrodite have all the tricks?" she thought. But when she opened the box, there was merely a puff of smoke, and Psyche fell to the ground.

Meanwhile, Eros, who had been in seclusion nursing the wound on his shoulder from the oil which Psyche had accidentally spilled on him that fateful night, was just about better. His mother had locked him in his room, but he managed to escape. He went right to Zeus and stated his problem. Now, Zeus was very fond of Eros, for Eros had given the Thunderer many pleasures; but Zeus also realized what a nuisance the young god could be, for, because of Eros, Zeus had gotten into his share of trouble. Therefore, he called an assembly of all the immortals, and he made an important proclamation. "Aphrodite, put aside your indignation. You will have nothing to be ashamed of. I will make this girl immortal and I will insist that there be a legal and binding marriage between your son and the girl."

This seemed pleasing to everyone. Eros went down to the Underworld, found Psyche still sleeping there, removed the smoke from her eyes and put it back into the box, took her overjoyed up to Olympus, and was married. There was a tremendous feast. Eros and Psyche sat together; nearby sat Zeus and Hera and then all the other gods and goddesses. Ganymede served Zeus, and Dionysus filled the cups of everyone else. Hephaistus prepared the meal; the Horae set the table with garlands of flowers; the Graces spread fragrances; the Muses sang; Apollo played the harp; Aphrodite danced; and good cheer prevailed.

And when Eros and Psyche finally did have their baby, they named it Pleasure.

Myths concerning love affairs are as common as myths dealing with transformations, and the two types are often inextricably connected. All one needs to do is to look at the stories in Chapter XII and at the summaries of the transformation myths in Appendix II and the connection will be clear. A very high percentage of the myths cited there could also be included under love affairs. One of the reasons is that the transformation is often a result of the type of love: a pure love will lead to a transformation that is beautiful; a sordid love will lead to one that is horrible; an unnatural love will lead to an unnatural transformation. A god may punish someone for not yielding or reward someone else for yielding. Mythology is indeed studded with love stories. They may be beautiful or violent or sordid or tragic; they may be natural or unnatural; they may be realistic or figurative or symbolic or aetiological. But they are omnipresent.

Trying to categorize the various types of love stories is dangerous, since categorization often becomes procrustean. Nonetheless, there are some prevalent types, although even these types overlap considerably. The following categories are meant merely to be suggestive and descriptive; they are not meant to be the final word on any of the stories.

a. Pure love — the type that any human might want for himself, such as the love between Philemon and Baucis, Perseus and Andromeda, Ceyx

220

and Alcyone. This type of love predicates total and selfless devotion. Life is not worth living without one's husband or wife. When Ceyx dies, all his soul can do is worry about Alcyone; and when she hears of his drowning, she plunges into the sea to join him. Naturally both are metamorphosed into birds and eternally fly together.

b. Familial love — the type of affection that one has for members of one's family or for very close friends, such as that of Patroclus for Achilles, Eos for her son Memnon, the sisters of Phaeton for their brother.

c. Prince Charming love — this type is uncommon in classical times but quite common in Hellenistic or in late Roman times when writers told romances. The Eros and Psyche story best illustrates this motif.

d. The Romeo and Juliet motif — again this type is not common in classical times but appears in later traditions. The Pyramus and Thisbe story is the best example.

e. The Beauty and the Beast motif — the story of Polyphemus and Galatea and of Pan and Syrinx are examples: the ugly monster and the innocent young maiden who is horrified by him.

f. Ill-fated love — such as Orpheus' for Eurydice or such as the love between Pyramus and Thisbe or Hero and Leander. In spite of the best of intentions and of deep emotional bonds, the love is frustrated.

g. Destructive love — such as Medea's for Jason or Phaedra's for Hippolytus. The lover loves so much that she will do anything to secure the object of her desires. When she fails, she usually destroys. Such a love is usually sent by the gods for one reason or another. Another type occurs when a mortal offends a god and the god punishes that person with a destructive love, such as Echo's for Narcissus, Pasiphae's for the bull, or Myrrha's for her father.

h. Triangle myths — a divinity is jealous because the object of his or her love loves someone else. Usually the subject of these two loves suffers. Hera punishes Semele and Io because of Zeus' love; she wreaks her vengeance upon Alcmena and Heracles, not upon Zeus; Zephyrus turns the discus against Hyacinth, not Apollo; Circe punishes Scylla, not Glaucus.

i. The Frame-up — this type is a variation of the previous two types. Here A loves B but B will not return A's love. A becomes angry and tries to frame B. When Hippolytus will not acknowledge Phaedra's love, she slanders him to Theseus. When Peleus (the later husband of Thetis) will not acknowledge the love of Acastus' wife, she makes up a story about him. Proetus' wife did the same to Bellerophon when he would not go along with her passion for him. In all three cases the wife lies to the husband, telling him that the third party has tried to seduce her, and invariably the husband then tries to kill that third party. This is often referred to as the "Potiphar's wife" motif, after the *Old Testament* story of Joseph.

j. Unnatural love — this type is usually a combination of some of the other types just mentioned. Rarely is unnatural love a positive quality;

221

most of the time it is destructive, such as Pasiphae's for the bull, Myrrha's for her father, and Nyctimene's for her father. Usually such passions are sent by the gods as punishments. One of the few unnatural loves that thrives is Pygmalion's for his statue; but then he has always respected Aphrodite, and she rewards his loyalty.

k. Figurative love — this type occurs when love is used to explain what was probably some natural phenomenon. Hylas, for instance, is said to have been pulled into a stream by a nymph who admired his beauty; in fact, he probably merely drowned for one reason or another.

★   ★   ★

There have been some very famous pairs of lovers or would-be lovers in classical mythology; The following list cites some of them; the stories have been told elsewhere in this volume:

Daphne and Apollo	Echo and Narcissus
Pyramus and Thisbe	Perseus and Andromeda
Psyche and Eros	Jason and Medea
Aphrodite and Adonis	Philemon and Baucis
Pygmalion and Galatea	Apollo and Hyacinth
Orpheus and Eurydice	Alcestis and Admetus
Peleus and Thetis	Hero and Leander
Zeus and Europa	Polyphemus and Galatea
Theseus and Ariadne	Pan and Syrinx

Keeping straight the myriad of love affairs among the gods is difficult, among the humans even more difficult, and among the gods and humans still more difficult. As a rule, however, it seems that a mortal woman pursued by a god does not usually suffer unless a goddess gets jealous and ruins the woman or unless the woman is arrogant, in which case she is sure to be ruined. But otherwise there seem to be two chief patterns. Either the mortal woman graciously or unknowingly accepts the god's advances and gives birth to a son that rises above mere mortals. Or else she flees the god and is merely transformed into a river or a tree or a bird or something similar.

The list in Appendix III may help in getting an overview of the gods' amorous pursuits. Not all the loves or passions have been cited, merely some of the more famous or significant ones. From that list one can make a few observations. 1. Zeus tends to be successful in his loves, although Hera often interferes. His offspring tend to be the founders of important cities. 2. Poseidon tends to breed monsters and generally unattractive or villainous sons. 3. Apollo tends to have offspring that are civilizing forces, offspring that in one way or another advance human refinement and culture. His loves, however, usually result in tragedy for either the woman or for her offspring. There is often a touch of misfortune or sadness connected with Apollo's loves. 4. The goddesses, on the other hand, tend not to show much erotic interest in mortals, but they do have favorites among mortal men, whom they watch quite solicitously. If they have affections they tend to save them for the gods. And woe be to the mortal who dares to presume upon a goddess: Ixion's desire for Hera, Tityus' for Leto, Orion's for Artemis all led them to destruction Almost the only mortal male to reap a productive harvest from union with a goddess was Anchises, who with Aphrodite fathered Aeneas.

★   ★   ★

Eros became Cupid to the Romans, and the Roman Cupid is the image that by and large has come down to us.

Eros features prominently in a lot of myths, for he is the one who prompts both gods and men to do outrageous things. But usually he is in the background. There is one story, however, in which he has top billing, and that is the story of Eros and Psyche. It is a long story — actually more a romance than a myth — told in the second century A.D. by Apuleius in his *Golden Ass*. The version told here is a drastic abridgement of the original, but even this sketch will indicate several of the motifs in folklore: the solicitous parents, the jealous and wicked sisters, the ingenuous and even simple-minded beauty who learns the hard way, the transition from innocence to experience, the mysterious lover who turns out to be a god/prince-charming, the vindictive mother-in-law, the attempt to destroy by means of assigning impossibly difficult tests or quests, the surmounting of these quests because of one's innate goodness, the folly of curiosity, the ambiguous prophecy, the benevolent father/king who serves as arbiter and eases all the ruffled feathers, the "and they lived happily ever after" conclusion. The story is fraught with ideas that appear over and over again in folk tales.

One can see from the tale of Eros and Psyche how emasculated the gods have become. They are a far cry from the majesty of the Olympians. They have charm but little dignity. And certainly there is nothing religious about them. Even the mighty Hephaistus is nothing more than a cook. The final scene can well remind us of aunts and uncles and cousins and various and sundry in-laws bustling around making preparations and adding final touches at a family wedding. Hera and Demeter remind us of elderly aunts who don't want to get involved. And even Zeus isn't much more than the wise old grandfather who takes everything in stride and who can usually solve all problems. And Psyche! She could come right out of a nineteenth-century English novel: the ingenuous, victimized, gullible, stupid, silly little innocent — almost a twin sister of Lucie Manette or Amelia Sedley. The story is marvelous entertainment but not much more.

Erich Neumann in his *Amor and Psyche* (Bollingen Series, Princeton) presents a sophisticated and lucid psychological interpretation of the story.

CHAPTER XVIII

PLATO: THE LITERARY MYTH

Plato (429-347 B.C.), one of the great philosophers and writers of the ancient Greek world, used and perfected the dialogue form as a vehicle for his ideas. While a discussion of that form or of those ideas, as he developed them in nearly thirty extant works, is far beyond the scope and purpose of this book, Plato is included here because of his unique use of myth. In several of his dialogues, he created new myths as a means of expressing ideas that he found difficult to express effectively in direct speech, and some of these myths have come down as a part of the heritage of western literature and art. Some of his myths borrow from ancient stories, while others are entirely new creations. Three examples of Plato's myths are included — perhaps the three most famous ones — and the chapter concludes with a list of references to several other myths in his dialogues.

Man's original form and the nature of love

In his dialogue Symposium, *Plato has the comic playwright Aristophanes tell the following story at a drinking party in honor of the playwright, Agathon. (198, C — 193, D)*

Man did not always look as he does now. In fact, originally he was quite different. Instead of just two sexes, there were originally three: there was the male and there was the female, but there was a third called the male/female, who had characteristics of both. The males came from the Sun, the females from the Earth, and the male/females came from the Moon, which has characteristics of both. A more important difference, however, was that all three sexes were globular in shape, with four arms and four legs. They had cylindrical necks topped with a head that had faces front and back and four ears. Each of the three sexes had two sets of genitals: two male, two female, or one male and one female. They propagated as grasshoppers or crickets do, the female laying eggs on the ground to be fertilized by the male.

These original humans were tremendously powerful and energetic. Usually they walked upright on their four legs, but when they wanted to move quickly, they stuck out all eight of their limbs and rolled like cartwheels — in this way they were capable of terrific downhill speeds. But along with their speed and strength, they also had a large dose of arrogance. Not satisfied to be mere mortals, they decided to storm the heavens — like Otus and Ephialtes — and assault the gods.

Zeus, when he learned of this plan, met in counsel with the other gods to decide what should be done about the mortals. The gods had a problem: on the one hand, they enjoyed the sacrifices and honors that they received from the mortals, so they didn't want to destroy them outright — but, on the other hand, they couldn't tolerate this outrageous behavior. After much soul searching, Zeus came up with a brilliant plan. He would cut each of the mortals in half; thus, there would be twice as many to make offerings to the gods, but each would be only half as strong. They would still be able to walk, but now on only two legs, and if they continued to be obstreperous, Zeus warned, they would be split again and would have to hop on one.

So, Zeus enlisted the aid of Apollo, and the two carried out the plan. Zeus did the splitting, and then Apollo patched up the parts. First he turned the remaining face so that it faced the open wound. Then he pulled the skin from the edges, stretching it over the belly, and tied it like a sack, thus leaving the navel. He smoothed most of the remaining wrinkles with a cobbler's tool — leaving just enough to be a reminder and a warning — and he roughly fashioned the chest. And once the operation was finished, each of the halves embraced the other, yearning to be reunited.

When Zeus looked down on the halved mortals, he realized that he had made one strategic miscalculation. The halves kept clinging to each other, and they were dying of starvation. They had no incentive to do anything but cling. If one half died, the other half went wandering, embracing others at random, hoping to find another half. Zeus felt sorry for the mortals and, deciding that he would have to do something for them, he came up with another idea. He moved the genitals, which were still grasshopper fashion on the backside, to the front. Thus, if a half male happened to embrace a half female, he might in the process conceive a child. If a half male embraced a half male, he would at least get some relief and could go on with the business of daily life. And when Zeus looked down again, he saw that his plan was a brilliant success. Mortals were again functioning and making offerings to the gods.

Now when we say that someone is in love, we mean that he is

225

seeking that primeval wholeness that was lost because of mortal sinfulness. Each of us seeks our other half; but we must always remember that there is the chance that we will be split again if we forget our places.

Appearance and reality: the allegory of the cave

Plato has Socrates develop the simile of the cave in a dialogue with a young man named Glaucon at the beginning of Book VII of the Republic. *The two are talking about the effect of education on our nature. (514, a — 517, a)*

Imagine a great, underground cavern with an entrance open to light all along one end of it. Men live in that cave under curious circumstances. Since childhood, they have been chained by their necks and feet so that they cannot move. Being unable to turn their heads, they can look only straight ahead. Some distance behind these men, and somewhat above them, a fire burns constantly. Between the fire and the prisoners, there is a roadway with a wall built along one side of it. Men go along this road, carrying on their shoulders all sorts of things: jars and statues and figures of animals made of wood and stone and other materials; but only the objects they carry rise above the wall. Some of the men talk as they go along the road, others are silent.

The chained prisoners can see nothing of themselves and nothing of those around them, but see only the shadows cast by the fire on the wall in front of them. On that wall they see shadows of the objects that are carried along the road behind them. And the cave has an echo so that when the men on the road speak, it sounds to the prisoners as if the shadows on the wall are speaking.

Now imagine what will happen if one of these prisoners is freed. Forced to stand up and walk toward the light, he will experience much discomfort. His stiff limbs will ache from lack of use, and he will be blinded by the brilliant light of day. In the glare, he will have trouble even seeing the objects, the shadows of which he had learned well in his former state. Even when his eyes adjust, if he is told that the objects he now looks at passing along the road on the shoulders of men are more real than the shadows he saw and knew before, he will have trouble believing that. He will even have trouble recognizing and naming the objects, though he had names for their shadows. He will be confused and will probably refuse to believe

226

those who tell him that these are reality, preferring to believe that the shadows he knows so well are the reality.

Imagine that this freed prisoner is dragged up out of the cavern into the bright light of day. It will take him some time to grow accustomed to the sights of the upper world. At first he will see shadows best, then he will be able to see reflections in the water, and finally he will see the objects themselves. At first, night will be more comfortable to him than day, and he will prefer the moon and the stars, but finally he will be able to tolerate the sun itself.

Imagine then what will happen if he returns to his old cave and tries to tell his friends, still chained in place, that they are only looking at shadows of reality. In the cave the prisoners have established honors and commendations for those who are quickest at identifying shadows, showing the relations between them, and predicting sequences. Surely the prisoners are going to be hesitant to give up what they know so well. Resisting his new knowledge, perhaps they will challenge him to a contest in identifying and evaluating shadows. His eyes now accustomed to the light of day, he will make a poor showing, and they will laugh at him. They will say that he returned with his eyes ruined and that one should beware of the ascent from the cave. If they could, they would probably kill the man who tried to release them and lead them up.

Atlantis: the lost island

In the Timaeus *(24, e — 25, d) Plato has Critias introduce the tale of the war between Athens and Atlantis. Critias says that Egyptian priests told the tale to a friend of his great-grandfather, and that the conflict was supposed to have taken place nine thousand years before. In the* Critias *(113, a — 121, c) Critias describes the civilization of Atlantis in some detail, but for unknown reasons the dialogue was never finished.*

Beyond the Pillars of Heracles there was once a huge island called Atlantis. Bigger than Libya and Asia put together, it was a tremendously rich and powerful island, and at one point in the distant past it waged war on the whole of Europe and Asia. From the Pillars of Heracles its armies conquered Libya as far as Egypt and Europe as far as Tyrrhenia, when they met the Athenians. Alone, the Athenians defeated them. But soon afterwards there was a great earthquake and flood which, though it lasted for only a single day, killed all the

227

Athenian soldiers and caused the entire island of Atlantis to sink into the sea, never to be seen again.

In the center of Atlantis was a very fertile and beautiful plain, and in the center of that plain was a low mountain. Evenor, one of the original earth-born men of Atlantis, lived there with his wife Leucippe and their daughter Clito. Just when Clito reached marriageable age, both her parents died. When the Olympian gods had drawn lots to divide their jurisdiction over the various parts of the earth, Poseidon had drawn Atlantis, and now he decided that he would have Clito as his own. Thus he built protection for the mountain, making it into an impregnable island. Around it he put alternate rings of water and land — three of water and two of land. He made food plants of all kinds grow there and provided fountains of both hot and cold water. Then he slept there with Clito and by her had five sets of twins.

Atlas was the oldest of the ten children of Clito and Poseidon, and the island and the ocean surrounding it were named after him. Though the island was divided up among the ten brothers, Atlas was the supreme ruler and lived on the acropolis Poseidon had created for his mother Clito. For many generations the descendants of Atlas ruled the island benevolently. There were abundant mines and forests on Atlantis. Wild and domestic animals grew in great numbers, and there was a profusion of fruit and grain. The island was entirely self-sufficient.

Atlas' acropolis was the most holy site on the island, and there a great trading port grew up. The people of the island bridged the rings of water, so that there was easy access to the city, and they dug a canal from the sea to the outer ring to make a safe harbor. Near the spot where Poseidon had lain with Clito, they built a gigantic temple to the god, sheathing it in silver. The figures on the pediment of the temple they sheathed in gold. The two springs provided bathing for all and irrigation for the crops. Because of this irrigation, the people were able to harvest two crops a year.

Though they had tremendous wealth, the people of the island were humble and virtuous from the start. They lived peacefully together and were satisfied with what they had, though they never took prosperity for granted. They understood that all things increase from virtue and mutual love. But as time passed and the initial infusion of divine blood in the people weakened with each new genera-

228

tion, the behavior of the people became less gentle. They began to take pride in their power and wealth and to covet the wealth of others.

Zeus saw what was happening to the people of Atlantis and was disturbed. He decided to discipline them and, gathering all the gods in his palace, he said to them . . . . (*Here Critias' story ends.*)

Other important myths in Plato:

Phaedo (107, d - 114, c) — Socrates on the afterlife.

Gorgias (523, a - 527, a) — judgment of the soul by Socrates

Protagoras (320, d — 322, d) — The sophist, Protagoras, tells of creation and the potential of living creatures and how politics came about.

Phaedrus (246, a - 257, b) — Socrates tells of the soul, like a charioteer with two horses, and of love.

Symposium — speeches on love: Phaedrus' (178, a - 180, b)
Pausanias' (180, d - 185, c)
Eryximachus' (186, a - 188, d)
Agathon's (195, a - 197, e)
Socrates' (203, b - 204, a)

Republic (Book X, 614, b - 621, d) — myth of Er.

CHAPTER XIX

ROMAN MYTHOLOGY

There is little truly Roman mythology. Most of the Roman stories of the gods are thinly disguised Greek myths. Likewise, the Roman heroes bear a remarkable resemblance to Greek heroes, except that the former are used more heavily for pseudo-historical purposes. Where the Greek myths often reflected a profound and important dimension of Greek religious life, the Roman myths were primarily decorative or used to illustrate some practical or historical problem.

The Italic tribes that moved into Italy from Central Europe in the second millenium B.C. brought with them gods who were not anthropomorphic but rather were vague forces that animated many aspects of nature and human experience. The Etruscans, however, who seem to have come to Italy from Asia Minor during the early years of the first millenium B.C., brought with them a lively, although death oriented, mythology. Conquering Latium in the seventh century, the Etruscans actually founded Rome by uniting the hill cities under one rule. Though the Etruscans are still a mysterious race to us, we do know that they found some aspects of Greek art and culture tremendously appealing. For example, they provided an important market for Greek painted vases, and many of the illustrations in this book come from Greek vases found in Etruscan tombs. The Etruscan kings seem to have imposed Etruscan and Greek culture on the Romans. In addition, the Greeks established colonies in southern Italy and Sicily starting in the eighth century B.C., providing another contact the Romans had with Greek culture.

By the time the Romans had overthrown the Etruscan kings at the beginning of the fifth century B.C., they had absorbed much that was Greek. They seem to have applied the names they had for their vague forces to Greek gods who came closest to representing those forces. They created few new stories to go with their gods but rather adopted the traditional Greek stories. Some of the most important equivalents are listed below:

Aphrodite	— Venus	Hephaistus	— Vulcan
Ares	— Mars	Hera	— Juno
Artemis	— Diana	Heracles	— Hercules
Athena	— Minerva	Hermes	— Mercury

Cronos	— Saturn	Hestia	— Vesta
Demeter	— Ceres	Hypnos	— Somnus
Dionysus } Bacchus }	— { Liber { Bacchus	Leto	— Latona
		Moirae	— Parcae
Eos	— Aurora	Muses	— Musae, Camenae
Erinyes } Eumenides }	— { Dirae { Furiae	Ouranos	— Coelus
		Persephone	— Proserpina
Eros	— Cupid	Poseidon	— Neptune
Gaia	— Terra	Rhea	— Ops, Magna Mater
Hades } Pluto }	— { Dis { Pluto	Selene	— Luna
		Zeus	— Jup(p)iter, Jove
Helios	— Sol		

The Romans could find no equivalent for Apollo, and thus he came into their mythology with his Greek name. His son Asclepius, whom we have already seen as the father of medicine, was imported, along with his cult, in the third century to deal with a particularly bothersome plague; the Romans corrupted his name to Aesculapius. On the other hand, there was one important Roman force for whom there was no Greek equivalent — **Janus**. He was envisioned, in anthropomorphic form, as a man with faces front and back. He was the spirit of the doorway. With his two faces he could see comings and goings. He was an ancient Italic force and seems originally to have been associated in some way with the new moon. The month of January is named after him.

Every people needs its foundation myth, and the Romans first created theirs in the story of Romulus and Remus. As the story goes, Procas once ruled the city of Alba Longa in the Alban Mountains, near the present Rome. When he died, he left his throne to his oldest son, the virtuous **Numitor**. But his second son, **Amulius**, contested his brother's right to rule and ultimately expelled him. Amulius, however, was not comfortable on his throne. Numitor had a daughter, Rhea Silvia, and Amulius, afraid that she might produce offspring who would seek revenge, devised a plan. Pretending that he was doing her a great honor, he had Rhea Silvia made one of the Vestal Virgins, thus insuring that she would never have children. But his plans were foiled when Mars came and lay with the girl, and she produced twins. Worried, and not prepared to believe that the twins were sons of Mars, Amulius had them put in a box and set adrift in the Tiber. The Tiber, however, flooded, and rather than floating out to sea as Amulius had planned, the box came to rest on one of the river's banks. There a she-wolf found the twins and fed them from her breasts.

231

Later the twins, named **Romulus** and **Remus**, were discovered by the shepherd Faustulus, who brought them to his wife Acca Larantia. The boys were brought up as the shepherd's sons and followed his profession. One day, after they had matured, the young men got into a quarrel with shepherds from Alba Longa. When the quarrel became heated, Remus was taken prisoner and brought to Amulius. The flocks belonged to Numitor, who was living under his brother's rule, so the captive was sent to him. Somehow Numitor realized that the shepherd was his grandson and together they plotted the overthrow of Amulius. Romulus, who had come to find his brother, aided in the implementation of the plot, and the two brothers returned Numitor to his rightful throne.

Ambitious young men, the two brothers decided, after restoring Numitor, that they should found a city that would far outshine Alba Longa. They decided that the place for the city was surely the spot where the she-wolf had found them; therefore, they returned to that place to make the necessary preparations. One problem faced them, however. Two people couldn't be founding fathers of a city. Thus, they decided to take auspices by watching birds to find out which of them would be the founder. Romulus stood on the Palatine Hill and Remus stood on the Aventine, and they both watched the skies. First Remus saw six vultures circling over the hills, but immediately afterwards Romulus saw twelve. Remus claimed that he would be the founder because he had seen the birds first; but Romulus said, no, he had seen more, and he immediately began to build his walls. The furious Remus jumped over his brother's new walls to mock him, and Romulus promptly killed him. No one was going to jump over his walls — then or ever after!

The new city needed settlers, and thus Romulus opened it to outcasts and lawless men expelled from other cities. It became an asylum. Though many men came, the nature of the population kept women and respectable men away. Clearly the city couldn't survive without women, so Romulus formulated a plan. He invited the neighboring people, the **Sabines**, to a festival in celebration of the founding of the city. But once the Sabine men and women were within the walls of the city, the Roman men attacked on a prearranged signal, chasing off the men and capturing the women. Thus the men found wives.

The Sabine men were outraged at this breach of hospitality. Even though the women communicated to their fathers and former husbands that they were quite happy with their new situations, the Sabine men decided to attack Rome. With the aid of the traitoress

Tarpeia, they were on the verge of taking the city when Romulus prayed to Jupiter, promising him a magnificent temple in the city if he would aid them. Jupiter heard the prayer and turned the tide of the battle. Ultimately the two peoples reached a reconciliation, and Titus Tatius, the king of the Sabines, ruled Rome with Romulus. Unfortunately, Tatius was soon killed in a feud, and from then on Romulus ruled on his own.

AENEAS AND ANCHISES. Attic Red-Figured Vase by the Altamura Painter, 5th Century B.C. The Trojan Aeneas carries his venerable father, Anchises, from the burning city. *Courtesy, Museum of Fine Arts, Boston.*

One day, after many years of ruling and after Rome had become an important city, Romulus went to the plain near the Lake of Capra to review his troops. While he was passing the men in review, a violent windstorm accompanied by an eclipse of the sun came upon them, and when it had passed, Romulus had disappeared. It was concluded that Romulus had been taken up to Heaven and thus he was later officially deified as the god Quirinus.

As the Romans became a more powerful force in the Mediterranean, they found the need for a more illustrious genealogy. **Aeneas,** the son of Aphrodite by **Anchises,** had been an important figure in Etruscan mythology. Aeneas' rescue of his father from the burning Troy was a popular theme in their art, but the popularity had passed with the passing of the Etruscans. The Romans, however, resurrected Aeneas and made him the father of the Roman people. Vergil's *Aeneid*, written during the latter half of the first century B.C., traced Aeneas' journey from Troy to Italy. After many difficulties, he finally arrived on mainland Italy, where he married Lavinia, the daughter of King Latinus, and founded the city of Lavinium. There he deposited the sacred Trojan images he had brought with him. His son, **Ascanius,** founded Alba Longa after Aeneas' death and Romulus and Remus were his descendants through Procas and Numitor.

One dimension of mythology that the Romans invented, independent of the Greeks, was the concept of emperor worship. In the final book of his *Metamorphoses,* Ovid writes of the deification of Julius Caesar, who claimed his descent from Aeneas. When Venus looked down and saw that Caesar was about to be murdered, she tried to veil him in the cloud she had used to hide Aeneas, his forefather, from Diomedes. But Jupiter stopped her and told her that it was Caesar's fate to leave the earth. He had completed his earthly tasks and now should join the gods in heaven. Thus, as he was killed, Venus met his soul and brought it with herself to join the gods. She knew, too, of the even greater deeds that his stepson, Augustus would do.

Julius Caesar was the first historical ruler to be deified — Romulus, also deified, had been a mythic ruler — though the deification took place after his death. Augustus was the first emperor to be deified during his lifetime and thus established a precedent that was to become an important dimension of Roman civic religion up to the acceptance of Christianity as the state religion in the fourth century A.D.

234

APPENDIX I

A catalogue of some of the monsters, creatures, menaces, and hostile forces often found in classical mythology.

AMAZONS. The Amazons were a breed of very wild women who lived in the area of the Black Sea. They were a highly warlike race, and from birth were trained to be aggressive and to cultivate what would usually be considered to be masculine qualities. When they had children, they kept only enough males to keep the species going and destroyed the others. They cut off one breast of their females so that they would not be obstructed when throwing the javelin or when shooting the bow. They kept the other breast only so that the women might feed their young. One of their queens was Hippolyte; the sign of her leadership was a girdle or belt from Ares, from which god the race of Amazons were descended. Heracles eventually killed her. In that expedition, Theseus, who was accompanying Heracles, carried off one of these Amazons and by her had a son, Hippolytus. Because of the abduction of one from their number, the Amazons invaded Athens but were beaten. In the Trojan War, Penthesilia, another Amazon queen, fought on the side of the Trojans and killed many Greeks. She was accidentally killed by Achilles, who after her death fell in love with her because of her beauty.

BASILISK. This was a type of serpent, but quite small — about six inches long. It had a white spot on its head, very much like a little crown; in fact, this creature was called the king of serpents, and its name reflects that belief: the Greek word *basileus* means "king." When the basilisk hissed, all other snakes would avoid it, for any creature that made eye contact with the basilisk supposedly died on the spot. It did not move as did other serpents, but, from the middle part of its body to the top, it was vertical, somewhat like a creeping "L" or "J." If it ever breathed upon a shrub, that shrub would be destroyed. It burned grass and split stones, so baneful was its power. It was even said that, if a horseman struck the basilisk with his spear, the venom from the creature would climb right up the weapon, killing both the man and the horse. The only defense against the basilisk was the weasel, for the basilisk could not stand the weasel's odor and would perish from it.

CENTAURS. Zeus and Hera, to test just how far Ixion would entertain his passion for Hera, designed a counterfeit of Hera, shaped

235

from a cloud. From Ixion's union with that cloud was born Centaurus. Centaurus, a person having no honor among men or gods and having passions as violent as his father's, consorted with horses. The result was the Centaurs, creatures who shared the characteristics of both their parents: they were half human and half horse. They were generally considered savage, violent, vulgar, and hostile to humans.

The enmity between Centaurs and men is said to have started at the marriage celebration of Pirithous, a natural son of Ixion. Being "step-brothers" of Pirithous, the Centaurs were invited. Being unaccustomed to wine, however, they drank too much and became drunk and rowdy. Eurytion, the worst of the Centaurs, tried to abduct the new bride, and a wild brawl ensued. The Lapiths, local inhabitants of the area, joined in the fight. Pirithous, his friend Theseus, and the Lapiths killed many of the Centaurs, and Eurytion got his ears and nose cut off.

On another occasion they almost tore apart Peleus, the son of Aeacus and later the husband of Thetis and father of Achilles. Peleus had been framed by the wife of Acastus, King of Iolcus. Acastus' wife had fallen in love with Peleus, but Peleus refused to acknowledge her advances. She then told Acastus that Peleus had tried to rape her. Acastus, unwilling personally to kill his guest, took Peleus on a hunting expedition. At night, he hid Peleus' weapons, deserted him, and instigated the Centaurs to destroy the man. Fortunately, Chiron stepped in at the last minute and prevented the murder.

On another occasion, Heracles was visiting the Centaur Pholus. When Pholus opened a jar of wine, the smell allured other Centaurs, who arrived with rocks and fir limbs. There was a fight, the Centaurs were beaten, and many of them took refuge with Poseidon.

Chiron was reckoned to be the best of the Centaurs, and he is quite prominent in mythology. Said to be the son of Cronos and Philyra, he was the oldest of the Centaurs, and the only relationship he bears to the other Centaurs was his man-horse appearance. When Cronos was lying with Philyra, Rhea suddenly sneaked up, and Cronos allegedly changed himself into a horse to avoid getting caught. Hence, Chiron's appearance comes from that bizarre metamorphosis of his father.

Chiron was known for his wisdom, kindness, goodness, and concern for humans. He was the one who brought up Asclepius and trained him in the art of healing, who trained Actaeon to be a hunter, who rescued Peleus from the attack of the Centaurs, who advised Peleus on how to woo Thetis, who tutored Achilles as a child, whose ashen spear Achilles used in the Trojan War, and who brought up the hero Jason. He was a particular friend of Apollo and, as might be expected, had the gift of prophecy. He was a highly cultured and versatile creature, totally unlike the race of Centaurs.

At the wedding feast of Pirithous, Heracles accidentally wounded Chiron with one of his poisoned arrows. The wound could not heal but, since Chiron was immortal, he could not die. Hence, he exchanged his immortality for Prometheus' mortality, and thus the Centaur died. He was then turned into a star in the constellation Centaurus.

CERBERUS has already been mentioned. Some ancient writers say that he had a hundred heads, others say fifty, but the number is usually reckoned to be three. He had the tail of a serpent and his back was covered with the heads of snakes. This mixture of serpent and dog guarded the portal of the Underworld. Anyone could enter, but he would tear apart anyone who tried to leave. Cerberus was also known for his thunderously loud bark.

CERCOPIANS (CERCOPES). The Cercopes were an evil group of people living either in Libya or in Asia Minor. They were treacherous, perfidious, and violent. It is often thought that they were vicious robbers who would prey upon anyone who entered their land. They, furthermore, were notorious blasphemers and liars. Zeus, being disgusted with them, changed them into ugly creatures bearing a resemblance to humans but not human. He shortened their limbs, flattened their noses, ridged their faces with wrinkles, covered their bodies with hair, took away their ability to speak but left them with the ability only to babble incoherently; in short, they became monkeys.

CALYDONIAN BOAR. When the King of Calydonia forgot to include Artemis in his yearly sacrifice, the goddess sent an enormous and vicious monster to ravage the land. It killed everyone whom it encountered, and no one could sow the land because either he would become prey to the boar or the boar would tear up the fields. Consequently, a hunting expedition was formed to kill the boar, an extremely famous expedition in Greek mythology. Everyone who was anyone was there: Meleager, Castor and Polydeuces, Theseus, Admetus, Jason, Pirithous, Peleus, Telamon, and Atalanta, just to name a few. Meleager finally killed the beast and gave its skin to Atalanta.

CHARYBDIS was one of the two dangerous rocks – the other was Scylla – between Sicily and Italy. Since terrible whirlpools surrounded this very high and craggy rock, Charybdis usually referred to the perilous whirlpool rather than to the rock itself.

CHIMAERA. The offspring of the giant Typhon and Echidna, the Chimaera was a monster that ravaged the country of Lydia and devoured all the cattle it could get. While just one creature, it had the strength of three, for it was three creatures in one. The head was that of a lion, the mid-pàrt that of a goat, and the tail that of a dragon. Furthermore, it breathed forth volumes of flames. The hero Bellerophon killed the Chimaera by riding his horse Pegasus into the air and shooting the beast from above. From this monster has derived the English word "chimerical" — i.e., fantastic, unbelievable, imaginary, characterized by unrealistic and impractical fantasies — and "chimera," a noun suggesting an idea or notion that is foolish, unrealistic, imaginary, and impractical.

CYCLOPS. The Cyclops were part of the original creation story, born together with the Hecatoncheires and the Titans from Ouranos and Gaia. At first cast into Tartarus by their father, they were eventually released by Zeus, and they gave the three major gods an important gift: to Zeus they gave thunder and lightning, to Hades they gave a helmet that made him invisible, and to Poseidon they gave a trident with which he could control the waters. They were huge creatures, very strong, with roughly the shape of a man but with one eye instead of two, located in the middle of their foreheads. Because of this single eye, they were often called "goggle-eyed." Later traditions show the Cyclops as workmen and assistants of Hephaistus in his foundry in the islands around Mount Etna and Sicily. Together with the god, they made weapons and armor and fineries for mortals and immortals; they were the ones who made Artemis' bow, arrow, and quiver. And, of course, they kept on fashioning Zeus' thunderbolts.

It is said that when Zeus struck down Asclepius with a thunderbolt for bringing someone back to life with his curative powers, Apollo was so angry at the death of his own son that he took revenge by killing one of the Cyclops.

Polyphemus was the most important of the Cyclops. He was the creature that Odysseus met and blinded. His eye was as large as a shield; he used a pine tree for a walking staff; he played a pipe made of a hundred reeds; he had a beard and a lot of body hair, especially on his shoulders. In view of his size, one wonders about his love for the Nereid Galatea. But Polyphemus did indeed fall in love with this nymph to such an extent that he threw part of a mountain on her mortal lover, Acis, and killed him. The youth was changed into the river that bears his name.

Homer describes the Cyclops as a lawless and antisocial group

238

who scorn Zeus and the other gods. They never met in assemblies, which to Homer represents the most telling symbol of their lack of civilization; they did not sow the land but rather merely tended their flocks in isolation from each other.

ECHIDNA. A daughter of Gaia and Tartarus, she was a monster, half nymph and half serpent. She lived in a deep cavern far from gods and men but would devour anyone who approached her. She was the most important for her association with Typhon as the mother of an array of monstrous creatures. See *Typhon.*

FURIES (ERINYES, EUMENIDES, DIRAE, FURIAE). Born from the drops of Ouranos' blood, the Furies were avenging spirits who relentlessly pursued people who had committed serious crimes, especially crimes against parents, murder, the violation of the guest-host right, and the violation of an oath. There were three of them: Alecto, the Relentless; Tisiphone, the Blood Avenger; and Megaera, the Grudge Bearer. They lived in the Underworld until they were summoned by a curse or by the gods. For a superb description of the avenging process, see the story of Athamas in Ovid's *Metamorphoses,* Book VIII, lines 430ff., and the play, the *Eumenides*, by Aeschylus.

GERYON. The son of the Oceanid Callirrhoe, Geryon was one of the mightiest of all mortals. From the waist down he was of one body but from the waist up he had the torsos and heads of three men. He and his two-headed dog, Orthos, born from Typhon and Echidna, guarded a flock of cattle. He was killed by Heracles.

GIANTS. There are several of them: Otus and Ephialtes, Typhon, the Hecatoncheires, the race of giants born from Ouranos' blood, Antaeus, the Cyclops, and Orion – to name just a few.

GORGONS. Daughters of Phorcys, these three sisters – Stheno, Euryale, and Medusa – could turn into stone anyone who looked at them. They were uncommonly ugly, with snakes on their heads instead of hair, tusks in their mouths instead of teeth, bronze claws instead of hands, and wings that allowed them to fly. Stheno and Euryale were ageless and immortal. See *Medusa.*

GRAEAE (GRAIAE). These three daughters of Phorcys were the sisters of the Gorgons, with whom they lived in the western extreme of the Ocean. They were born old and were immortal. They had only one eye and one tooth among themselves, which they had to share mutually. They protected nymphs who had a pair of winged sandals and who guarded Hades' helmet of invisibility. Their names were Enyo, Pephredo, and Dino.

GRIFFIN. The griffin looked like a lion but had the beak and wings of an eagle; it was even said to have had the spots of a leopard.

Griffins were supposed to be very fond of gold and to protect it wherever they found it, usually hoarding it in their own dens. They lived in the far North, near the area where Boreas had his cave, and they fought frequently with the one-eyed Arimaspians who tried to steal their gold.

HARPIES. The Harpies were sisters of Iris, the Rainbow. Their name means "robbers" or "those who seize." There were two stories concerning them. The first concerned the daughters of Pandarus who, left orphaned, were favored by the gods. For some reason the Harpies snatched these daughters and gave them to the Furies to serve them. The second, much more famous, concerns the Harpies and the Argonauts. Phineus, the son of Agenor, had been given the gift of prophecy by Apollo. When he divulged secrets of Zeus, the god took away his sight and sent the Harpies to torment him. Every time he would try to eat, the Harpies would swoop down upon him and, taking whatever food they wanted for themselves, would leave a film of reeking slime on the rest. They would leave unpolluted just enough food for Phineus to survive. Being sent by Zeus, they could not be killed, but Iris later interceded with Zeus to remove them from Phineus. They are described as part woman, part bird, with long claws and beaks, who could fly as quickly as lightning.

HECATONCHEIRES. These three giants had fifty heads and a hundred hands; their names were Briareus, Gyes, and Cottus. Their story in the myths of creation is told in Chapter I.

HYDRA. Another offspring of Typhon was the Hydra. Bred in a swamp, it plundered both the animals and the people of Lerna. It had one huge body with nine heads, eight of which were mortal and the ninth, in the middle, immortal. If one head were removed, two new ones would grow. If attacked, a huge crab would come to its assistance. The Hydra was killed by Heracles.

LADON was the dragon that guarded the Golden Apples. It had a hundred heads. Some say that Heracles killed or tricked it, others say Atlas killed or tricked it.

LAESTRYGONIANS. These were a race of cannibals who lived on the coast of Sicily or in the islands around Sicily. They are described as being more giants than men. They threw huge rocks and speared men the way one might spear a fish.

MEDUSA. One of the three Gorgons, Medusa was the only one who was not immortal. When Perseus beheaded her, Pegasus, a winged horse, was born. Such a birth is appropriate, for Poseidon had been the father, and Poseidon is closely associated with horses. Later traditions say that originally Medusa was a very beautiful woman

A GRIFFIN ATTACKS AN ARIMASPIAN. Attic Red-Figured Cup, 4th Century B.C. A Griffin assaults an Arimaspian who has tried to steal its gold. *Courtesy, Museum of Fine Arts, Boston.*

who incurred the wrath of Athena; she was supposed to have had especially beautiful hair. There are two explanations for Athena's wrath: 1. Medusa and Poseidon had their affair in one of Athena's temples; 2. Medusa had said that she was as beautiful as the goddess. Regardless, the goddess punished her by changing her beautiful hair into snakes and by causing anyone who looked at her to change into stone. Athena is said to have placed Medusa's head on her shield. Even after her death, her head was able to turn people into stone, and it is even said that just a lock of her hair could accomplish the same end.

241

MINOTAUR (ASTERION). When King Minos of Crete did not keep a promise made to Poseidon, the god punished him by instilling an unnatural passion for a bull in Minos' wife Pasiphae. She fell in love with this bull and gave birth to a creature that was half human and half bull, the Minotaur, whose actual name was Asterion. His face was that of a bull but the rest of him was normal. He was inclosed in a place called the labyrinth, a maze of passageways in which it was easy to get lost. He feasted on Athenian youths, who were sent as tribute to Minos. He was eventually killed by Theseus.

PEGASUS. This winged horse was the son of Medusa and Poseidon. He was born when Perseus beheaded Medusa. Pegasus was one of the few creatures beloved by the gods, and he served faithfully both men and gods. At first he was a wild horse. Then Bellerophon, with the aid of Athena, tamed and harnessed the horse. Riding Pegasus, Bellerophon managed to fight the Amazons and to kill the Chimaera. Eventually, when Bellerophon became too headstrong, too proud of his flying horse, he tried to ride the horse up to the heavens, but the horse threw him; he fell and spent the rest of his life lame, scorned by man and god, alone, and morose. Meanwhile Pegasus became the official horse of the gods. By striking his hoof on Mount Helicon, he created the famous Hippocrene fountain and therefore became a favorite of the Muses, for this was one of the fountains of inspiration. He sometimes appeared with Eos, the Dawn, on her rounds, but most of the time he was with Zeus on Olympus, bringing to Zeus his thunderbolts.

The **PHOENIX** was a bird that brought itself back to life. It was a very rare bird, seldom seen by man. It was the size of an eagle and had brilliant colors, especially around its neck. The rest of its body was purple, its tail was a sky-blue, and its plumage was of gold and crimson. There was a crest around its throat, and its head had a cluster of feathers. It ate very little, feeding usually only on drops of frankincense and on the dew of shrubs. When it had lived for five hundred years, it made a nest with pieces of aromatic shrubs and died. From its body a new bird would be born, which would also live for five hundred years. When the new bird was strong enough, it took its father's body to the temple of the Sun in Egypt.

PLANCTAE. In the same area as Scylla and Charybdis were the Planctae, or "Wandering Rocks." They were similar to the Symplegades; but, whereas the Symplegades guarded the entrance to the Black Sea, the Planctae guarded the Strait of Messina between Italy and Sicily. One of the two rocks seemed so lofty that it touched the sky; its side was completely perpendicular to the surface of the water; therefore, it was unscalable. One of the two rocks had burning fire at its surface, and the air was so smoky that sunlight was not visible. When anything would come between these two rocks, they would dash together and crush it.

PYGMIES. The Greek word *pugme* denotes a measure of length, from the knuckles of one's hand to the elbows. The Pygmies were people of about that length. They lived along the banks of the Nile and veered out toward the borders of the Ocean itself. Their major enemy and greatest fear were the Cranes. In fact, it is said that one Pygmy queen was so conceited and vain that she ignored the gods and was changed into a crane, a perpetual enemy of her own kind. Every spring, the Pygmies went *en masse* to the sea shore, seated on goats and rams; they had with themselves a supply of arrows and would use them to destroy all the nests and the young of cranes that they could find. This venture would take about three months and was essential to their well-being; otherwise, they would be infested by the cranes. They built their huts out of mud and feathers or egg-shells.

SCYLLA. In the Mediterranean Sea not far from the northern coast of Sicily were two huge rocks, the dwelling of Charybdis and Scylla. Scylla was a monster with one torso but twelve thin feet and six very long necks; on each neck was a head with three rows of razor sharp teeth. She lived in a cave, and whenever sailors came by her, she would snatch them off their ship and eat them. Her faces were said to look like dogs' faces.

Scylla was once a beautiful woman, according to some traditions. Glaucus, a minor sea divinity, being madly in love with her but being rejected, went to Circe for help. Circe herself fell in love with him. When Glaucus remained true to his love for Scylla, Circe became so jealous that, combining her magic with the spells of Hecate, she turned the girl into the six-headed monster.

Scylla and Charybdis have been identified as being situated in the Strait of Messina, through which ships had to pass if they wanted to get from Italy to Sicily. Since they had to choose between the dangers of Scylla and the dangers of Charybdis, they were in a situation in which they could not win. Hence our idiom "the Scylla and Charybdis of a problem" indicates that we are in a dilemma and that, whatever alternative we take, that alternative is undesirable.

SIRENS. There were three Sirens, daughters of the River Achelous and one of the Muses. Inheriting qualities from both their parents, they lived on an island and had the gift of magnificent and alluring song. Whenever someone heard their music, he would be irresistibly attracted to it, losing all interest in what he was doing, being impelled only to seek the source of the sound. One of them played the lyre, another sang, and the third played the flute. From the waist down, they looked like birds; the rest of them were attractive women with wings. How they got their wings is a disputed question. One tradition says that, companions of Persephone, they asked wings from the gods so that they might more easily look for the missing girl. Others say that the Sirens were the ones who were changed into birds for having challenged the Muses to a contest and having been defeated.

We now use the word "siren" to describe a woman who is so alluring that she leads people to their own destruction. There is even a story that says that some Centaurs, when they were fleeing from the brawl at Pirithous' wedding, were so mesmerized by the Sirens that they forgot to eat and starved.

SPHINX. A daughter of Typhon and Echidna, the Sphinx was part lion and part woman, often with claws and wings. Hera sent the Sphinx to plague Thebes. It would ask a riddle of anyone who wanted to enter or leave the city. If the person did not answer the riddle correctly, the Sphinx would devour him. The riddle was, "What walks on four feet in the morning, on two feet at noon, and on three feet in the evening?" The answer was "Man" and, when Oedipus correctly answered it, the Sphinx perished.

SYMPLEGADES. Sometimes called the Rocks of Cyanae, these were two rocky islands at the entrance of the Bosporus leading to the Black Sea. Whenever anything came between these two rocks, they would clash together and destroy it. Hence, they are often referred to as the "Clashing Rocks." They were often confused with the Planctae, rocks that were similar but off the coast of Sicily.

TYPHON. The full story has been told in Chapter III. Typhon was a giant born of Earth and Tartarus, the hugest creature ever to walk the earth. He declared war on the Olympians and was eventually consigned by Zeus to Mount Etna, where his eruptions are still evidenced. He mated with his sister Echidna and produced a host of monsters: the Chimaera, the Nemean Lion, the dog Orthos (see *Geryon*), Ladon, the Sphinx, the eagle that mutilated Prometheus' liver, Cerberus, and the Hydra of Lerna.

UNICORN. The unicorn, a very fierce animal, had the body of a horse, the feet of an elephant, the tail of a bear, and the head of a deer. It had a deep voice and one black horn in the middle of its forehead about five feet long. It is said that this animal could not be captured alive. In the Middle Ages it became regarded as symbol of virtue and purity.

244

From the preceding list of anomalies, one can make a few observations. First of all, there is no consistency among them. Almost every giant is described as the largest creature ever to walk the earth; almost every dragon is the worst or the meanest or the most vicious; t!. Clashing Rocks are now in the Bosporus, now off the coast of Italy; the Sphinx is the daughter of the Chimaera or of Echidna, of Orthos or of Typhon; Cerberus had fifty heads or three heads or a hundred heads. The fact that there is much discrepancy among details would not have bothered the ancient mind; what was important was what the anomaly represented: the danger, the fear, the temptation, the strangeness, the violence, or the irritations that one can experience in this world. That these qualities have some universality is seen by the fact that so many of these anomalies have their counterparts in our own vocabulary: a woman can be an Amazon or a Harpy or a Gorgon or a Siren; a man can be Cyclopean; an impractical idea or a wild story is chimerical; the Scylla and Charybdis of a dilemma are the two equally unattractive alternatives; an enigmatic person is sphinx-like; and a small person is a pygmy.

Secondly, many of these monsters can be interpreted as merely figurative or imaginative representations of actual phenomena. The smoky and fiery Planctae was probably a volcanic island; the volcanic eruptions and the shaking of the earth from the eruptions of Mount Etna were attributed to the giant Typhon, trying to free himself from the mountain that Zeus had thrown upon him; Charybdis was probably an actual whirlpool-geyser; the Cyclops' hurling rocks from Mount Etna nicely portrays the flying of rocks in a volcanic eruption; and gigantic walls made of huge interlocking rocks at Tiryns in the Peloponnesus and at other various Mycenean sites were explained as being built by the Cyclops; the Laestrygonians may have been an actual cannibalistic race; the fight between the Centaurs and the Lapiths may have been a figurative way of expressing the rivalry between two peoples of northern Greece: a primitive, rough, uncouth, unsophisticated group of people who lived in the hills and tended horses versus a more sophisticated or advanced group that kept those boors away from the civilized areas. Even the fanciful Chimaera has been explained as a semi-dormant volcanic mountain; lions would live on the higher elevations; goats grazed on the grassy areas in the middle; and snakes inhabited the rocky areas at the bottom.

Thirdly, many of these phenomena can be seen to represent actual human qualities. The Furies, for instance, may be the pangs of conscience or guilt that can affect a person when he has violated a

245

taboo or done something terrible. The Sirens may be the temptation and the instinct of curiosity that can lead us into trouble. Other of the phenomena may have resulted from the romanticizing of actual menaces at some period in history; one can quite easily imagine an actual lion in Nemea, an actual snake in Lerna, or some actual birds of prey who became legendized into Harpies.

Finally, we should never dismiss the fairy-tale element in some of these creatures. All humans like a good story, and many of the creatures listed above certainly add spice to an adventure story.

APPENDIX II

A Catalogue of Some of the Famous Transformations in Ovid's *Metamorphoses*

Book I

Lycaon. When Zeus visited King Lycaon, the king cut up a hostage and offered him as a meal to test whether Zeus was a god. Zeus punished Lycaon by turning him into a wolf. See Chapter V.

Daphne. Running from Apollo's amorous pursuits, this nymph asked her father, the Peneus River, to disguise her. She was transformed into a laurel tree. See Chapter XVII.

Io. When Hera was about to catch Zeus in the midst of an interlude with Io, Zeus changed her into a cow to avoid detection. See Chapter XVII.

Syrinx. She asked assistance from her sisters, the Naiads, to avoid the advances of Pan. They then changed her into reeds. Pan cut these reeds and fastened them together, thereby forming the Pipes of Pan. See Chapter X.

Book II

Cycnus. There are many figures named Cycnus in Greek literature. This one was a friend of Phaeton's. When Phaeton, driving the Sun's chariot, plunged to his death, Cycnus mourned so intensely that Apollo turned him into a swan. Phaeton's sisters, also in mourning, were turned into trees. See Chapter VIII.

Callisto. Hera changed her into an ugly bear because Zeus was showing her too much attention. Then one day, her son Arcas, while out hunting, was about to kill the bear not realizing that it was his mother. To prevent such a tragedy, Zeus changed both Arcas and Callisto into constellations, *ursa major* and *ursa minor.*

Nyctimene. She was changed into an owl because of an incestuous relationship with her father.

Ocyrrhoe. She began to go into too much unpleasant detail when predicting the fate of Asclepius. In order to silence her, the gods changed her into a mare.

Battus. He saw Hermes steal Apollo's cattle. When Apollo questioned him, he told the god what he had seen. Hermes punished him by changing him into a black flint or touchstone.

Book III

Actaeon. This young hunter accidentally saw Artemis while she was bathing, and she punished him by turning him into a stag. He was then pursued by his own hounds and torn to shreds.

Echo. The nymph Echo used to distract Hera from catching Zeus in the midst of his assignations. She would detain the goddess with all sorts of chit-chat. When Hera discovered the ploy, she changed the nymph into an echo. See Chapter XII.

Narcissus. He was changed into a flower as he was pining away, in love with his own image. See Chapter XII.

Book IV

Leucothoe. Leucothoe's father buried her alive when he discovered that she had been having a romance with Helios. Helios out of pity changed her into a frankincense tree. Then he punished her sister, Clytie, for her gossiping about the romance, by changing her into a sunflower.

Daphnis. This shepherd on Mount Ida was turned to stone for not accepting the love of a nymph. Other traditions say that he had promised never to love anyone else but one day broke his promise. Sometimes he is said to have been blinded rather than to have been turned into stone.

Hermaphroditus. The nymph Salmacis, having finally secured the handsome youth in her arms, prayed that they might always be joined together. Her prayer was answered and the two bodies became one.

Ino and **Melicertes.** Ino and her husband Athamas took care of the infant Dionysus, disguising him as a girl so that Hera might not be able to find the child. When Hera discovered what was happening, she drove the couple mad. Ino threw her son Melicertes into boiling water and then jumped off a cliff with the boy into the sea. Aphrodite then prevailed upon Poseidon to change each of the two into a sea deity: Ino became Leucothea and Melicertes became Palaemon.

King Atlas. Atlas, remembering an oracle that said that his golden fruit would be picked by a son of Zeus, suspecting Perseus to be that person, tried to drive him out of his kingdom. Perseus showed him the head of the Medusa and he became a mountain.

Book V

Cyane. Cyane was a nymph who grieved so miserably after the abduction of Persephone that she was changed into a fountain.

Stellio. When Demeter was hunting for Persephone, she disguised herself as an old woman. A boy began insulting her on one occasion, not knowing she was a goddess. Demeter turned him into a lizard.

Ascalaphus. He saw Persephone eat the pomegranate seeds when she was in the Underworld for the first time. For divulging this information to Hades, Demeter punished him by pinning him under a huge stone. When Heracles later removed this stone, Ascalaphus was changed into an owl.

Arethusa. This nymph, fleeing from the advances of the River Alpheus, asked Artemis for protection. Arethusa is said to have fled to Syracuse in Sicily and there to have been changed into a fountain. The Spring of Arethusa still exists. It was sometimes thought that the Alpheus pursued her to Sicily by burrowing an underground channel.

Lyncus. King Lyncus of Scythia tried to kill Triptolemus, who was spreading the rites of Demeter. Demeter changed the perfidious king into a lynx.

Book VI

Arachne. She challenged Athena to a sewing contest. She won the contest but the subject of her embroidery featured scenes illustrating the most compromising behavior of the gods. Offended at her choice of topics, Athena changed her into a spider.

Niobe. She boasted she was better than Leto and was turned into stone. See Chapter VIII.

Procne, Philomela, and **Tereus.** For the story of their respective transformations, see Chapter XII.

Book VII

Ants. Aeacus, King of Aegina, prayed that Zeus would repeople his land with as many citizens as he saw ants before him. Zeus changed each ant into a person, and these new people formed the race of Myrmidons.

Book VIII

Nisus and **Scylla.** Scylla, daughter of King Nisus of Megara, fell in love with King Minos of Crete, who was at the time making war on Megara. She cut off a lock of her father's hair and gave it to Minos. Minos took the city but then sailed without her. She clutched onto his ship and was changed into a bird, while her father, having been changed into a sea-eagle, tore her from the boat.

Ariadne. When Ariadne was in tears after the departure of Theseus from Naxos, Dionysus turned her crown into a constellation in order to immortalize her.

Perdix. Perdix was the nephew of the master-craftsman Daedalus. Jealous of his nephew's skill — for the boy had invented the saw and the mathematical compass — Daedalus threw the six-year-old boy out a window. Athena, who appreciated the cleverness of the boy, changed him into a partridge.

Philemon and **Baucis.** For their transformation, see Chapter V.

Book IX

Galanthis. Galanthis, servant of Alcmena, when she heard her mistress' pains in trying to give birth to Heracles, deceived the goddess of childbirth. For this deception she was changed into a weasel.

Lotis. Lotis was changed into the lotus flower in order to avoid the advances of Priapus.

Byblis. To avoid the amorous passion for his sister Byblis, Caunus, the grandson of the Meander River, tried to escape her. She followed him all over the world. Finally, grief stricken, she cried herself to death and her tears turned into a fountain.

Book X

Cyparissus. For the story of his transformation, see Chapter XII.

Hyacinthus. Apollo dearly loved Hyacinthus. One day when they were together throwing the discus, Apollo accidentally killed the youth and turned his blood into the flower called the hyacinth.

Myrrha. See the story of Adonis in Chapter VII.

Hippomenes and **Atalanta.** Hippomenes did not thank Aphrodite for her help in getting Atalanta as his wife by tricking her into losing a footrace. Deciding to use him as a warning to others, Aphrodite filled him with such a passion that he committed forbidden acts with Atalanta in a shrine of Cybele. In punishment, the two of them were transformed into lions who pulled Cybele's chariot.

Pygmalion's statue. See the story of Pygmalion in Chapter XII.

Book XI

Daedalion. Chione gave birth to twin sons, Autolycus by Hermes and Philammon by Apollo. Taking too much pride in her sons, she slighted Artemis, who pierced her with an arrow. Chione's father, Daedalion, driven mad by her death, jumped off Mount Parnassus and was turned into a hawk by Apollo.

Alcyone and **Ceyx**. Ceyx, King of Thracis, perished in a shipwreck. His wife, Alcyone, daughter of Aeolus, about to plunge into the sea, was changed into a bird. The gods, taking pity on her in her grief, changed her husband also into a bird so that they might always fly together.

Aesacus. Aesacus of Troy fell in love with the nymph Hesperia. In fleeing from him, she stepped on a snake and died. Full of sorrow and guilt, Aesacus jumped off a cliff and was changed into a diving bird by Tethys, who pitied him.

Cycnus. Achilles after several attempts finally killed the Trojan warrior, Cycnus, who was changed into a swan by Poseidon.

Book XII

Caenis. After Poseidon seduced Caenis of Thessaly, he granted her any wish. She chose to be turned into a man so that she might never again be molested. The god granted Caenis' wish and made him invulnerable.

Book XIII

Daughters of Anius. The four daughters of King Anius of Delos had been given exceptional gifts by Dionysus: the skill to make all kinds of crops grow. When Agamemnon heard about them, he tried to force them to feed the Greek army. They escaped. When soldiers were about to retake two of the daughters, they prayed to Dionysus, who saved them by turning them into doves.

Glaucus. Glaucus, seeing some fish that he had caught become revitalized and jump back into the sea, wondered whether the grass caused their new energy. He ate the grass, became mad, and plunged into the sea, where he was turned into a minor sea god.

Book XIV

Scylla. Circe had fallen in love with Glaucus, but he was in love with Scylla. Circe in revenge turned the nymph into a monster.

Cercopes. Zeus changed the Cercopes into monkeys because of their foul habits and their crimes.

Odysseus' men. Since Odysseus' men had been acting like pigs, Circe turned them into pigs.

Vertumnus. Vertumnus, a Roman god of fruit trees, could change himself in whatever shape he wished. When his love for Pomona, another divinity of fruit trees, was constantly rejected, he disguised himself as an old woman. The old woman then encouraged Pomona to accept Vertumnus' love. She eventually did so.

Anaxarete. Anaxarete cruelly and rudely scorned the love of Iphis. When he hanged himself in desperation over her hard heart, she remained just as cold. As she was watching his funeral procession, she was turned into a stone statue.

Book XV

Egeria. Artemis took pity upon her as she inconsolably mourned the death of her husband Numa. As she wept, she became turned into a fountain.

Julius Caesar. When Caesar was killed, Aphrodite changed his soul into a star so that he might forever shed light upon Rome.

APPENDIX III

A Catalogue of some of the Love Affairs of the Gods

ZEUS with divinities   **offspring**

    Metis   Athena

After Metis had become pregnant by Zeus, Zeus heard that a child of hers would be stronger than its father. To avoid that possibility, Zeus swallowed Metis and later himself gave birth to Athena through his head.

Themis	the Horae and Moirae (Fates)
Eurynome	the Graces (Charities)
Demeter	Persephone
Mnemosyne	the Muses
Leto	Apollo and Artemis
Hera	Hebe, Ares, and Eileithyia (goddess of childbirth)
Maia	Hermes

with mortals

    Semele   Dionysus

Hera, jealous of Semele, tricked her into getting her lover to reveal himself in all his majesty. When he did, she was consumed by the force of his lightning and thunder.

    Alcmena   Heracles

Zeus pretended to be Amphytrion, Alcmena's husband.

    Leda   Castor and Polydeuces (Pollux), Helen, Clytemnestra

Zeus appeared to Leda as a swan. His sons Castor and Polydeuces, known as the Dioscuri, or twins of Zeus, remained together throughout life. Helen became the wife of Menelaus and then was abducted to Troy by Paris. Clytemnestra married Agamemnon and then killed him when he returned from the Trojan war.

Danae	Perseus

Hearing from an oracle that his grandson would surpass him, Acrisius put his daughter Danae into a chamber, but Zeus came to her in the form of a shower of gold and fathered Perseus.

Europa	Minos, Rhadamanthus, Sarpedon

Zeus disguised himself as a bull, got Europa on his back, and took off with her throughout much of Europe. Minos and Rhadamanthus had careers in Crete and eventually became judges in the Underworld. Sarpedon eventually became King of the Lycians.

Aegina	Aeacus

Known in life for his justice, honor, piety and peacemaking abilities, Aeacus was made one of the judges of the Underworld. Zeus carried off Aegina to an island that later took her name. Sisyphus happened to see the abduction and told Aegina's mortal husband; this blabbing got Sisyphus into serious trouble.

Antiope	Amphion and Zethus

Antiope is not the Amazon wife of Theseus but rather a pivotal figure in the story of the House of Labdacus. Imprisoned by her uncle and aunt, Lycus and Dirce, she escaped and told her sons of the cruelty shown her. They killed Lycus and Dirce and took over Thebes. Then Amphion married Niobe. When Amphion died, Laius reigned over Thebes.

Electra	Dardanus

This is not the famous Electra, daughter of Agamemnon and Clytemnestra. This Electra was one of the Pleiades. Her son Dardanus founded Troy.

Taygete	Lacedaemon

Taygete was one of the Pleiades. Lacedaemon founded Sparta.

Callisto	Arcas

Callisto was a nymph who incurred Hera's jealousy, who prevailed upon Artemis to kill her in the hunt. When Zeus discovered Callisto dead, he turned her and her son into constellations, the *ursa major* and the *ursa minor*. Arcas was the youth whom Lycaon cut up to serve to Zeus, who was visiting him, for he wanted to test Zeus' powers. Zeus restored the boy, and Arcas later founded the Arcadians.

Dia	Pirithous

Zeus disguised himself as Ixion, husband of Dia. Because of this, he later was more than indulgent to Ixion when Ixion killed his father-in-law. Pirithous became the very close friend of Theseus.

Io	Epaphus

The story of Zeus and Io has been told in Chapter XVII. Epaphus became a king of Egypt and founded the city of Memphis. His daughter Libya gave her name to Libya, or Africa.

Laodamia	Sarpedon

Laodamia was a daughter of Bellerophon. Sarpedon was a noble and valorous Trojan ally who was killed by Patroclus in the Trojan War.

HERA and Zeus	Ares, Hebe, Eileithyia

The wedding night of Hera and Zeus supposedly lasted three hundred years.

——	Hephaistus

Hera was indignant when Zeus gave birth to Athena without her; so she decided to bear a child without his assistance. When the deformed Hephaistus was the result of her labor, she threw him off Olympus.

——	Typhoeus (Typhon?)

This was Hera's first solo attempt to outdo Zeus. What she got was a monster.

HERMES and Aphrodite   Hermaphroditus

The nymph Salmacis fell in love with this beautiful youth. When she finally got him in an embrace, she prayed that the gods would always keep them that way. They did: the two bodies merged into one, a combination male-female.

?   Pan

This goat-man was smelly and coarse and vulgar and lascivious, but those who knew him were very fond of him. Pan became the patron of shepherds and country life. See Chapter X for more details.

Chione   Autolycus

Autolycus was father of Anticlea, the mother of Odysseus. He was known for his wrestling, and he taught the young Heracles to wrestle. He stole some cattle from Eurytus in Euboea; when Eurytus' son Iphitus was looking for the cattle, he came upon Heracles. When Iphitus suggested that Heracles might have committed the theft, Heracles threw him off a cliff, and for that he had to live with Omphale for a year.

Herse   Cephalus

Herse and her sister Aglauros were important in the history of Athens, for they were the ones to whom the baby Erichthonius was entrusted.

?   Myrtilus

The mother here is disputed. Hermes' son Myrtilus played a small but important part in the history of the house of Atreus, for he was the one who sabotaged Oenomaus' chariot in the race between Oenomaus and Pelops.

ARES and Aphrodite   Phobos (Fear) and Deimos
                                      (Terror), Anteros, Harmonia

Anteros is the god who punishes those who do not acknowledge Eros, who turn their back on Eros, or who ignore Eros' arrows. Harmonia married Cadmus of Thebes.

256

Cyrene   Diomedes

This is not the fearless Diomedes of the Trojan War but King Diomedes of Thrace. Heracles stole his horses and fed him to his own horses.

HEPHAISTUS and Atthis   Erichthonius

Erichthonius, born secretly and entrusted to Herse, Aglauros, and Pandrosos, was a legendary founder of Athens. The three women were given a chest and told never to open it; when their curiosity won the day, they saw a serpent in the basket. They were so frightened that they committed suicide.

Anticlea   Periphetes

She is not the Anticlea who mothered Odysseus. Periphetes was one of the robbers that Theseus met and killed on his way to Athens. Periphetes was the "Club Man."

ATHENA did not bear children but she favored Heracles, Odysseus, Perseus, Erichthonius (a legendary founder of Athens), and Bellerophon.

APHRODITE and Anchises   Aeneas
                   Hermes   Hermaphroditus
                   Ares   Phobos, Deimos, Anteros,
                                   Harmonia

Among Aphrodite's favorite mortals were Pygmalion, Aeneas, Phaeton, and Adonis. Aphrodite engineered many loves but was not particularly active herself.

DEMETER and Zeus   Persephone
                 Poseidon   Arion

When Demeter was looking for Persephone, Poseidon saw her and wanted her. She changed herself into a mare to avoid him; he changed himself into a horse and had her. Arion was born from that union. Arion became the horse of Adrastus, who was one of the Seven Against Thebes and escaped only because of the swiftness of Arion.

POSEIDON and Amphitrite　　　　　Triton, Rhode

Rhode married Helios and founded Rhodes. Amphitrite is little more than a personification of the sea. Triton is a "merman," part man and part fish.

Medusa　　　　　Pegasus, Chrysaor

Pegasus was the famous winged horse who assisted Bellerophon and who was later adopted by Zeus as his personal thunderbolt bearer.

Demeter　　　　　Arion
Gaia　　　　　Antaeus

Antaeus was the famous wrestler who gained his strength from contact with the earth and whom Heracles killed.

Thoosa　　　　　Polyphemus

Polyphemus was the famous Cyclops whom Odysseus blinded.

Tyro　　　　　Neleus and Pelias

Poseidon took the shape of her husband. Neleus became a king of Pylos and Pelias was the evil uncle of Jason in Iolcus and father of Alcestis.

Aethra　　　　　Theseus

Poseidon assumed the shape of her husband, King Pittheus of the Troezen. Some say, however, the King Aegeus of Athens was actually Theseus' father.

Libya　　　　　Agenor and Belus

Agenor fathered Cadmus and Europa and was King of Tyre. Belus was the father of Aegyptus and Danaus. A more detailed genealogy of the descendants of Agenor and of Belus accompanies the story of the House of Labdacus in Chapter XV and the story of Perseus in Chapter XVI.

Melia	Bebryces

Bebryces was King of Bithynia. He challenged all visitors to a boxing match. Polydeuces killed him when the Argonauts landed at Bithynia.

Iphimedeia	Otus and Ephialtes

These were the twin giants who grew six feet taller and two feet broader each year. They challenged the gods, piled Mount Pelion on Mount Ossa, were beaten, and were consigned to Tartarus.

Anippe	Busiris

This king of Egypt used to butcher all visitors. He was killed by Heracles.

?	Cercyon

He settled in Eleusis and forced all travelers to wrestle with him. Theseus killed him.

?	Sinis

Sinis lived in the Isthmus of Corinth. He would tie all travelers to two pine trees that had been bent together, release the trees and thus kill the poor victim. Theseus rid the world of Sinis.

Alcyone	Arethusa

Alcyone was one of the Pleiads. Arethusa was changed into a fountain when she was fleeing the advances of the River Alphaeus.

Chione	Eumolpus

Eumolpus' life was one disaster after another. He, however, is credited with founding the sacred rites and mysteries at Eleusis.

Theophane	a ram

When Theophane was fleeing some suitors, Poseidon changed her into an ewe and himself into a ram. She bore the ram which grew the Golden Fleece.

259

DIONYSUS, like Aphrodite, effected many births, particularly among humans, but he himself fathered very few offspring. Priapus resulted from his union with Aphrodite and he had a few children by Ariadne. But he was not an active father in classical mythology.

APOLLO and Coronis   Asclepius

Asclepius became the patron of medicine.

       Cyrene   Aristaeus

Aristaeus, a fertility god, became a patron of those involved with agriculture. A story about him appears in Chapter X.

       Evane   Iamus

Iamus was a famous soothsayer.

       Urania   Linus

This is not the Linus who taught music to Heracles. This Linus inherited the gift of music from his parents, challenged his father to a duel, and was destroyed by his father.

       Creusa   Ion

This Creusa is not the mother of Aeneas but rather the daughter of Erechtheus. Ion founded the Ionians.

       Chione   Philammon

Philammon was a very famous musician who was connected with the oracle at Delphi.

       Deione   Miletus

Miletus founded the city that bears his name.

Apollo actually had innumerable love affairs, but not very many of them are significant.

APPENDIX IV

A Note on Methodology

Since, as we have mentioned, few myths exist in their entirety in any one primary source, we often have to piece together details from several different sources in order to get a complete story. The purpose of the following remarks is to help the reader interested in pursuing the original sources.

Perhaps the best reference tool available is the Loeb Classical Library, published by the Harvard University Press. Each volume presents the text in the original language with an accompanying translation and provides a very thorough index, and these indexes are invaluable.

The two works of Apollodorus, the *Library* and the *Epitome*, are the best place to begin any research. Sir James Frazer's notes and cross references in the Loeb edition are superb: Frazer not only gives the variations for the myths but he also cites the sources for those variations. Some of the sources will be available only in large university libraries, and a few of them — such as Hyginus' *Fabulae,* Tzetzes' *Commentary on Lycophron,* and the various Scholiasts — exist only in the original Latin or Greek; but these esoteric sources are usually not essential.

After Apollodorus, the most important sources for details are the works of Homer, Hesiod, Pindar, the Greek tragedians, and Pausanias. Ovid is a rich source and often tells a full story, but his version of a myth is often idiosyncratic.

The following list includes the original sources used in the preparation of this volume.

Greek Authors

Aeschylus: the tragedies
Apollodorus: the *Library* and the *Epitome*
Apollonius of Rhodes: The *Argonautica*
Callimachus: the *Hymns* and the *Epigrams*
Diodorus of Sicily: Books I- V
Euripides: the plays
Herodotus: *History*
Hesiod: *Works and Days, Theogony, Shield of Heracles*
Homer: *Iliad* and *Odyssey*
Homeric *Hymns*

Lucian: *Dialogues*
Lycophron: *Alexandra*
Lyric, Elegaic, and Bucolic poets
Nonnos: *Dionysiaca*
Pausanias: *Description of Greece*
Pindar: *Odes*
Plato: Dialogues
Plutarch: *Lives* and *Moralia*
Scholiasts on Homer
Sophocles: the tragedies
Theocritus: the *Odes*
Tzetzes: *Commentary on Lycophron*
Xenophon: *Memorabilia*

Latin Authors

Apuleius: *The Golden Ass*
Catullus: *Poems*
Cicero: *De Natura Deorum*
Claudian: *Gigantomachia*
Horace: *Odes*
Hyginus: *Fabulae*
Livy: *History*
Lucan: *Pharsalia*
Lucretius: *De Rerum Natura*
Ovid: *Metamorphoses, Fasti, Heroides*
Pliny the Elder: *Natural History*
Tibullus: *Elegies*
Valerius Flaccus: *Argonautica*
Vergil: *Aeneid* and *Georgics*

Bibliography of Secondary Sources

Dodds, E.R., *The Greeks and the Irrational,* Berkeley, 1968.
Grant, Michael, *Myths of the Greeks and Romans,* Cleveland, 1962.
Graves, Robert, *The Greek Myths,* Baltimore, 1971.
Guthrie, W. K. C., *The Greeks and their Gods,* London, 1968.
Henle, Jane, *Greek Myths: A Vase Painter's Notebook,* Bloomington, 1973.
Kerenyi, C., *The Gods of the Greeks,* London, 1974.
Kerenyi, C., *The Heroes of the Greeks,* London, 1974.
Kirk, G.S., *The Nature of Greek Myths,* Baltimore, 1974.
Larousse New Encyclopedia of Mythology, New York, 1968.
Lesky, Albin, *Greek Tragedy,* London, 1967.

Neumann, Erich, *Amor and Psyche,* Princeton, 1973.
Nillson, Martin P., *A History of Greek Religion,* New York, 1964.
Nillson, Martin P., *Mycenean Origins of Greek Religion,* Berkeley, 1973.
Otto, Walter F., *Dionysus: Myth and Cult,* Bloomington, 1965.
Otto, Walter F., *The Homeric Gods,* Boston, 1964.
Parke, H.W., *Greek Oracles,* London, 1972.
Pinsent, John, *Greek Mythology,* New York, 1969.
Reinhold, Meyer, *Past and Present: The Continuity of Classical Myths,*
        Toronto, 1972.
Rose, H.J., *A Handbook of Greek Mythology,* London, 1965.
Smith, William, *A New Classical Dictionary,* New York, 1873.

A Time Chart for the Major Sources of Classical Myths

		Greek writers	Latin writers
B.C.	900 800 700	Homer Hesiod	
	600	Lyric, elegaic, bucolic poets	
	500	Pindar Aeschylus, Bacchilydes	
	400	Herodotus Sophocles, Euripides, Plato	
	300	Theocritus, Lycophron, Callimachus	
	200	Apollonius	
	100	Diodorus	Cicero, Lucretius, Catullus Vergil, Horace, Livy, Ovid, Tibullus
A.D.	1	Apollodorus(?)	Lucan
		Plutarch	Pliny the Elder Valerius Flaccus
	100		
	200	Lucian Pausanias	Apuleius
	400	Nonnus	Claudian

INDEX OF SELECTED SOURCES

The following listing does not include every primary source used in the preparation for the stories in this book. It includes by and large only those works which are available in translation on the trade market or in the Loeb Classical Library series. Sir James Frazer's notes in the Loeb edition of Apollodorus will direct the reader to the more esoteric sources. Furthermore, his index is an exceptionally useful one.

CHAPTER I: CREATION OF MATTER

The story: *Theogony* 116 ff., Apollodorus, I, i, 1-4. **Alternate versions:** *Metamorphoses,* I, 1 ff., *Iliad,* XIV, 201 ff. **Birth of Aphrodite:** Homeric Hymn "To Aphrodite." **The Furies:** Aeschylus, *The Eumenides.* **Offspring of Night:** Cicero, *De Natura Deorum,* III, xvii. **Atlantian creation myth:** Diodorus, III, 56 ff.

CHAPTER I: REIGN OF TITANS

The story: *Theogony,* 453 ff., Apollodorus, I, i, 4 ff. **Prometheus' role:** Aeschylus, *Prometheus Bound,* 212 ff. **Cronos' stone:** Pausanias, X, 24.6. **Zeus' infancy:** Callimachus, "Hymn to Zeus" and Ovid's *Fasti,* V, 112 ff. **Division of universe:** *Iliad,* XV, 187 ff. **Story of Atlas:** Diodorus III, 60. **Story of Cronos:** Diodorus, III, 61. **Zeus, Crete, and Curetes:** Diodorus, V, 65 ff.

CHAPTER II: ZEUS

Diodorus, V, 70 ff. **Early mates:** *Theogony,* 886 ff., Apollodorus, I, iii, 1 and 6. **Aegis:** *Iliad,* II, 446 ff., and XVII, 593 ff. **Zeus' power:** *Iliad,* VIII, 30 ff. **Division of the universe:** *Iliad,* XV, 190 ff.

CHAPTER II: HERA

Treatment by Zeus: *Iliad,* I, 567 ff. and XV 18 ff. **Tricks Zeus for Poseidon:** *Iliad,* XIV. **Renewed virginity:** Pausanias, II, 38.2. **Hebe:** Pindar, *Nemean Ode* VII, 1-5.

CHAPTER II: POSEIDON

Description: *Iliad,* XIII, 10 ff. **With Demeter:** Pausanias, VIII, 25.3. **Contest in Athens:** Apollodorus, III, xiv, 1, *Metamorphoses* VI, 75 ff., Herodotus, VIII, 55. **Walls of Troy:** Pindar, *Olympian* VIII and *Aeneid,* II, 608 ff. **Triton:** *Metamorphoses,* I, 331 ff., Pindar, *Pythian* IV, 24 ff., Apollonius, *Argonautica,* IV, 1551 ff. **Tritons:** Pausanias, IX, 21.1. **Proteus:** *Odyssey,* IV, 365 ff. Vergil, *Georgics,* IV, 418 ff., Lucian, *Dialogues of the Sea Gods,* IV, "Menelaus and Proteus," *Metamorphoses,* XI, 221 ff. **Amphitrite:** Apollodorus, III, xiii, 5.

CHAPTER II: DEMETER

Homeric Hymns "To Demeter." Callimachus, "Hymn to Demeter." Apollodorus, I, v, 1 ff. *Theogony,* 969 ff. *Odyssey,* V, 125 ff. Ovid, *Fasti,* 613 ff. *Metamorphoses,* V, 341 ff. Diodorus, V, 2 ff. and V, 68 ff. **Plutus:** Diodorus, V, 77.

CHAPTER II: HESTIA

Homeric Hymn "To Aphrodite." Homeric Hymn "To Hestia." Plato: *Phaedrus,* 246e. Ovid, *Fasti,* VI, 319 ff.

CHAPTER II: APOLLO

Birth: Homeric Hymn "To Apollo." Callimachus, "Hymn to Delos." Apollodorus, I, iv, 1 ff. **Tityus:** *Odyssey,* XI, 576 ff. Pindar, *Pythian* IV, 90 ff. **Python:** Callimachus, "Hymn to Apollo." Homeric Hymn "To Apollo." Plutarch, *De Defectu Oraculorum*, 421. **Niobe:** *Iliad*, XXIV, 599 and *Metamorphoses*, VI, 146 ff. **Marsyas:** Pausanias, II, 22.9 and Pindar, *Pythian* III. Diodorus, III, 59. *Metamorphoses*, VI, 383 ff. **Hyperboreans:** Herodotus IV, 33. **Asclepius:** Pindar, *Pythian* III. *Metamorphoses* II, 598 ff. Apollodorus, III, x, 3-4. Diodorus, IV, 71.

CHAPTER II: ARTEMIS

Callimachus: "Hymn to Artemis." **Actaeon:** Apollodorus, III, viii, 2 and *Metamorphoses*, III, 138 ff. **Orion:** Apollodorus I, iv, 3. **Her worship:** Euripides, *Hippolytus*, especially 57 ff. **Callisto:** Apollodorus III, viii, 2 and *Metamorphoses*, II, 405 ff.

CHAPTER II: HERMES

Birth and early exploits: Homeric Hymn "To Hermes." Apollodorus III, x, 1-2. *Metamorphoses*, II, 676 ff. Horace *Odes*, I, 10. **Hermaphroditus:** *Metamorphoses*, IV, 285 ff. **Io:** Apollodorus, II, i, 3 ff. Aeschylus, *Prometheus Bound*. *Metamorphoses*, I, 583 ff. Aeschylus, *Suppliants*. **Pan:** Homeric Hymn "To Pan." **Attributes:** Diodorus, V, 75.

CHAPTER II: ATHENA

Birth: Pindar, *Olympian* VII, 35 ff. Homeric Hymn "To Athena." Apollodorus I, iii, 6. *Theogony*, 886 ff. **Pallas:** Apollodorus, III, xii, 3. **Arachne:** *Metamorphoses*, VII. **Tiresias:** Callimachus, Hymn V. Apollodorus, III, vi, 7. **Erichthonius:** Apollodorus, III, xiv, 6 and Euripides, *Ion*, 20 ff. and 267 ff. **Contest:** Apollodorus, III, xiv, 1. **Attributes:** Diodorus, V, 73.

CHAPTER II: HEPHAISTUS

Birth: *Theogony*, 928. Homeric Hymn "To Apollo," 300 ff. **With Thetis:** *Iliad*, XVIII, 395. **Fall from Olympus:** *Iliad*, I, 590 ff. **Throne incident:** Pausanias, I, 20.3. **Attributes:** Diodorus, V, 74.

CHAPTER II: APHRODITE

Birth: *Theogony*, 180 ff. Homeric Hymn "To Aphrodite." **Mother Dione:** *Iliad*, V, 370 ff. **Anchises story:** First Homeric Hymn to Aphrodite. Apollodorus, III, xii, 2. **Judgment of Paris:** *Iliad*, XXIV, 25 ff. Apollodorus, *Epitome*, III, 1. **Hephaistus' trap:** *Odyssey*, VIII, 266 ff.

CHAPTER II: ARES

Zeus' hate: *Iliad*, V, 861 ff. **Otus and Ephialtes:** *Iliad*, V, 385 and *Odyssey*, XI, 305 ff. **Areopagus:** Apollodorus, III, xiv, 2.

CHAPTER II: DIONYSUS

Semele: Pindar, *Olympian* II, 27. Pausanias, II, 35.5. Nonnos, VII, 190, Apollodorus, III, iv, 3. **Ino:** Apollodorus III, iv, 3 ff. *Metamorphoses*, IV, 416. Euripides, *Medea*, 1283 ff. **Lycurgus:** Apollodorus III, v, 1. *Iliad*, VI, 130 ff. **Pentheus:** Euripides, *Bacchae*. *Metamorphoses*, III, 511. Nonnos, XLIV ff. **Melampus:** Apollodorus, II, ii, 2. **Ikarios:** Apollodorus, III, xiv, 7 and Nonnos, XIII. **Pirates:** Homeric Hymn "To Dionysus." Apollodorus III, v, 3. Nonnos, XLV, 105. **Minyas:** *Metamorphoses*, IV. **Daughters of Proetus:** Apollodorus II, ii, 2. **Ariadne:** Hesiod, *Theogony*, 948 ff. Euripides, *Hippolytus*, 399 ff. **Persephone:** Nonnos, VI, 121 and XLVIII, 29. **Miscellaneous details:** Diodorus of Sicily, III, 62 - IV, 7.

CHAPTER III: MONSTERS AND REBELLIONS

Giants: Apollodorus, I, vi, 1 ff. Horace, *Odes*, III, iv, 49 ff. Pindar, *Pythian* VIII, 12 ff. *Metamorphoses* I, 150 ff. **Typhon:** *Metamorphoses* V, 318 ff. *Theogony*, 820 ff. Pindar, *Pythian* I, 13 ff. Apollodorus I, vi, 3. Aeschylus, *Prometheus Bound*, 351 ff. **Sons of Aloeus:** Apollodorus I, vii, 4. *Odyssey*, XI, 305 ff. *Iliad*, V, 385 ff. **Rebellion against Zeus:** *Iliad*, I, 399 ff. Diodorus V, 51.

CHAPTER IV: PROMETHEUS AND PANDORA

Hesiod, *Theogony,* 506 ff. and *Works and Days,* 42 ff. Apollodorus, I, vii, 1. Plato, *Protagoras,* 320D. Aeschylus, *Prometheus Bound.* Ovid, *Metamorphoses,* I, 76 ff. Pausanias, X, 4.4.

CHAPTER V: DETERIORATION

Fullest account in *Metamorphoses* I, 89-415 and VIII, 620 ff. **Zeus' nod:** *Iliad,* I, 524 ff. **Ages of Man:** Hesiod, *Works and Days,* 109 ff. **Golden age under Saturn:** Tibullus, I, iii and Diodorus, III, 61. **Deucalion and Pyrrha:** Apollodorus, I, vii, 2 and Pindar, *Olympian* IX, 41 ff.

CHAPTER VI: UNDERWORLD

Descriptions: *Theogony,* 720 ff. *Works and Days,* 169 ff. Pindar, *Olympian* II, 61 ff. *Odyssey,* IV, 561 ff., X, 508 ff., XI, 13 ff., XXIV, 1-22. *Iliad,* XXIII; *Aeneid,* VI. **Charon:** Lucian, *Dialogues of the Dead,* IV. **Burial:** Sophocles, *Antigone*; *Iliad,* XXIII, 69 ff. **Judges:** Apollodorus, III, xii, 6 and III, i, 2; Diodorus, IV, 60 and V, 78 ff. **Hecate:** *Theogony,* 411 ff.; Theocritus, Ode II. Apollonius, *Argonautica,* III and IV *passim.* **Sinners:** Lucretius, *De Rerum Natura,* III, 978 ff. **Tantalus:** Pindar, *Olympian,* 1, 36 ff. Apollodorus, *Epitome,* II, 1. *Odyssey,* XI, 582 ff. Euripides, *Orestes,* 4 ff. **Sisyphus:** Apollodorus, III, xii, 6 and I, ix, 3. *Odyssey,* XI, 593 ff. Theognis, *Maxims,* 712 ff. **Ixion:** Apollodorus, *Epitome,* I, 20. Pindar, *Pythian* II, 21 ff. Lucian, *Dialogues of the Gods,* VI. **Tityus:** *Odyssey,* XI, 576 ff. **Danaids:** Apollodorus, II, i, 4-5. Horace, *Odes,* III, xi. Aeschylus, *Suppliants.* Ovid, *Heroides,* XIV. **Pirithous:** Diodorus, IV, 63.

CHAPTER VII: DEATH AND RESURRECTION

Orpheus: *Metamorphoses* X, 1-105 and

XI, 1-84. Vergil, *Georgics* IV, 456 ff. Pausanias, X, 30, 4-12. Apollonius, *Argonautica,* I, 492 ff., 534 ff., IV, 891 ff., 1392 ff. **Aphrodite and Adonis:** *Metamorphoses,* X, 299-736. Apollodorus III, xiv, 4. Bion, *Idyll* I, "The Epitaph of Adonis." Theocritus, *Idyll* XXX, "The Death of Adonis." **Alcestis:** Euripides, *Alcestis.* Apollodorus, I, ix, 14-15.

CHAPTER VIII: THE FALL

Orion: Apollodorus, I, iv, 3 ff. Aratus, *Phaenomena,* 634 ff. Diodorus, IV, 85 ff. Ovid, *Fasti,* V, 537 ff. **Phaeton:** *Metamorphoses,* II, 1-401. **Niobe:** *Metamorphoses* VI, 148 ff. *Iliad,* XXIV, 602 ff. Apollodorus III, v, 6. **Salmoneus:** *Aeneid* VI, 585 ff. Apollodorus I, ix, 5 ff. Diodorus IV, 68, 1-2. **Bellerophon:** *Iliad,* VI, 155 ff. Apollodorus II, iii, 1-2. Pindar, *Olympian* XIII and *Isthmian* VII, 43 ff.

CHAPTER IX: ABSTRACT DIVINITIES

Themis: Diodorus V, 67. Apollodorus I, iv, 1. Euripides, *Iphigenia in Tauris,* 1259 ff. Aeschylus, opening of *Eumenides.* **Muses:** Diodorus, IV, 7. *Theogony,* 36 ff. Pausanias IX, xxxiv, 3 and xxix ff. *Metamorphoses* V, 250 ff. and 662 ff. Apollodorus, I, iii, 3. **Mount Helicon:** Pausanius IX, xxviii. **Charities:** Pausanias IX, xxxv. *Odyssey* VIII, 362 ff. *Passim* in Pindar, especially *Olympian Odes. Theogony,* 907 ff. **Horae:** *Theogony,* 901 ff. Homer, second "Hymn to Aphrodite." Theocritus, *Idyll* XV, 105 ff. **Moirae:** *Theogony,* 216 ff. and 904 ff. *Passim* in Pindar, *Olympian* II and *Nemean* VII.

CHAPTER X: POWERFUL FORCES

Gaia: *Theogony* 116 ff. Homeric Hymn "To the Earth." **Antaeus:** Lucan, *Pharsalia,* IV, 589 ff. Pindar, *Isthmian,* IV, 52 ff. Ovid, *Ibis,* 391 ff. Apollodorus II, v, 11. **Rhea and Cybele:** Pausanias VII, 10 ff. Ovid, *Fasti,* IV, 181 ff. Catullus, Poem

LXIII. *Metamorphoses,* X, 104-5, Diodorus III, 58. Lucretius, *De Rerum Natura,* II, 610 ff. **Pan:** *Metamorphoses,* I, 694 ff. Homeric Hymn "To Pan." **Priapus:** Ovid, *Fasti,* VI,·319 ff. and II, 391 ff. Diodorus IV, 6. **Aristaeus:** Pindar, *Pythian* IX, 5 ff. Apollonius, *Argonautica,* II, 500 ff. Ovid, *Fasti,* I, 363 ff. Vergil, *Georgics,* IV, 281 ff. Diodorus IV, 81 ff.

CHAPTER XI: POWERS OF EARTH, SEA, SKY

Eos: *Metamorphoses,* XIII, 575 ff. Homeric Hymn "To Aphrodite," 218 ff. Apollodorus, I, iv, 4 and *Odyssey,* V, 121 ff. **Helios:** Diodorus, V, 56. *Metamorphoses* II, 1-366. **Rhodes:** Pindar, *Olympian* VII, 54 ff. **Hesperides:** Apollonius, *Argonautica,* IV, 1396 ff. *Metamorphoses,* IV, 637 ff. **Aeolus:** Apollodorus, *Epitome,* VII, 10. *Odyssey,* X, 1-27. *Aeneid,* I, 50-68. **Boreas:** *Iliad,* XX, 223 ff. **Zetes and Calais:** Apollonius, *Argonautica,* I, 211 ff. *Metamorphoses,* VI, 677 ff. **Zephyrus:** Ovid, *Fasti,* V, 195 ff. Lucian, *Dialogues of the Gods,* XIV. **Satyrs:** Pausanias I, 23.5 ff. **Silenus:** Lucian, "The Assembly of the Gods." Euripides, *Cyclops.* Catullus, LXIV, 251-264. **Oceanus, Pontus and offspring:** *Theogony,* 333 ff. and Apollodorus I, ii, 2 ff., II, iv, 2. **Thetis:** *Iliad,* XVIII, 393 ff., VI, 130 ff. Pindar, *Isthmian* VIII, 29 ff., *Nemean* IV, 57 ff., *Nemean* V, 25 ff. *Metamorphoses,* XI, 217 ff. Catullus, LXIV. Apollonius, *Argonautica,* IV, 865 ff. **Pleiades and Hyades:** Ovid, *Fasti,* IV, 169 ff., V, 164 ff.

CHAPTER XII: TRANSFORMATION MYTH

The stories in this chapter are found in Ovid's *Metamorphoses* and/or Apollodorus.

CHAPTER XIII: PROPHETS AND ORACLES

Delphi: Plutarch, *Oracles at Delphi, "E"*

at Delphi, Obsolescence of Oracles. **Tiresias:** Apollodorus, III, vi, 7; Callimachus, *Hymn to Athena,* 68 ff. Pindar, *Nemean,* I, 58 ff.; *passim* in Sophocles *Oedipus* and *Antigone.* **Melampus:** Apollodorus, I, ix, 11 and II, ii, 2; Herodotus, II, 49 and IX, 34, **Helenus:** Apollodorus, *Epitome,* V, 10. **Calchas:** *Iliad,* II, 299 ff. and Apollodorus, *Epitome,* VI, 2 ff. **Cassandra:** *Epitome,* V, 22 and Aeschylus, *Agamemnon.* **Laocoon:** Vergil, *Aeneid,* II, 199 ff. **Sibyl:** *Aeneid* VI.

CHAPTER XV: HOUSE OF ATREUS

The story: Diodorus, IV, 73 ff. **Tantalus:** Pindar, *Olympian,* I, 35 ff. **Pelops:** *Epitome,* II, 3-9; Pindar, *Olympian,* I, 70 ff. Pausanias, VIII, 14. **Stymphalos:** Apollodorus, III, xii, 6. **Atreus & Thyestes:** Apollodorus, II, 10. **Agamemnon and Menelaus:** *Epitome,* III, 1-5; VI, 23; *Odyssey,* III, 193. **Cassandra:** Apollodorus III, xii, 5. See also the tragedies listed at the beginning of the chapter.

CHAPTER XV: LABDACUS

The story: Apollodorus III, i. ff; and Diodorus, IV, 64 ff. **Cadmus:** *Metamorphoses,* III, 1-137 and IV, 563 ff. **Europa:** *Metamorphoses,* II, 836 ff. **Miscellaneous details:** Pausanias, II, 6.1 ff. and IX, 5.4 ff. Other sources cited in text.

CHAPTER XV: TROJAN HOUSE

Apollodorus, III, xii and II, vi, 4; Homeric Hymn "To Aphrodite," 202 ff. *Iliad,* XXIV, 218 ff. *Metamorphoses,* X, 155 ff. Also see works listed in the text.

CHAPTER XVI: PERSEUS

The story: Apollodorus, II, ii, 1 ff., Pindar, *Pythian Ode,* XII, *Metamorphoses,* IV, 610-V, 249. **Danae:** Sophocles, *Antigone,* 944 ff., and Simonides, fragment on Perseus. **Gorgons and Graiae:** Hesiod, *Theogony,* 270 ff. Pindar, *Pythian* X, 29 ff. **Acrisius:** Pausanias, II, 16.2 ff.

CHAPTER XVI: HERACLES

The story: Diodorus, IV, 8-39 and Apollodorus, II, iv, 5-II, vii, 1. **Zeus and Alcmena:** Hesiod, *Shield of Heracles*, 27 ff. **Heracles' birth:** *Metamorphoses*, IX, 273 ff. **Infant Heracles:** Pindar, *Nemean* I, 33 ff., Theocritus XXIV. **Nemean lion:** Theocritus, XXV. **Stymphalian birds:** Apollonius, *Argonautica*, II, 1046 ff., and Pausanias, VIII, 22.4-6. **Laomedon:** *Iliad*, XXI, 441 ff., and Lucian, *De Sacrificiis* IV. **Golden apples:** *Argonautica*, IV, 1396 ff. **Olympic Games:** Pindar, *Olympian* III and X. **Admetus:** Euripides, *Alcestis.* **Cacus:** Ovid, *Fasti*, I, 545 ff., and Propertius IV, 9. **Scythians:** Herodotus IV, 9-10. **Termerus:** Plutarch, *Theseus*, 11. **The six Heracles:** Cicero, *De Natura Deorum*, III, xvi. **Pleasure and Virtue:** Xenophon, *Memorabilia*, II, 1, 21 ff.

CHAPTER XVI: JASON

The framework of the story is from Apollodorus, I, ix, 1-28 and Diodorus, IV, 40-56. Apollonius, *Argonautica* gives a vivid account of the expedition to Colchis. Pindar, *Pythian* IV, comments on the significance of the expedition. Euripides' *Medea* and Ovid, *Heroides*, XII develop Medea's personality. Valerius Flaccus *Argonautica* and *Metamorphoses*, VII, give additional details. Diodorus III, 52 ff., gives details about the Amazons.

CHAPTER XVI: THESEUS

The story: Plutarch, *Theseus*, Diodorus, IV, 59 ff., Apollodorus III, xv, 6 ff., and *Epitome*, I, 1 ff. **Supporting details:** Pausanias: I, 39.3, I, 22.2, I, 17.4, II, 1.4, II, 32.3 and V, 10.8; *Odyssey*, XXI, 295 ff. and XI, 321 ff.; Euripides, *Hippolytus;* Bacchylides, Poems 17 and 18; Ovid, *Metamorphoses*, VII, 425 ff., VIII, 155 ff., XII, 219 ff., *Heroides*, X, *Ars Amatoria*, I, 525 ff.

CHAPTER XVII: LOVE

The stories of Daphne, Pyramus, and Zeus/Io are in *Metamorphoses*. Aeschylus, *Prometheus Bound* also devotes many details to Io. Hero and Leander is in Ovid, *Heroides*, XVIII and XIX and in Musaeus. Eros and Psyche is from Apuleius, *The Golden Ass*, IV, 28 ff.

CHAPTER XIX: ROMAN MYTHOLOGY

The *Iliad* (for the fall of Troy) and the *Aeneid* (for the aftermath of the Trojan War) are essential. See also Livy, Book I, and *Metamorphoses*, Books XIII, XIV, and XV.

APPENDIX I: MONSTERS

Amazons: Apollodorus, II, v, 9; Callimachus, *Hymn to Artemis*, 237 ff.; *Argonautica*, II, 966 ff.; Herodotus IV, 110-117; Diodorus, III, 52 ff. **Basilisks:** Pliny, *Natural History*, VIII, 33. **Centaurs:** Pindar, *Pythian* II; *Odyssey*, XXI, 293 ff.; Apollodorus, III, v, 4 and *Epitome*, I, 20-21; *Metamorphoses*, XII, 210; Diodorus, IV, 69. **Chiron:** Pindar, *Pythian* III and IV, *Nemean* III; *Argonautica*, II, 1231 ff.; Apollodorus XXX, x, 5 and II, v, 4; Ovid, *Fasti*, V, 379 ff. **Cerberus:** *Theogony* 767 ff. and Apollodorus II, v, 12. **Cercopes:** *Metamorphoses*, XIV, 91 and entry in Suidas' lexicon. **Charybdis:** *Odyssey*, XII, 223 ff. and *Epitome*, VII, 20-23. **Chimaera:** Apollodorus II, iii, 1-3 and *Iliad*, VI, 178 ff. **Cyclops:** Callimachus, *Hymn to Artemis*, 46 ff.; *Odyssey*, Book IX; Theocritus, *Idyll* II and *Metamorphoses*, XIII, 738 ff. **Echidna:** *Theogony*, 295 ff. **Furies:** Aeschylus, *Eumenides*, especially 39 ff., and 299 ff.; *Metamorphoses*, VIII, 430 ff. **Griffin:** Pausanias, I, xxiv, 5-6; Pliny, *Natural History*, VII, 2. **Harpies:** *Argonautica*, II, 178 ff. and *Odyssey*, XX, 65 ff. **Pegasus:** Pindar, *Olympian* XIII; *Isthmian* VII; *Iliad*, VI, 199 ff.; Aratus,

Phaenomena, 216 ff. **Phoenix:** Herodotus, II, 73; *Metamorphoses,* XV, 391 ff.; Pliny, *Natural History,* X, 2. **Planctae:** *Odyssey,* XII, 55 ff.; *Argonautica,* IV, 922 ff. **Pygmies:** *Iliad,* III, 6 and *Metamorphoses,* VI, 89 ff.; Pliny, *Natural History,* VII, 2. **Scylla:** *Epitome,* VII, 20-21; *Odyssey* XII; *Argonautica,* IV, 824 ff.; *Metamorphoses,* XIII, 730-XIV, 74. **Sirens:** *Epitome,* VII, 18-19; *Argonautica,* IV, 898 ff.; *Metamorphoses,* V, 552 ff.; *Odyssey,* XII. **Symplegades:** *Argonautica,* II, 317 ff. **Typhon:** *Metamorphoses,* V, 341 ff.; *Theogony,* 295 ff. **Unicorn:** Pliny, *Natural History,* VIII, 31.

GENERAL INDEX

Note 1: A few names not mentioned in the text are included in this index as a quick reference.

Note 2: Since proper names have been transliterated, spelling will often vary from one translation to another. Readers who cannot find a particular name under one spelling may find it under another.

The following lists some of the letters that are frequently interchangeable:

C and K, as in Circe/Kirke
           Cronos/Kronos

X and CH and KH, as in Xronos/Chronos
           Achaia/Akhaia

AE and AI, as in Hephaestus/Hephaistus
           Phaeacia/Phaiacia

AE and E, as in Aegyptus/Egypt
           Aetna/Etna

OE and OI, as in Oedipus/Oidipus
           Moerae/Moirae

-OS and -US, as in Ouranos/Ouranus
           Menelaos/Menelaus

OU and U, as in Ouranos/Uranos

EI and I, as in Eileithyia/Ilithyia

U and Y, as in hubris/hybris
           Rhadamanthus/Rhadamanthys

-ES and -S, as in Aloades/Aloads

I and J, as in Deianira/Dejanira

Note 3: An asterisk after a page reference indicates an illustration.

Arcas, grandson of Lycaon; son of Callisto, 27, 247, 255

Ares, 12, 13, 32, 33*, 36, 38-39, 41, 42, 51, 52, 80, 85, 90, 127, 145, 180, 188, 235, 256-257

Arete, wife of Alcinoos; mother of Nausicaa; queen of Phaiacians, 189

Arethusa: 1) daughter of Hesperus, 118
2) nymph, changed into a fountain, 249

Arges, a Cyclops, 1, 5

Argives, name for Greeks

Argo, Jason's ship, 82, 187 ff., 191*

Argolis, area in Peloponnesus

Argos, 1) Agamemnon's kingdom, 163 ff.
2) builder of *Argo,* 187

Argus, 1) Odysseus' dog
2) 100-eyed creature, 30, 214-215*

Ariadne, daughter of Minos; aided Theseus, 48, 153, 200-201, 249

Arimaspians, 240, 241*

Arion, a horse, exceptionally fast, fathered by Poseidon; saved Adrastus after the expedition against Thebes, 14, 257

Arisbe, 161

Aristaeus, 27, 108-109, 112

Arnaios, bully in *Odyssey*; sometimes called Irus

Artemis, 11, 19, 20, 21, 22, 23, 25 ff., 26*, 31, 51, 52, 85, 86, 88, 91, 94, 104, 146, 148, 174, 204, 210, 237

Ascalaphus, 178, 249

Ascanius, Aeneas' son; sometimes called Iulus, 234

Asclepius, physician, 21-22, 24, 89, 91, 205, 231, 238

Asculapius, Roman name for Asclepius

Asopus, river and river god, 79

Asphodel, 77

Assaracus, son of Tros, 160

Astaeus, 7

Asterion, 242, name for Minotaur

Asterius, 152

Astraea, abstraction of Justice, daughter of Themis

Astraeus, 110, 120

Astyanax, child of Hector and Andromache

Astydamia, wife of Acastus; sometimes called Hippolyte; tried to frame Peleus, 221, 236

Atalanta, 1) huntress in Arcadia, 187
2) daughter of Schoeneus of Boeotia, 250

Ate, 96, 97

Athamas, son of Aeolus; brother of Sisyphus; married Nephele and later Ino, 45, 72, 184-185, 239, 248

Athena, 10, 15, 23*, 31 ff., 33*, 39, 48, 50, 55, 56, 89, 95, 111*, 153, 166, 167, 168, 171, 173*, 174, 175*, 178, 180, 191*, 241, 257

Athens, 15-16, 198 ff., 202, 203-209

Atlantis Island, 227-229

Atlas, a Titan, son of Iapetus, 1, 5 ff., 14, 93, 118, 178

Atlas Mountains, 169, 248

Atlas, son of Poseidon, 228

Atreus, king of Mycenae; father of Agamemnon and Menelaus, 143, 146-148

Atropos, one of the Fates, 3, 100; *also see* Fates

Attis, 106-107

Augean Stables, 174

Augeas, king of Elis, 174

Augustus, 234

Aulis, town in Boeotia where the Greek forces met to sail against Troy, 148

Aurora: Roman name for Eos (*q.v.*)

auspices, 131

Autolycus, Odysseus' grandfather; well known thief, 256

Automedon, Achilles' charioteer

Auton(o)e, 1) mother of Actaeon; daughter of Cadmus, sister of Agave, 27, 108, 154
2) one of Penelope's maids

Avernus, Italian entrance to Underworld

Cernian stag, 174
Ceto, sea divinity, 120
Ceyx, 221, 251
Chaos, 1
Charicle, Tiresias' mother, 34
Charities (Graces), 11, 37, 97, 99, 100, 220
Charon, Underworld ferryman, 74, 75*, 76, 77
Charon's coin (Charon's obol), 74
Charybdis, whirlpool, 237, 243, 245
Chimaera, creature, 95, 238, 245
Chione, 250
Chios, island in Aegean
Chiron, noble Centaur, son of Cronos, 21, 27, 108, 114, 115, 174, 184, 185, 187, 188, 236-237
Chloris, goddess of flowers and spring; Latin, Flora, 111
chronos, time, 6
Chrysaor, monster, 15, 167
Chryseis, Agamemnon's mistress. When she was restored to her father, Agamemnon appropriated Achilles' mistress Briseis, and thus began the rift described in the *Iliad*.
Chryses, priest of Apollo; Chryseis' father
Chrysippus, son of Pelops; abducted by Laius, 146, 155
Cicones, tribe of people looted by Odysseus
Cilix, 152
Cimmerians, 199
Cinyras, father of Adonis, 84-85
Circe, enchantress, 189, 190, 243, 251
Cithaeron Mountain, 170
Clashing Rocks: *see* Symplegades
Clio, a Muse, 98
Clito, 228
Clotho, one of the Fates, 3, 100
Clymene, 1) Titaness; wife of Iapetus; daughter of Oceanus;
    2) Phaeton's mother
Clytemnestra, daughter of Leda; wife of Agamemnon, 148-150, 149*
Clytie, nymph; perished from frustrated love for Apollo, 248

Clytius, 160
Cnossus, city in Crete
Cocalus, Sicilian king who sheltered Daedalus, 202
Cocytus River, 77
Coeus, Titan, 1, 7, 19
Colchis, land on east coast of Black Sea, 176, 188 ff.
Colossus at Rhodes, 118
Corinth, 41
Coronis, 1) Asclepius' mother, 21
    2) one of Hyades, 118
Corybantes, Phrygian attendants of Cybele, 106, 107
Cottus, hundred-handed giant, 1, 5
cranes, 243
Cratos, personification of Strength, brother of Bia(s), 77
cremation, 75
Creon, 1) king of Thebes, son of Menoeceus, brother of Jocasta, 156-157, 171, 208
    2) king of Corinth, father of Glauce, 192
Crete, 4, 106, 136, 190, 199-200, 203
Cretheus, father of Pelias and Aeson; founded Iolcus, 72
Creusa, 1) wife of Aeneas, daughter of Priam and Hecuba, 162
    2) daughter of Erechtheus, 260
Crisa, old name for Delphi, 21
Crius, a Titan, 1, 7
Crommynian sow, 197
Cronos, Titan, 1 ff., 4 ff., 10, 18, 58, 64, 65, 66, 104, 188, 236
Ctessipus, suitor of Penelope
Cumae, Italian town, 135
Cupid: Roman equivalent of Eros
Curetes, 4, 106
Cyane, friend of Persephone, 248
Cybele, 106-107, 250
Cyclades, islands in the Aegean Sea
Cyclops, 1, 3-4, 5, 22, 37, 90, 163, 238, 245
Cycnus (Cygnus): 1) son of Ares, 180
    2) friend of Phaeton, 93, 247
    3) Trojan warrior, son of Poseidon; said to have been invulnerable, 251

4) son of Apollo

Cynthia, name for Artemis, who was said to have been born on Mt. Cynthus on Delos.

Cyparissus, 127, 128, 129

Cyprus, island favored by Aphrodite, 2, 37, 84, 121

Cyrene, 1) mother of Aristaeus, 108
  2) mother of Diomedes of Thrace, 42

Cythera, island, 2, 37

Cytherea, name for Aphrodite, 2, 37

Cyzicus, name of city and island in Propontis

D

Daedalion, 250

Daedalus, 199-202, 250

Damastes: see Procrustes

Danaans, names for Greeks, 72

Danae, mother of Perseus, 165 ff., 166*, 254

Danaides: see Danaus

Danaus, king of Argos; father of fifty daughters, 80, 163

Daphne, nymph, 210-211, 247

Daphnis, shepherd; son of Hermes, poet and flautist, 248

Dardanelles, see Hellespont

Dardanus, founder of Troy; son of Zeus and Electra, 159

Dark Age, 136

Dawn: see Eos

Deianera, wife of Heracles, daughter of Oeneus, 181

Deidameia, 205

Deidamia, parent with Achilles of Pyrrhus and Neoptolemus

Deimos, fear, 39, 42

Deiphobus, son of Priam; married Helen after Paris was slain; killed by Menelaus; important Trojan warrior, 132

Delos, island, 19, 25

Delphi, city and site of oracle, 11, 19, 21, 24, 49, 97, 102, 135-136, 153, 155, 172, 184, 195, 199

Delphyne, monster, 51

Demeter, 4, 11, 14, 16 ff., 88, 89, 102, 145, 159, 218, 248-249, 257

Demodocus, blind poet in Alcinoos' palace

Demophon, 1) son of Theseus, 203, 208
  2) son of Celeus of Eleusis, nursed by Demeter, 17

Deucalion, 69, 72, 209

Dia, wife of Ixion, 80, 205

Diana: Roman name for Artemis

Dictys, brother of Polydectes of Seriphos, 165-168

Dido, queen of Carthage

Dike, 1) one of the Horae, 100
  2) abstraction of Justice, 11

Dino, one of the Graiae, 239

Diocles, 17

Diomedes, 1) king of Thrace, savage son of Ares, 42, 176
  2) rugged Greek warrior, son of Tydeus; wounded Ares and Aphrodite

Dione, 1) one of Hyades, 118
  2) name for Aphrodite, 41

Dionysus, 9, 18, 36, 42 ff., 44*, 51, 79, 89, 98, 106, 107, 116, 118, 125, 136, 201, 220, 248, 260

Dioscuri, "sons of Zeus"; name for Castor and Polydeuces, 153

Dirae: see Furies

Dirce, wife of Lycus; abused Antiope and was punished by being tied to a bull. Her body was thrown in a stream which took her name, 155

Dis, Roman equivalent of Hades

Dodona, oracle, 10, 135, 187

Dolios, loyal servant of Laertes

Dolon, Trojan spy

Dorians, one of the four major Greek peoples, 72

Doris, wife of Nereus, 119

Dorus, founded the Dorians; son of Hellen, 72

Dryad, nymphs, 112
Dryas, son of Lycurgus. Lycurgus killed him in a moment of Dionysus-inspired madness, 46

E

Earth: *see* Gaia
Echidna, monster, 239, 244
Echion, Pentheus' father, 154
Echo, a nymph, 122-125, 248
Egeria, a nymph, 252
Eidothea, sea nymph, daughter of Proteus
Eileithyia (Ilithyia) goddess of childbirth, 13, 19, 33*, 169
Eirene (Irene), 1) one of the Horae, 100
    2) personification of peace, 11
Electra, 1) one of the Pleiades; mother of Dardanus and Iasion, 17, 119, 159, 254
    2) an Oceanid, mother of Iris and Harpies, 119, 120
    3) daughter of Agamemnon, sister of Orestes, 150
Electryon, 169
Eleusinian Mysteries, 18, 49
Eleusis, 16, 102, 204
Elis, city and area in western Peloponnesus
Elpenor, one of Odysseus' companions; fell from a roof and died
Elysian Fields: *see* Elysium
Elysium, 76, 77
emperor worship, 234
Enceladus, a giant, 50
Endymion, 117
Enyo, 1) one of the Graiae, 239
    2) Roman war goddess, bloodthirsty
Eos, the Dawn, 50, 90, 109*, 110, 111*, 160, 161*, 242
Epeus, builder of Wooden Horse
Ephialtes, giant son of Aloeus, 52

Epigone, sons of the Seven against Thebes, 157
Epimetheus, Prometheus' brother, 54 ff.
Epopeus, 154-155
Erato, a Muse, 98
Erebus, the Underworld, 1, 39, 76, 77
Erechtheus, legendary Athenian King, 16, 209
Erginus, king of Orchomenos, 170-171
Erichthonius, 1) son of Dardanus, 159
    2) son of Hephaistus, legendary early Athenian king, 35, 209, 257
Eridaunus River, 93
Erigone, 48
Erin(n)yes: *see* Furies
Eriphyle, wife of Amphiarus, whom she betrayed, 157
Eris, goddess of Strife, 39, 114
Eros, 1, 3, 39, 40*, 41*, 42, 189, 210, 216-220
Erymanthian Boar, 174, 175*
Erysicthon, 209
Eryth(e)ia, 1) Geryon's island, 177
    2) daughter of Hesperus, 118
Eteocles, son of Oedipus, brother of Polyneices, 156-157
Etna (Aetna) Mt., 51, 245
Etruscans, 230, 234
Eudora, one of the Hyades, 118
Euhemerus, *see* Introduction
Eumaeus, Odysseus' faithful swineherd
Eumenides: *see* Furies
Eumolpus, 259
Eunomia, one of the Horae, 100
Eupeithes, father of Antinoos
Euphrosyne, a Grace, 99
Euripides, dramatist, 37, 47, 143, 154, 209
Europa, sister of Cadmus; mother of Minos and Rhadamanthus, 152-153, 254
Eurus, the East Wind, 110
Euryale, 1) a Gorgon, 166
    2) Orion's mother
Euryalus, Phaiacian who challenged Odysseus
Eurybia, 7, 120

Eurycleia, Odysseus' nurse
Eurydice 1) Ilus' wife, 160
    2) Orpheus' wife, 79, 82-83, 109
    3) Creon's wife
Eurylochus, companion of Odysseus
Eurymachus, perfidious suitor of Penelope
Eurynome, 1) mother of Charities, 11, 119
    2) one of Penelope's maids
Eurystheus, 169 ff., 175*
Eurytion, 1) Geryon's herdsman, 177
    2) A Centaur, 206, 236
Euterpe, a Muse, 98
Evadne: *see* Capaneus
Evander, Italian chief
Evenor, 228

F

Fates (Moirae, Parcae), 3, 11, 22, 86, 97, 100, 101, 131
Father Time, 6
Faunus, Roman god of forests and rustic life
Faustulus, 232
Flora, Roman goddess of flowers; identified with Chloris
Fortuna: *see* Tyche
funeral pyre, 75
Furies (Erin(n)yes, Eumenides), 2, 3, 77, 97, 100, 141, 159, 239, 245

G

Gaea: *see* Gaia
Gaia, the Earth, 1 ff., 10, 15, 16, 20, 24, 32, 35, 50, 54, 69, 91, 102, 104, 118
Galanthia(s) (Galanthis), Alcmena's maidservant, 169, 250
Galatea, 1) Pygmalion's wife, 122
    2) courted by Polyphemus, 114, 238
Galli: *see* Corybantes
Ganymede, son of Tros, 13, 141, 159-160, 220

Ge: *see* Gaia
Geryon, monster, 177, 182, 239
ghosts, 76, 77
giants, 50, 179, 239
Gigantomachia, battle of giants, 50
Glauce, Jason's second wife; sometimes called Creusa, 192
Glaucus, 1) sea god, 187, 243, 251
    2) Bellerophon's grandson and ally to Troy in Trojan War.
    3) son of Minos; as a child he fell into a vat of honey and drowned. The seer Polyidus restored him to life.
Golden Age, 64
Golden Fleece, 82, 185 ff., 259
Gorgon, 165-166, 239
Graces: *see* Charities
Graeae (Graiai) (Graiae), 166-167, 239
Griffin, 239-240, 241*
guest-host relationship, 2, 66, 71, 76, 139
Gyes, one of the Hecatoncheires, 1, 5

H

Hades, 4, 5, 6, 9, 13, 16 ff., 24, 29, 51, 73 ff., 82, 83, 177, 178-179, 206
Haemon, Creon's son: Antigone's fiancé
Halcyone: *see* Alcyone
Halitherses, Greek soothsayer
Hamadryads, nymphs, 112
Harmonia, Cadmus' wife, 39, 42, 154, 157
Harpies, 120, 188, 240
Hebe, daughter of Hera, 12, 13, 159, 181
Hecate, 17, 78, 189
Hecatoncheires, 1, 3-4, 5, 240
Hector, Priam's oldest son; killed Patroclus and was in turned killed by Achilles, who dragged his body thrice around Troy, 161
Hecuba, Priam's second wife, sometimes called Hecabe, 161-162

Helen, Menelaus' wife; daughter of Leda & Zeus, 39, 148, 206, 207
Helenus, prescient son of Priam, 132
Heleus, 169
Helicon Mt., 98, 172, 242
Helios, the Sun, 17, 32, 38, 39, 50, 91-93, 117-118, 177, 192, 248
Hellas, 138
Helle, daughter of Athamas, 184-185
Hellen, son of Deucalion and Pyrrha; founded the Hellenes, 72
Hellenistic Period, 138
Hellespont, 185
Hemera, the Day, 1
Hephaistus, 9, 12, 13, 32, 34, 36-37, 38-39, 56, 57, 90, 91, 115, 154, 180, 188, 190, 220, 255, 257
Hera, 4, 11, 12, 13, 16, 19, 20, 23, 27, 28, 29-30, 34, 36, 39, 45, 46, 50, 51, 52, 53, 80, 107, 114, 123, 156, 169, 172, 176, 181, 185, 189, 192, 205, 214-215*, 218, 235-236, 248, 255
Heracles, 9, 13, 15, 50, 57, 79, 81, 87-88, 103, 160, 170 ff., 171*, 173*, 175*, 187, 195, 206, 235, 237, 256
Hercules, *see* Heracles
Hermaphroditus, 30, 31, 248
Hermes, 17, 19, 28 ff., 33*, 35, 39, 45, 51, 52, 56, 57, 70, 74, 80, 107, 112, 166, 167, 180, 214, 215*, 247, 256
Hermione, daughter of Menelaus who married Achilles' son Neoptolemus
herms, 51
Hero, 213
Heroic Age, 65
Herse, sister of Aglauros and daughter of Cecrops, 35, 209, 257
Hesiod, 58, 64, 74
Hesione, Laomedon's daughter, 177
Hesperia, a nymph; also sometimes used as a name for Italy.
Hesperides, daughters of Hesperus, 82, 118
Hesperus, the Evening Star, 110, 118
Hestia, 4, 9, 18, 31, 42, 108
Hicataon, 160

Hieromneme, 160
Hippocrene, fountain on Helicon, 98, 242
Hippodamia, 1) daughter of king Oenomaus; wife of Pelops, 145-146, 165
    2) wife of Pirithous, 205-206
    3) one of Penelope's maids
Hippolyte, 1) an Amazon, 176, 203, 235
    2) wife of Acastus, sometimes called Astydamia, 221, 236
Hippolytus, Theseus' son, 14, 25, 38, 203-205, 209
Hippomenes, won Atalanta in race, 250
Hippotas, 117
Homer, 49, 143, 162, 239
Horae, the Seasons, 11, 37, 97, 99-100, 220
host: *see* guest-host relationship
Hyacinth(us), 111, 221, 250
Hyades, 118
Hyas, 118
hybris (hubris), 22, 96, 140, 167, 183
Hydra, nine-headed monster, 240, 172-173
Hylas, friend of Heracles, 187, 222
Hymen, god of marriage
Hyperboreans, 20, 23, 178, 179
Hyperion, Titan; sometimes a name for the Sun, 1, 117
Hypermnestra, daughter of Danaus, 80, 163
Hypnos, god of sleep, 78
Hypsip(p)yle, queen of Lemnos, 187

I

Iamus, 260
Iapetus, Titan; father of Prometheus, 1, 7, 72
Iasion, mate of Demeter; son of Electra, father of Plutus, 17-18, 159
Icarius, 1) Penelope's father
    2) Icarius, of Attica, 48

Laodamia, wife of Protesilaus. She loved him so much that she accompanied him to the Underworld.

Laodice, attractive daughter of Priam who was consumed by the Earth

Laomedon, king of Troy, father of Priam, 15, 160, 177

Lapiths (Lapithae), 205-206, 207* 236, 245

Lares, household gods of Romans

Latona: Latin equivalent of Leto (q.v.)

Laurel tree, 211

Lavinia, Aeneas' second wife, daughter of King Latinus, 234

Leander, 213

Learchus, son of Athamas, 45

Leda, mother of Helen, Clytemnestra, Castor, and Polydeuces, 147-148, 253

Lemminkainen, 89

Lemnos, island in north Aegean, 36, 90, 187

Lenai, 44

Leocritos, suitor of Penelope

Lernean Hydra, 172

Lesbos, island in Aegean

Lethe River, 76, 77

Leto (Latona), mother of Apollo and Artemis, 11, 19-20, 22, 23, 24, 93

Leucothea (= Ino), a sea nymph, 46, 248

Leucothoe, 248

Liber: Roman equivalent of Dionysus

Libya, 152, 163

Linus, Heracles' tutor, 170

Loki, Norse god, 59

Liriope, mother of Narcissus, 122

Lotis, 107, 250

Lotus, a plant that, when eaten, numbs one's desires and initiatives

Loxias, epithet of Apollo, especially regarding his function as a prophet

Lucifer, the Morning Star, 110

Lucina, Roman equivalent of Eileithyia

Lucretius, 66

Luna, Roman equivalent of Selene

Lycaon, king of Arcadia, 67, 71, 247, 255

Lycia, region in Asia Minor

Lycomedes, king of Scyros, 208

Lycurgus, king of the Edones, 46, 49

Lycus, Theban regent, 154-155

Lynceus, husband of Hypermnestra, 163

Lyncus, 249

Lyrus, 160

M

Machaon, Greek physician, son of Asclepius

Maenads, wild female followers of Dionysus, 23*, 43*, 44, 107

magic, 131

Maia, one of the Pleiades, mother of Hermes, 28, 119

Manes, 77

Mantho, daughter of Tiresias, prophetess, 93

Marpessa, chose the mortal Idas over the god Apollo

Mars, Roman equivalent of Ares

Marsyas, 22, 23*, 129-130

Medea, 78, 188 ff., 195, 198

Medon, herald in Odysseus' palace, faithful and loyal

Medus, son of Medea, 192, 194

Medusa, 15, 165-167, 178, 240-241

Megaera, a Fury, 2

Megapenthes, 1) son of Menelaus
2) son of Proetus, 168

Megara, 1) wife of Heracles, 171-172, 180
2) city east of Corinth

Melampus, a prophet, 47, 132

Melanion, beat Atalanta in a footrace; in other versions of the story, it is Hippomenes (q.v.) who beat her.

Melanippus, Theban warrior; killed by Tydeus

Melanthios, goatherd; disloyal to Odysseus

Melantho, disloyal maid of Odysseus and friendly to Eurymachus

Meleager, adventurer from Calydon, son of Oeneus, 187, 237

Meliad nymphs, 112

Melid nymphs, 112

Melian nymphs (Meliae) 3, 4, 112

Melicertes, became the sea god Palaemon, 45, 248

Melpomene, a Muse, 98

Memnon, 110, 111*

Memphis, 152

Menelaus, son of Atreus and king of Sparta; brother of Agamemnon; husband of Helen, 147

Menestheus, 1) 206-208
2) Greek leader in Trojan War

Menoeceus, father of Jocasta and Creon; another Menoeceus is a grandson of this Menoeceus.

Menoetes, herdsman in Underworld, 179

Menoetius, Patroclus' father

Mentes, Greek captain whose body Athena appropriates in the *Odyssey*

Mercury: Roman equivalent of Hermes

Merope, 1) one of the Pleiades, 119
2) Oedipus' foster mother at Corinth, 155
3) courted by Orion, 90

Mestor, 169

Metaneira, mother of Triptolemus, 17

Metis, abstraction of wisdom, 4, 10, 32, 253

Midas, king of Phrygia, 22, 125-127

Miletus, son of Apollo and founder of the city of Miletus, 153

Minerva: Roman equivalent of Athena

Minos, king of Crete, 25, 76, 152-153, 199-202, 242, 249

Minotaur, 199-200, 242

Minyans, Greek people who originally settled in Thessaly and later moved into Boeotia, 187

Minyas, legendary founder of Minyans, 47

Mnemosyne, Titaness; abstraction of memory; mother of Muses, 1, 11, 97

moira, lot; fate; destiny, 96

Moirae: *see* Fates

Momus, 3, 116

Moon: *see* Selene

Mopsus, Greek prophet, 134

Morpheus, divinity of sleep and dreams; son of Hypnos.

mother earth: *see* Gaia

mountains, 1

Muses, goddesses of inspiration, 11, 84, 97-99, 108, 220, 242, 243

Mycenae, Agamemnon's home; city in southeast Peloponnesus, 146-147

Mycenean Age, 137

Myrmidons, fierce and ruthless Greek warriors, 76, 249

Myrrha (sometimes called Smyrna), mother of Adonis, 38, 84-85

Myrtilus, charioteer; son of Hermes, 145-146, 256

N

Naiads, nymphs, 112

Nana, 106

Narcissus, 122-125, 248

Nausicaa, Phaician princess; daughter of Alcinous and Arete

Naxos, island, 200-201

nectar, drink of the gods, 9, 19

Neleus, Nestor's father

Nemean Lion, 172

Nemesis, divinity of retribution, 96, 97, 123, 148

Neoptolemus (sometimes called Pyrrhus), son of Achilles; killed Priam and his son Astyanax

Nephele, 1) wife of Athamas, 184-185
2) cloud created by Zeus to trap Ixion, 236

Neptune: Roman equivalent of Poseidon

Nereid nymphs, 68, 112-114, 167

Nereus, an old man of the sea, 112-114, 120, 178

Nessus, a Centaur, 181

Nestor, son of Neleus; long-winded king of Pylos

Night (Nyx), 3, 39

Pandora, 56 ff.

Pandrosus, daughter of Cecrops, 35, 209, 257

Paphos, city on Cyprus favored by Aphrodite, 122

Parcae: Roman equivalent of Fates parents, respect for, 2, 66, 76, 139

Paris (sometimes called Alexander), son of Priam and Hecuba; Trojan warrior, 39, 115, 148, 162

Parnassus Mountain, 69, 98

Pasiphae, wife of Minos, 153, 199, 242

Patroclus, friend of Achilles; killed by Hector

Pedasus, horse of Achilles

Pedile, one of the Hyades, 118

Pegasus, winged horse, 15, 95, 167, 240, 242

Peiraeus, companion of Telemachus

Peisistratus, son of Nestor who accompanied Telemachus to Sparta

Peleus, king of Myrmidons in Thessaly; brother of Telamon; father of Achilles; son of Aeacus, 39, 114-115, 187, 236

Pelias, king of Iolcus, 86, 185, 190-192

Pelion, mountain in Thessaly, 52

Pelopia, mother of Aegisthus, 147

Pelops, son of Tantalus, 79, 145-146, 155

Penelope, Odysseus' wife; daughter of Icarius

Peneus River, 210-211, 213

Penthesileia, Amazon queen, 235

Pentheus, Theban king; son of Agave, 46-47

Pephredo, one of the Graiae, 239

Perdix (sometimes called Talos), nephew of Daedalus, 199, 250

Periphetes, robber, 196

Persephone, daughter of Demeter; queen of Underworld, 11, 16 ff., 48, 73, 78, 79, 81, 82, 85-86, 88, 89, 178, 206, 219

Perses, 1) son of Crius, 120
  2) son of Perseus, 168

Perseus, son of Danae, 49, 165 ff., 166*

Phaea, 197

Phaecia, Paradisic land ruled by Alcinoos and Arete

Phaedra, wife of Theseus; stepmother of Hippolytus, 38, 153, 203-205, 209

Phaeto, one of the Hyades, 118

Phaeton, son of Helios, 91-93

Phemius, poet at Ithaca

Philammon, 260

Philemon, 70-72

Philoctetes, Greek warrior deserted by the Greeks in the Trojan War; eventually became reconciled and killed Paris, 181

Philoetius, loyal herdsman of Odysseus

Philomela, daughter of Athenian king Pandion, 127-128, 209

Philyra, name of an island and of a nymph; mother of Chiron, 236

Phineus, 1) king of Salmydessus; son of Agenor; blind prophet, 188, 240
  2) brother of Cepheus, 167-168, 169

Phlegethon (Pyriphlegethon) River, 77

Phobus, 39, 42

Phoebe, Titaness, mother of Leto, 1, 7, 19

Phoebus, epithet for Apollo to stress his brightness and radiance

Phoenix, 1) Egyptian bird, 88, 242
  2) son of Agenor, brother of Europa, 152
  3) Greek warrior, son of Amyntor

Pholus, a Centaur, 174, 236

Phorcys, sea god, 120, 239

Phrixus, son of Athamas, 184-185

Phrygia, land in Asia Minor, 106-107

Phyllis, killed herself when she despaired that Theseus' son Demophon no longer loved her

Picus, turned into a woodpecker for rejecting Circe

Pieria Mountain, 97

Pierides, the Muses, 98

U

Ulysses: Roman equivalent of Odysseus
Underworld, 17, 73 ff., 83, 178; *also see* Tartarus
Unicorn, 244
Urania, a Muse, 98
Uranus: *see* Ouranos

V

Venus, Roman equivalent of Aphrodite, 234
Vergil, 162
Vertumnus, Roman vegetation god, 251
Vesta: Roman equivalent of Hestia
Vestal Virgins, women who devoted themselves to the service of Vesta and who consequently took an oath of chastity
Vulcan: Roman equivalent of Hephaistus

W

Wooden Horse, 134

X

Xanthus, 1) alternate name of Scamander River
  2) horse of Achilles who at one point in the Trojan War spoke to Achilles
Xuthus, 72

Z

Zagreus, 48, 49
Zelos, abstraction of Jealousy, 77
Zephyrus, the West Wind, 110, 111, 216, 221
Zetes, son of Boreas, brother of Calais, 111, 187, 188
Zethus, twin of Amphion, 155
Zeus, 4, 6, 8*, 9, 10 ff., 33*, and *passim* throughout book